Trust and Honesty

Trust and Honesty

America's Business Culture at a Crossroad

Tamar Frankel

OXFORD

UNIVERSITY PRESS

2006

OXFORD
UNIVERSITY PRESS

Oxford University Press, Inc., publishes works that further
Oxford University's objective of excellence
in research, scholarship, and education.

Oxford   New York
Auckland   Cape Town   Dar es Salaam   Hong Kong   Karachi
Kuala Lumpur   Madrid   Melbourne   Mexico City   Nairobi
New Delhi   Shanghai   Taipei   Toronto

With offices in
Argentina   Austria   Brazil   Chile   Czech Republic   France   Greece
Guatemala   Hungary   Italy   Japan   Poland   Portugal   Singapore
South Korea   Switzerland   Thailand   Turkey   Ukraine   Vietnam

Published by Oxford University Press, Inc.
198 Madison Avenue, New York, New York 10016

www.oup.com

Oxford is a registered trademark of Oxford University Press

Library of Congress Cataloging-in-Publication Data
Frankel, Tamar.
Trust and honesty : America's business culture
at a crossroad / Tamar Frankel.
p. cm.
ISBN-13 978-0-19-517173-0
ISBN 0-19-517173-X
1. Corporation law—United States—Criminal provisions.   2. Fraud—
United States.   3. Breach of trust—United States.   4. Corporations—
United States—Corrupt practices.   I. Title.
KF9351.F73 2005
345.73'0263—dc22   2005001659

4 6 8 9 7 5 3

Printed in the United States of America
on acid-free paper

Preface

W<small>HEN</small> I <small>WAS</small> <small>YOUNGER</small>, I used to take a long walk after my birthday festivities. The gifts were examined and enjoyed, the candles were blown, and the cake was eaten. It was time for reflecting. As I walked, I used to ask myself: What has happened to me during the past year, and where was I heading? The many things that happened—both good and bad—were unanticipated. I took them in stride without much thought. They became part of my life and I adjusted to them, often unknowingly. Now it was time to bring these events and my own behavior to the fore. It was time to think about them consciously. As I grew older, I recognize that this walk need not take place on birthdays only. From time to time, it is important to stop and take stock.

This book invites you, the reader, to take this kind of a long walk. Where was trust and honesty in America in the past, and where it is going? But wait! Is this walk necessary? Who would object to trust and honesty? After all, reputation for honesty is valuable and advantageous. Everyone knows that trust and honesty are important in both personal and business relationships.

And yet, why does talk about these virtues sound like the "Sermon from the Mount," a "holier than thou" speech? Why does it "feel" divorced from "reality" and why is seeking trust and honesty viewed by some people as "hopeless"? There is a nagging suspicion that reality is not about being honest but about seeming to be honest; that reality is about discovering what is behind the façade of honesty, because surely such a façade exists. It is tiring and tiresome to live in such a reality, with innuendoes and vague signals raising anxious concerns that what we see is not what truly is.

Just the other day, I received a card to be opened immediately, by "American Senior Alliance," P.O. Box 100125, Marietta, GA, 30061-9900. It notifies senior citizens of changes in the law, offers help, and seeks information. Tucker Sutherland, editor of *Senior Journal*, suggests that this organization "should be viewed with caution" because "no one has been able to locate this company." He advises "seniors not respond to the mailing" (see the website available online at [http://seniorjournal.com NEWS/ Features/4-111-30AmSrAllicanc.htm.]. This card was received a year ago, but fraudulent e-mails seeking information "to update" my accounts (which I do not have) continue to arrive. And little has changed, except that we might become jaded and used to this. Seniors and citizens must be careful; check and recheck actions and publications by "strangers." Do not trust—verify! This is a tiring, tiresome, and "hopeless" reality.

And yet, we have some power over our reality. We are the ones who shape our relationships with others. And even though we cannot dictate the behavior of everyone, we can influence how we, as well as others, would behave: We are not merely followers but also leaders. Make no mistake about it. We might imitate the behavior of others, but others follow our behavior, be they our children, our students, our spouses, our peers, and sometimes our superiors and the public. Our reaction to the above advertising may change the behavior of the people who wrote the advertising and the behavior of seniors generally. If this is a sham organization, people need not wait for the government to find the senders of the advertising, and to punish them for trying to defraud helpless people. If the millions of potential victims decide to help enforce trust and honesty, they present a formidable force that can do part of the job. Few can become policemen. But many more can work hard to change attitudes, both their own and others.

This book is about the empowerment of those who would like to see America moving toward a higher level of trust and honesty. It invites the reader to take the long walk and reflect on where America is today, where America is going, and—if the direction is wrong—what the reader can do about it.

Acknowledgments

Books offer new ideas and draw on existing ideas. I am grateful to so many: the writers whose books and articles I read, and the colleagues who offered me their thoughts and suggestions, and helped to bring this book to fruition. Professors Diego Gambetta, Colin Mayer, and Avner Offer of Oxford University and Professor Peter Tufano of the Harvard Business School opened new doors to the insights of other disciplines. Professor Larry Cunningham of Boston College, Professor Duncan Kennedy of the Harvard Law School, Mr. Rajeev Bhattacharya, and Dean Ronald Cass and my colleagues at the Boston University Law School contributed their knowledge, understandings, and, best of all—their supportive criticism. Ann Rutledge and Ed and Mary Weyhing offered their very helpful reactions.

I am indebted to my assistants, who during the past three years have worked hard in research: Bill Hecker, John Brooks, Nowles Heinrich, Brett Leland, and Kate Long.

I owe an enormous debt of gratitude to Paul Donnelly, formerly editor at Oxford University Press. His probing and suggestions and his wise guidance were invaluable. My thanks to Niko Pfund, publisher at Oxford, and to Terry Vaughn, excutive editor, and Catherine Rae of Oxford University Press.

When I am tired and discouraged, I am sustained by the thoughts of my two children, Anat Bird and Michael Frankel, and contact with them and with my grandchildren Guy and Assi Yalif, Paul, Liat, Gil, and Arik Bird. Thinking of them and talking to them gives infinite joy and energy. A special place in my life and work belongs to my husband, Ray. He has always offered unbiased opinions and wonderfully warm and steady support. To all I am very grateful.

Contents

Trust and Honesty

Introduction

THE INITIAL TITLE of this book was "Abuse of Trust." Then news about frauds, which started as a trickle, grew to a downpour. And as I continued my research, it became clear that something different from the past and more basic has been happening to America. It is that America is *becoming used to* abuse of trust and deception. It is that American culture has been moving toward dishonesty, regardless of whether fraud has been actually rising. And that became the focus and title of this book.

Culture reflects the habits of society; at its base is a set of assumptions that we take for granted about how people behave. Like habits, culture develops with repetition, and with increasingly automatic behavior. This behavior becomes more comfortable and predictable. Eventually it is "understood without saying."

What convinced me of this culture trend? There is no comprehensive study on all people's sentiments. There is no decisive database that compares today's fraud in America with fraud in the past. But newspapers, magazines, court cases, and studies point to spreading and rising fraud in America. Deception covers the population in all walks of life: management and employees; Main Street and Wall Street corporations; lawyers, accountants, and physicians. More individuals cheat in healthcare and insurance claims. More young people cheat in school examinations and in sports. More job applicants cheat on their resumes. More people and businesses defraud more vulnerable consumers. Fraud has contaminated science, journalism, newspaper management, the professions, and the financial infrastructure. Chapter 1 in part I of this book documents these findings, and the counterarguments that there is nothing new in the recent developments.

Events alone, however shocking, do not change a culture, unless they affect general attitudes. I found evidence of a move toward greater acceptance of dishonesty as a "way of life" and toward justifications—"dishonesty is not that bad." There are even attempts by some leaders and their advocates to redefine fraud out of existence. For example, there are arguments that shareholders are not the owners of corporations. Therefore, directors can serve other interests without breaching their duties to the shareholders. The final stage in this process would be a culture in which dishonesty is taken for granted, and no one can imagine any other order of things or alternative behavior. If America reaches this final stage, then what we consider to be fraudulent behavior today will be the natural and smart way to behave. America is not yet there, but it is moving in that direction.

The change in culture, like the change in habit, does not happen overnight. It evolves. Between assumptions that harden into an automatic habit and no assumptions at all, there is a direction that culture takes. American culture has been moving in the direction of dishonesty for some time. It took more than three decades to plant and nurture the seeds that produced the fruits of the 1990s. Chapters 5–8 show the shifting balance between temptations and opportunities to defraud on the one hand and the barriers against abuse of trust on the other. During the past 30 years, and especially in the 1990s, these temptations and opportunities have risen while the barriers have fallen.

The regulation of trusted persons was diluted. The prohibitions on abuse of trust and fraud were weakened. Lawyers, businesspersons, government regulators, and legislators denigrated the law to a greater extent than before. The markets were put on a higher pedestal than before. Self-interest and individualism were exalted at the expense of commitment to society. The professions, such as physicians and lawyers who should have acted in the public service first and sought compensation second, turned into businesses whose first and foremost goal is sale for profit. Moral behavior—withstanding temptation even if there are no police around—is no longer a virtue. And, as the materials in chapters 8–11 demonstrate, the enforcement and punishments of white-collar criminals have been weak and reporting of abuse of trust even weaker.

Culture, trust, deception, and their synonyms mean relationships, as chapters 2–4 analyze. We may speak metaphorically of a person who trusts his self-control or deceives himself. But in this book, *trust* and *mistrust, honesty, dishonesty, cheating,* and *deceiving* mean relationships among people. Throughout the book I use these synonyms interchangeably—*honesty* and *trust*, and their opposites: *dishonesty*, and *distrust, deception,* and *fraud.* These words have different flavors but point to a direction. Honesty relates to integrity and openness toward other people, while dishonesty represents the opposite: deceit, corruption, shame, cheating, and duplicity toward others. Trust is based on belief in other people, while distrust and mistrust represent the opposite: disbelief, doubts, and suspicions of others.

As the large number of these synonyms shows, people's relationships are not identical. There are gray areas between clear-cut situations on which most, if not all, people would agree. There are gray areas between unqualified trust and unquestioned abuse of trust, between absolutely honest and truthful communication and clear deceit. Within these areas, one can move in small steps, one at a time, from honesty to dishonesty. One can shift in small steps, one at a time, from truth to deception. And one can slip and creep, in small steps, from trustworthiness to abuse of trust.

The rise and spread of dishonesty can be slow and gradual. Like aging, it can be hard to see the difference unless you come across an old picture and face the change. The comparison can shock, as one recognizes the old self. A picture of today's culture can shock, as one recognizes the current direction of America and its maturing into a culture of dishonesty.

Does all this seem obvious to you, the reader? Do you remember recent episodes in your everyday life that point to the danger of a dishonest culture? Do you recall in the workplace and among friends the admiration for people who know how to use dishonesty (or shades of dishonesty) to their advantage and "get away with it?"

Still, you may ask: "Why should I care? How does this story affect me? So what if smart people know how to finagle benefits for themselves at the expense of stupid people, or just devise a new misleading way to catch unaware buyers in the net? Let the people beware."

You should care, because dishonesty and mistrust are not free. Their cost can destroy the foundation of our economy and prosperity. See the signs of mistrust around you. There was a time when the doctor's advice was sufficient for both patient and doctor. Now the patient seeks a second opinion, and the doctor and the hospital require the patient to sign waivers of all sorts. The patient will mistrust the doctor; the doctor will mistrust the patient. Blaming the litigation bar and the high insurance costs, doctors have begun to investigate new patients to determine their "litigation past," and some doctors refuse to treat litigation lawyers. All these special protections cost the parties, the doctors, and, in the final analysis, the economy. Mistrust corrodes the wheels of exchange and commerce and contaminates trusted professional services. We can still recognize the symptoms. When they become automatic habits, we will accept them without thought or recognition. And we will pay the price without remembering the alternatives.

Some people may say: "Even suppose all this is true, what can one person do? Besides, no matter what we do, nothing will change." But this is not the American way. Whether things will change depends not only on the leadership but also on the citizens. In this country, leaders are not anointed. They rise from among the population. The population decides.

Make no mistake about it. America will continue to have its con artists, rogue brokers, and powerful white-collar abusers of trust. That will not change. What should change are the general attitude and the tolerance of dishonesty. What should change is the direction of America's culture to an *aspiration to honesty,* an aspiration that "goes without saying." Attitude and aspiration redirect and transform culture.

America needs a better balance of pressures and a healthier perspective. Ideologies and rigid dogmas should give way to a middle ground. There is a balance between self-interest on the one hand and morality and altruism on the other; between taking and giving; between individualism and a commitment to society; between rigid ideology and an ideal of honesty—even if it can never be fully reached. People are not only self-interested; society is not only a market, and relationships are not only an exchange. Moral people who withstand temptation are not stupid. Their attitudes are crucial to a prosperous society. Greed is not good. It destroys the greedy persons and those around them. Law is not the enemy of business. It is the enemy of *crooked business*. Law does not necessarily undermine free markets and competition. It can protect free markets from *competition by deception*.

Most Americans practice this balance. Most Americans are honest and compassionate—they take but also give; they are self-interested but also committed to others and to America. How come they are moving toward a society and a leadership that fails to resemble them? How come too many Americans, including the younger generation, have begun to accept less honesty?

One explanation is rooted in the behavior of most Americans. Gradually and increasingly, the people have abdicated their power to political, financial, and academic leaders who have not been in sync with the public's inclinations. The honest majority of Americans have remained passive. The fraudulent minority has grown, taken the lead, exploited, and corrupted.

Therefore, the American people can redirect America's culture if they get involved. If Americans have had enough of financial abuse and exploitation, and if they are concerned about the effect of mistrust and fraud on their children, the population, and the economy, they can demand of their leaders and of each other more honesty and less cynicism, more trust and less doubting. Rather than follow, Americans can lead this country to reject the actions, attitudes, theories, and assumptions that brought us the 1990s.

PART I

The Eroding Trust, Truth, and Culture of Honesty

The Spreading Abuse of Trust and Deception

ABUSE OF TRUST has spread throughout America. It has covered corporations and individuals; sellers and consumers; leaders and followers; young and mature. It has touched activities that had been "clean" and self-regulating, such as science and journalism. And it seems that many of these abuses have been on the rise.

THE DISCOVERIES OF SCANDALOUS BEHAVIOR IN THE 1990S

In 2001, America woke up to the astonishing discovery of Enron Corporation's failure. Mimi Swartz and Sherron Watkins reveal a pattern of mistakes, arrogance, and deception leaving behind the fundamentals of business and emerging as fraudulent images that mimic truth [Swartz & Watkins]. Since the Enron discovery, embezzlement, fraud, and incredible avarice—sometimes heartless and grasping—have been uncovered in other corporations, springing and spreading from the country's largest firms to large mutual funds, insurance brokers, securities analysts, and securities brokers, and involving, directly or indirectly, a number of their top management.

The news kept pouring in. In 15 months, WorldCom padded its accounts to the tune of $3.9 billion. The company also developed a practice of "rolling revenue," that is, registering the same sale many times over to inflate the revenues and its stock price. At the same time, the practice depleted the company's assets by paying the salespersons "rolling" commissions, that is, multiple commissions for the same sale.[1] Xerox Corporation overstated its profits by $1.4 billion.[2] The Federal Home Loan Mortgage Corporation (Freddie Mac) understated its gains by about $5 billion.[3]

There were allegations that large corporations defrauded each other. Among these allegations was that WorldCom has been rerouting telephone calls, and defrauding its competitors of hundreds of millions of dollars during a nine-year period.[4] This accounting fraud was alleged to amount to over $9 billion.[5] Boeing Corporation won a large contract with the Air Force by using documents that had been stolen from

Lockheed (a bidding competitor for the contract). And HealthSouth officials pleaded guilty to charges of fraud.[6]

Large contractors corrupted government officials. Boeing was further accused of having received proprietary pricing data from Darleen Druyun, an Air Force official who later went to work for Boeing.[7] Darleen Druyun, who controlled a $30 billion annual procurement budget of the military, pleaded guilty to a federal charge of conspiracy to obstruct justice. She tried to cover up the fact that she brokered an executive position with Boeing Corporation paying $250,000 a year when she signed, on behalf of the Air Force, a $20 billion contract for Boeing.[8] Boeing's chief financial officer "pleaded guilty to illegally negotiating an executive job" for Druyun "while she still had authority over billions of dollars in Boeing contracts." He promised to "help federal prosecutors investigate ethical issues at the highest levels of the company," and he might face a six-month prison sentence.[9]

Other large corporations have violated the government bidding rules. Since 1990, General Electric paid about $1 billion in fines for 87 alleged or actual violations. "Lockheed Martin has paid over $426 million for 84 alleged or real misdeeds. Boeing has 50 counts on its record and $378 million in payouts. Northrop Grumman, Raytheon, United Technologies, General Motors, Textron and TRW are not far behind."[10] Halliburton, a large oil company, was accused of overcharging the U.S. army by about $61 million for gasoline in Iraq.[11] A month later, the firm was accused of overcharging the U.S. government for meals served to American troops in Iraq and Kuwait.[12] A large corporation corrupted officials in other countries. Xerox Corporation was accused of making "improper payments" to the tune of $600,000 to $700,000 to government officials in India in order to increase sales in that country.[13]

Citigroup and J. P. Morgan were accused of helping Enron Corporation to hide manipulations of its financial statements. These two financial institutions paid $305 million to settle a case against them. The Canadian bank CIBC was fined $80 million for helping Enron's financial machinations.[14] On June 22, 2004, came the news of price-fixing investigations in the chemical industry: "Corporate Whistle-Blowers Win Prosecutors' Amnesty, Help Widen Scope of Probes." A two-year-old investigation revealed "just the tip of the iceberg" and has been broadened considerably. The fines have risen from $5 million, which was the maximum for a single Sherman Act criminal count 10 years ago, to $10 million or more against 40 corporate defendants and one individual. The five largest fines ranged from $110 million to $500 million.[15]

In mid-2003 came the discoveries of abuses by mutual fund advisers, who prided themselves on being "clean." For decades, that pride was earned. But in the 1990s, fund managers offered insider information and allowed preferred customers to profit from transactions in fund shares at the expense of other long-term fund investors. Fund managers and advisers benefited from these practices in various ways, and some personally participated in the practices. Investigations into mutual funds' abusive trading practices were followed by charges of fraud, resignations, and dismissals.[16]

A *Wall Street Journal* "Scandal Scorecard" listed 14 of the largest mutual fund complexes, including banks, that disclosed improper behavior and were either sanctioned or facing sanctions. The *Journal* noted that the Securities and Exchange Commission (SEC) was investigating Alliance Capital Management, American Express, Bank of America, Bank One, Charles Schwab, Federated Investors, Fred Alger Management, Janus Capital, Loomis Sayles, Morgan Stanley, Pilgrim, Baxter & Assoc., Prudential/Wachovia, Putnam Investments, and Strong Capital.[17] In 2004 came revelations of wrongdoing in the giant insurance brokerage firms. These included agreements among bidders to feign bidding and fix prices, as well as collecting pay for recommending insurance companies to clients.[18]

"Business as Usual" or Epidemic of Corruption?

"The headline-making cases are symptoms of a broader disease, not exceptions, and a regulatory apparatus that isn't up to the challenge." "'A few bad apples? Looks like we've got the whole peck here,' said retired judge Stanley Sporkin, the SEC's enforcement chief in the 1970s."

> Every decade has king-size corporate villains. In the 1970s, Robert Vesco was indicted for looting the Investors Overseas Services mutual funds. In the 1980s, arbitrageur Ivan Boesky and junk-bond inventor Michael Milken went to jail. But the scope and scale of the corporate transgressions of the late 1990s, now coming to light, exceed anything the U.S. has witnessed since the years preceding the Great Depression.

In the words of Henry McKinnell, chief executive officer (CEO) of the large pharmaceutical maker, Pfizer, "I've never seen anything of this magnitude with companies this large."[19]

Types of Fraud

Deception has spread across the whole population. It permeates the healthcare field, including healthcare providers and insurance claimants, employees and management within organizations, shoppers, job applicants, students in examinations, journalists in their publications and journals in their circulation numbers, scientists in their research materials, competing athletes, politicians and government employees, and even the victims of fraud themselves. Rising fraud is reported in foreign countries as well. Here are some of the discoveries in a nutshell.

Fraud in Healthcare. Healthcare has provided a fertile area for defrauding the government. The abusers include physicians, hospitals, and pharmacists. For example, a podiatrist was indicted for fraudulently billing Medicare to the tune of $630,000 during a four-year period. He charged for procedures he never performed and for treatment of patients who were dead.[20] Steven Quinn of the *Dallas Morning News* reported the story of Tenet Corporation, as of 2005. In 2002, federal and state authorities began an investigation of this corporation in connection with physicians in Redding, California. These physicians conducted cardiac procedures believed to have been unnecessary. In 2003, Tenet reached a $54 million settlement with the authorities and an approximately $390 million settlement with plaintiff patients. As of 2005, Tenet is on trial for violating kickback statutes and for illegally offering physicians relocation packages. The U.S. Attorney's office and the SEC are investigating other violations.[21] The public was defrauded as well. Bogus professional organizations have been offering consumers fraudulent health insurance plans that are too good to be true. The plans are extraordinarily cheap, offer a broad coverage, including preexisting conditions, and require little or no medical prescreening. Consumers then receive one or a few services and after that—nothing.[22]

Healthcare fraud is costly. "At least $1 in $20 spent on health care is stolen. That would be $83 billion [in 2003], up from $57 billion only five years ago." Malcolm Sparrow estimated the cost of Medicare frauds at $50 to $75 billion a year.[23] The estimate of the General Accounting Office was higher, at $100 billion.[24]

Insurance Frauds. Insurance fraud is enormously expensive and has long plagued the country. It is costly to both insurance companies and the insured. And it is on the increase, the Coalition Against Insurance Fraud has reported. In the year 2002, nearly 99,000 insurance fraud complaints were filed with state insurance fraud bureaus, "the highest number ever recorded," and in 2002, there were 2,535 insurance fraud convictions resulting from fraud bureau investigations, an increase of 31 percent from 2001. The states spent 48 cents per resident to fight insurance fraud based on 2003 budget figures, an increase from previous years.[25] According to the National Insurance Crime Bureau, an organization supported by property-casualty insurers, "insurance fraud costs Americans about $30 billion each year . . . $200–$300 in higher insurance premiums for the average household."[26] The Coalition Against Insurance Fraud reports that the total cost of insurance fraud is "nearly $1,000 per family."[27] The National Insurance Crime Bureau estimates that at least "10 percent . . . of property/casualty insurance claims are fraudulent."[28] And yet, in an Insurance Research Council survey of U.S. adults, a third said that it is all right to exaggerate insurance claims.[29]

Fraudulent claims are made by individuals, as well as by organized rings that stage accidents and produce fake evidence of treatment of nonexistent victims. For example, in New York in August 2003, 85 physicians, psychologists, chiropractors, attorneys, medical clinic owners, and others were indicted in the largest no-fault insurance fraud scheme ever prosecuted in New York State.[30]

The cost of these frauds is borne mainly by the policyholders. According to the New York State superintendent of insurance, "up to $177 of [a New Yorker's] . . . motor insurance bill is due to insurance fraud."[31] As of 2002 New Jersey had the highest average motor premium of $1,027.71 a year, but the bill for New York motorists was only slightly lower, at an average cost of $1,014.96 a year, according to a report of the National Association of Insurance Administrators, quoted by the Insurance Information Institute.[32] Britain is not far behind, according to a survey by the Association of British Insurers, reported in *Claims* magazine.[33]

On the other hand, in the Insurance Research Council survey, Elizabeth A. Sprinkel, who heads the organization, sounded a note of hope. American attitudes may be changing. Although a third of the surveyed persons believed that padding the insurance claim is fine, policyholders are beginning to understand that their "little frauds" may raise their own premiums. In the survey, almost all those who were surveyed understood this point and recommended prosecution to those who bring fraudulent claims.[34] This changing attitude may serve as a guide for other frauds that have become commonplace. It also shows that awareness of the cost can have the effect of changing attitudes and reducing the cost of fraud.

Check Frauds. The Federal Bureau of Investigation and the American Bankers Association Deposit Account Fraud Survey reported check frauds as the fastest growing problem (together with identity theft). The American Bankers Association reported that attempted check fraud at American banks almost doubled to $4.3 billion annually from 1999 to 2001 (although the actual losses increased only slightly);[35] and check fraud losses are expected to increase by 2.5 percent annually, according to a report by *American Banker,* as noted by the National Check Fraud Center.[36] Further, the FBI Financial Institution Fraud and Failure Report of 2002 reported that even though the number of investigations related to failed financial institutions decreased by 91 percent from July 1992, "the number of major FIF [financial institution fraud] investigations has remained substantial," and swindles by outsiders have increased. These swindles are "[replacing] bank insider abuse as the dominant FIF problem confronting financial institutions."[37] Therefore, fraud has greatly increased as a percentage of problems at financial institutions, and each instance of fraud or attempted fraud is becoming more expensive.

Technological advances and available personal information make check fraud and counterfeit negotiable instrument schemes easier, while the complexity of the activities makes detection more difficult.[38] The American Bankers Association reported banks' losses from check fraud at $698 million in 2001, and the total amount involved in attempts at check fraud that year was $4.3 billion.[39] The Check Fraud Working Group, a subgroup of the federal government's interagency Bank Fraud Working Group, reported in 1996 that 2,000 large corporations lost an average of over $360,000 per year to check fraud,[40] and the FBI estimated that total annual check fraud costs to commercial banks and other institutions were between $12 and $15 billion.[41]

Consumer Fraud. On August 5, 2004, the Federal Trade Commission (FTC) released a consumer fraud survey that showed that 11.2 percent of the adult population (nearly 25 million Americans) were the victims of fraud during the year that was studied. The more vulnerable victims were poor minorities and people in debt. The 10 listed frauds are advance-fee loan scams, buyers' clubs, credit card insurance, credit repair, prize promotions, Internet services, pyramid schemes, information services, government job offers, and business opportunities. "The results of our survey indicate that fraud in the U.S. is a serious problem," said Howard Beales, the director of FTC's Bureau of Consumer Protection.[42]

Identity Theft. Together with check fraud, identify theft is one of the fastest growing crimes in America. It was named "the cybercrime of the millennium" [Newman]. There are hundreds of databases containing detailed information about people's lives, including buying habits. The manufacturing of fake credit cards and driver's licenses is rampant. People are already transparent. They have little choice [Brin: 331–333]. The information about people is available; it can be used to defraud.[43]

In June 2004, Fraud Watch International published a white paper on "phishing" scams, in which the fraudsters trick consumers into revealing their personal information by posing as an official organization and requiring verifications of the personal information. This information is then used to steal bank accounts and utilize credit cards. In April 2004, such scams increased by 250 percent over the *previous month.* In May 2004, "phishing" increased by 215 percent over the reported attacks in April 2004. There is a consensus that these attacks have dramatically increased since they first appeared in mid-2003.[44]

Employee Fraud. In 1999 two studies—by the Institute of Internal Auditors and the Institute of Management and Administration, and by Michael G. Kessler—indicated that employee fraud is increasing.[45] This conclusion was affirmed by a later study by the accounting firm KPMG and by the 2002 report entitled "Fraud: The Unmanaged Risk," by the accounting firm of Ernst & Young. According to the latter report, 85 percent of the worst frauds were perpetrated by employees of the defrauded corporations.[46] Another KPMG report noted that internationally, external fraud is more costly, but inside employee fraud is far more common.[47] Presumably, employees might have more opportunities to defraud but are under greater controls, threat of potential sanctions, and constraints of corporate culture. Outsiders may have fewer opportunities, depending on their access to the corporations, but are subject to far weaker controls, sanctions, and controlling culture. With the rise of outsourcing, the balance of control and opportunity may change.

Shoppers' Pilfering and Energy Theft. Shoplifting is increasing, although the rise seems to be more related to the economy and other factors than to societal attitudes toward fraud. A leading authority on shoplifting, Will Cupchik, noted that shoplifting rises during the holiday seasons;[48] as compared to the previous year, shoplifting "[was] expected to increase $1-billion nationwide [during the 2002] holiday season, according to a study by Retail Forward, a Columbus, Ohio-based marketing firm.

Arrests consistently fell from 1996–2000, but grew . . . when the economy turned in 2001, FBI statistics show."[49] According to the 2001 National Retail Security Survey Final Report, shoplifting costs American retailers over $10 billion per year.[50] The buyers, the shareholders of the retailers, and the government treasury foot this bill. Energy theft is a related innovative fraud. The thieves link to the source of energy, such as a lamppost, and divert it to their homes or businesses. Ingenuity is boundless. The companies respond with new technological devices to prevent the diversion.[51] These cost as well.

Employment Applicants' Deception. There is an increasing trend by job applicants to use deceptive information in their resumes and applications. A survey by ADP Screening and Selection Services found that 51 percent of the company's 3 million employment, education, or credential reference checks showed discrepancies in the information they provided, with 10 percent showing "serious" discrepancies.[52] The survey noted an increase from the previous year, in which 44 percent of reference checks showed discrepancies.[53] More than 25 percent of job applications contain misrepresentations. Presumably, demand produced a 1999 book for "do-it-yourself" employers: Don't Hire a Crook! [DeMey & Flowers, 9]. False diplomas offered on the Internet may signify the demand of job applicants for diplomas. One typical spam advertisement reads: "Does that position require a university degree? We'll sell you a REAL one!" "There are no required tests, classes, books, or interviews!" "Get a Bachelors, Masters, MBA, and Doctorate (PhD) diploma!" "Receive the benefits and admiration that comes with a diploma!" "No one is turned down!" And "Confidentiality assured!" A 24-hour telephone number is provided as well.[54] With dozens of resumes for new positions, large employers cannot spend the resources to check the truthfulness of all the facts. If they check, or employ outside firms to check, the costs to the firms will rise, and some of these costs may be passed to others. This is the price of justifiable mistrust. The cost to the applicants may be high as well, once their fraud is discovered. The cost to the successful buyers of false diplomas may be even higher. They may be exposed to extortion, especially after they gain a lucrative position. And this practice is not limited to puffing up academic credentials for white-collar jobs. Other common lies on job applications include hiding drug rehabilitation, incarceration, or illness.[55]

Students' Cheating. In November 26, 2003, the *New York Times* published a story of cheating in one of the more prestigious high schools in Connecticut. Students used ingenious techniques like typing materials on the interior of a water bottle, and sophisticated high-tech devices: "Calculators loaded with computerized study guides . . . electronic messages exchanged between students taking the same exam during different periods." Traditional forms of cheating were not missing, for example, "physics homework parceled out between friends" and peeking over another student's work during the exam. Cheating has become "routine."[56]

Studies by the Center for Academic Integrity at Duke University suggest that cheating on exams is generally on the rise.[57] It seems that students who come from a "privileged background" are more prone to cheat, perhaps because these students have a greater sense of entitlement, or because of the tremendous pressure exerted on these students to succeed and to gain acceptance to Ivy League universities.

According to a 2002 survey of 12,474 high school students by the Josephson Institute of Ethics, 74 percent admitted cheating during a test in school at least once during the past year, compared to 61 percent in 1992, and 37 percent said that they "would be willing to lie" to "get a good job," compared to 28 percent in 2000.[58] College students did not fare much better. A 1999 survey by Donald L. McCabe of Rutgers University, the founder and first president of the Center for Academic Integrity at Duke University, shows that on most campuses, over 75 percent of the students have cheated at some point. Another survey by McCabe shows that Internet plagiarism has been on the rise between 1999 and 2001. The number of students who admitted to using information from the Internet without proper attribution rose from 10 percent to 41 percent. In 2001, 68 percent of students "suggest[ed] this was not a serious issue."[59] According to an article in the *New York Times*, Donald L. McCabe's study showed similar results.[60]

Similarly, a September 2003 study commissioned by the Business Software Alliance (BSA) showed that "software piracy among [college] students is a problem just waiting to emerge." Only 23 percent of students believe that piracy is "outright wrong," and "students do not believe that [piracy is] being discouraged" by professors and administrators.[61] While a June 2003 BSA study showed that software piracy is declining in the United States and around the world,[62] there are concerns that student attitudes may lead to a future increase in piracy.[63]

Journalists' and Scientists' Fraud. Problems of fraud have emerged in reports by journalists. The *New York Times* reporter Jayson Blair resigned after the newspaper discovered that he had copied articles from other newspapers and made outright fabrications in others.[64] In August 1998, the *Boston Globe* suspended columnist Mike Barnicle for using a comedian's jokes without attribution and for allegedly making up a story about two young cancer survivors. The *Globe* also asked for the resignation of Patricia Smith for fabricating characters and quotations in her articles.[65] The management of a newspaper was also contaminated. According to a news report, *Chicago Sun-Times* officials artificially inflated their circulation numbers, presumably in order to attract more advertising.[66] Needless to say, these cases raise great concern. The press in the United States serves a uniquely important role and has a privileged position and strong protection under the Constitution.

Other fallen idols are the scientists. In the past, scientists rarely attempted to publish fraudulent results. After a scientist declares a discovery, others are hard at work to replicate the results. If they cannot, the discovery might be discredited. This community verification process discourages fraud. Yet a number of such frauds have appeared recently. In 2002, Jan Hendrik Schon was fired from Bell Labs after an outside review found that he falsified data at least 16 times from 1998 to 2001.[67] This was the first case of scientific fraud in the history of the laboratory.[68] The story of physicist Victor Ninov of Lawrence Berkeley National Laboratory is similar. Ninov claimed to have discovered "superheavy" element 118. Four years later, it was found that he had based the claim on fabricated research. He was fired. Robert P. Liburdy of Lawrence Berkeley Laboratory resigned after he was discovered to have intentionally falsified data to support his conclusions regarding cellular effects from "electronic and magnetic fields." There may be many reasons for such frauds, including personality traits, drive for renown, and competition for financing. In the opinion of R. Eugene Mellican, the rise of scientific frauds is rooted in the cultural transformation of science during the 1990s.[69] The community verification process may have been weakened if, for example, replicating experiments requires costly instruments or if today's scientists are more committed to their own work than to testing the work of others. But regardless of the reasons, these frauds seem to be on the rise.[70] In November 2004, *Scientific American* told the story of the connection between scientists in the National Institutes of Health (NIH) and pharmaceutical companies. In 2003, the *Los Angeles Times* disclosed improper payments to the scientists at the NIH. Later, congressional investigations revealed that a drug of a certain company was "derailed" after the researcher in charge received a significant amount of money from a competitor pharmaceutical company. The NIH has reacted vigorously, in an attempt to balance the demand of leading scientists for higher compensation with the power of pharmaceutical companies to influence the scientists' findings and evaluations.[71]

Dishonest Athletes—Young and Old. Problems in the International Olympics Committee. The use of performance-enhancing drugs, including steroids, is now believed to be common in sports. Sandy Grady was cited as saying: "We [are] in the middle of a Steroid Era."[72] Although many scientists are developing drugs to help patients of serious diseases, these drugs can also enhance athletes' performance, and athletes may take advantage of such drugs, regardless of health and legal consequences. Dr. H. Lee Sweeney was cited as saying: "There are going to be scientists willing to set up illegal clinics to treat athletes who want genetic enhancement if they pay enough money."[73] Organizations that govern sports activities prohibit steroid use, because athletes should compete on personal ability only. Therefore, the board of directors of *USA Track & Field* voted for a lifetime ban for any athlete who tests positive for steroids, and for a ban on the athlete's coach as well. The National Football League, major league baseball, National Basketball Association, and National Hockey League have established testing athletes for drugs, and the National Collegiate Athletic Association will soon begin. Nonetheless, the use of drugs appears to have spread from professional athletes to young amateurs. As many as 1.1 million people between the ages of 12 and 17 may have taken performance-enhancing supplements and drugs, according to a survey released by the Blue Cross and Blue Shield Association. In 2005 Congress held hearings on this issue, showing that it considered the situation to be serious.[74]

Not all parents have been good models. Some bent the rules and cheated to advance their children's chances of winning in sports competitions. A father of a Little League player lied about his son's age to gain an advantage for his son over younger competitors. Another father prepared for his child oranges injected with amphetamines "to enhance his son's sports performance." "A group of fathers rigg[ed] their kids' homemade racing cars at the All American Soap Box Derby to increase their speed." There are psychological reasons for this behavior, such as the parents' over-identification with their children, or the parents' attempts to relive their own lives, or their desire to seek the best for the children.[75] Winning was the main objective. Fraud was the means. And regardless of the reasons, this attitude seems to be more acceptable today.

The scandals in the International Olympic Committee are described in a book by Dick Pound, *Inside the Olympics: A Behind-the-Scenes Look at the Politics, the Scandals, and the Glory of the Games.* For my purpose it is sufficient to quote the *Economist*'s words about this book: "[Dick Pound's] insider knowledge informs his compelling book about the development of the modern Olympics and the erosion of its ideals by greed, corruption and scandal."[76]

Dishonest Politicians and Government Employees. Political frauds are not missing from this picture. On June 21, 2004, John Rowland, a popular governor of Connecticut, resigned. He was charged with receiving bribes, and with lying by denying that he received bribes. Impeachment seemed inevitable, and a poll showed that 69 percent of the voters wanted him out of office. The editorial in the *Wall Street Journal* viewed this case as a signal that "the price of dishonesty in politics is going up."[77] Judges were not immune. The *Economist* reported in October 2003 on "Judges for Sale" in Brooklyn, New York.[78]

In Lawrence, Massachusetts, a voting machine accepted the votes of "ghost" voters, that is, people who had left the city but not the city's registration list. Those who controlled the machine were suspected of controlling the voting results.[79] A mayor of Mendota, California, and a former employee engaged in voting fraud.[80] Recently, the Defense Department's inspector general reported that the Pentagon's auditors themselves spent 1,139 person-hours in 2001 altering documents in anticipation of an internal review, putting the documents in the appropriate form.[81] The activity was considered waste rather than fraud. Yet it raises concern regarding the honesty of the government personnel and their approach to true reporting—especially when those charged to keep others honest are not meticulously honest.

In addition to the time wasted in putting the reports into shape, there may be another reason for condemning the practice. Even assuming that the employees corrected the documents in order to comply with the requirements of form and not in order to change the substance, the corrections were designed to gain a more favorable review. On the way, corrections can lead to some embellishments. And if many documents needed corrections, the picture they represent should have remained intact for the reviewers to judge. Sprucing up true documents has a flavor of deception, for it conceals their prespruced appearance, which seems to have some importance.

Dishonest Victims. Fraudulent schemes can offer the victims a share of the benefits from deceiving others. These are Ponzi schemes in which the con artists promise very high returns from a business that is impossible to verify, and pays existing investors from the money paid by new investors. In such a case, the initial investors gain at the expense of the later investors. If the investors know or suspect such a scheme, they participate indirectly in the frauds.[82]

Victims can use fraud to retaliate as a protection against those who attempt to defraud them. An article by Dan Damon of the BBC, "Turning the Tables on Nigeria's E-Mail Conmen," describes Mike (not his real name), who is a "scambaiter," and the e-mail correspondence in which he used precisely the same technique as the scammer to bait the scammer. When a scammer "prince" approached Mike, with one of the notorious "Nigerian letters," Mike responded with a story of his own. Using the identity of Father Hector Barnett of the Church of the Painted Breast, he told an incredible story that nonetheless whetted the appetite of the scammer. Mike offered the scammer what seemed to be "easy money"—$18,000—in connection with a friend called "Minnie Mowse." Having diverted the scammer from the original scheme, Mike then asked and received $80 in the process. He ended the affair with a sad story of how the money was gone.[83] The victim and victims' protector may be justified in paying the con artists in their own coin. The point is that victims may resort to the same method of fraud when they have no other means of self-protection.

Reports of Rising Fraud. In an introduction to KPMG's *Fraud Survey 2003,* the national partner in charge of KPMG's Forensic Division wrote: "Organizations are reporting a rise in fraud, responding with expanded fraud measures both reactive and preemptive, and planning further actions for the future." After interviewing "more than 450 executives in medium-sized industries and in state and federal government agencies," the survey found that 75 percent of the surveyed companies reported an instance of fraud, an increase of 13 percent since 1998. The rate of fraudulent financial reporting more than doubled since 1998. Middle-management fraud has risen perhaps because of opportunities, coupled with lower moral and cultural controls within the organizations.[84] The greatest percentage increase is in asset theft and expense accounts abuse.[85] Employee fraud is most prevalent, but financial reporting and medical and insurance fraud are more costly by a large order of magnitude.[86]

The 2002 report of the Association of Certified Fraud Examiners on occupational fraud and abuse covered 663 occupational fraud cases. These cases caused the total loss of $7 billion. The report projected a rise in occupational fraud.[87]

The accounting firm Ernst & Young opened the foreword to its 2002 Report, "Fraud: The Unmanaged Risk," with the words: "Fraud is not a new thing." Yet the first sentence in the following paragraph says: "Fraud risk is higher than ever before." The report lists a number of factors contributing to the rise: the complexity of the organization, accounting issues, and the economy in recession. One may take exception to the last explanation, because much fraud occurred in the 1990s, when the economy was flourishing. But the conclusions of the report correspond with those of the other recent studies that fraud is on the rise.

Global Expansion of Fraud

The dangers that accompany deception and abuse of trust loom large around the globe. For example, at the end of 2003, serious fraud was uncovered in a European Community semigovernment institution. The *Daily Mail* (London) noted that the European Community failed to end fraud in a large unit of the European Community.[88] Fraud of a magnitude larger than the Enron Corporation was discovered in the giant corporation Parmalat. This fraud involved persons at the apex of the government and corporate Italy. Contributing to the fall of this giant corporation are little-understood and less-explained complex financial transactions (collateralized debt obligations).[89]

A 2003 PricewaterhouseCoopers survey of economic crime interviewed CEOs and other senior executives of the top 1,000 companies in 50 countries, including Australia, Belgium, Canada, the Czech Republic, Denmark, France, Germany, Hong Kong, India, Japan, Netherlands, Norway, South Africa, Spain, Switzerland, the United Kingdom and the United States. The survey suggests that there is significant global economic crime. Asset misappropriation is the most widely reported. Sixty percent of all the victims cited misappropriation as the more expensive of the frauds they have experienced.[90] A survey of U.S. economic crime by the law firm of Wilmer, Cutler & Pickering concluded that over 84 percent of the CEOs and senior executives of U.S. *Fortune* 1000 companies believed that the risk of fraud would be the same or greater in the five years after 2003.[91]

These numbers do not paint the whole picture. They only signal some rise of fraud.[92] The true number of frauds and their cost is unknown. KPMG's *International Fraud Report* of April 1996 emphasizes this point. It notes that "fraud is big business internationally. Reported losses are in excess of US$1 billion and no country is immune to the depredations of the fraudster." The report assumes that the $1 billion is the "tip of the international fraud iceberg" and that the losses are higher, in light of the limited sample and reluctance of the participants to provide detailed information.[93]

Prosecutions of corporate frauds have risen in recent years. According to one news report,

the SEC opened 570 investigations [in 2001]. That's more than in any of the previous 10 years—but just 10 more than in 1994. More than 150 companies restated their earnings in each of the past three years, an acknowledgment that they had misinformed investors. That's more than triple the levels of the early 1990s, but represents only one of every 100 publicly traded companies.[94]

The 2004 numbers are higher. According to Huron Consulting Group's *Annual Review of Financial Reporting Matters*, 414 companies restated their financial statements in 2004, an increase of 28 percent from the 323 reported in 2003.[95] That number constituted 4 percent of the publicly traded companies. Huron's *Review* noted that 330 companies restated their earnings in 2002; 270 restated their earnings in 2001; and 233 restated their earnings in 2000. The report noted "a rising trend in the number of periods contained in each restatement."[96] One earlier example is Goodyear, which restated its earnings three times in a six-month period.[97]

THE FAILURE OF THE PRIVATE-SECTOR PROTECTORS OF TRUST

Accountants, Lawyers, Boards of Directors, Rating Agencies, Brokers, Investment Bankers, Analysts

The private sector guarantors of trust in the corporate and financial markets have failed to detect and prevent the frauds of the 1990s. Lawyers, accountants, and investment bankers are expected to act as the verifiers of truth. Boards of directors act as internal compliance mechanisms and institutional controllers of abuse of trust. The Enron Corporation debacle was shocking not only because of its magnitude, the involvement of top management, and the lax supervision of its board of directors. It was shocking also because it demonstrated the glaring failure of the lawyers, accountants, analysts, investment and commercial bankers, regulators and even the media to dampen these activities.

Enron Corporation's case demonstrated a "massive failure in the governance system," according to Robert E. Litan of the Brookings Institution. "You can look at the system as a series of concentric circles, from management to directors and the audit committee to regulators and analysts and so forth. This was like a nuclear meltdown where the core melted through all the layers," Litan told the *New York Times*.[98] "The institutions that were created to check such abuses failed. The remnants of a professional ethos in accounting, law and securities analysis gave way to getting the maximum revenue per partner."[99]

The rating agencies that rate corporate bonds failed to discover fraud. The rating agencies overlooked the serious financial conditions of giants like WorldCom and Parmalat. Standard & Poor's lowered Enron Corporation's rating from "investment" to "speculative" only a few days before the company officially became bankrupt on September 2, 2001. In December 2003, Standard & Poor's lowered the rating of Parmalat by 10 notches from investment (BBB) down to "dump" (CC) only two days before the company went bankrupt. Ten days later, it lowered the rating to D level (default) and refused to continue working with the company. The rating agencies affirm that there was nothing they could do, because the companies deceived them as they deceived all other investors. Globalization of the securities markets requires interaction among the rating agencies and cooperation with those who compile the rating. If the coordination is weak, the rating could be flawed.

Rating agencies are also beset by conflicts of interest. The agencies are paid not by the investing public but by the very same issuers of the securities that the agencies are rating. In addition, rating affects market prices. Therefore, the agencies have "insider information" about their future rating, and those who know could benefit by trading on this information.[100]

Accountants failed to detect fraud. Some helped their clients to defraud others. A few defrauded clients. The accounting firm Arthur Andersen dissolved after it shredded documents relating to the investigation of Enron Corporation. Before its dissolution, the firm also was involved in a real estate debacle that resulted in payments to the state of Connecticut[101] and a $90 million legal settlement to 6,800 investors who were suing the firm for faulty financial advice that cost them millions.[102] Richard P. Scalzo, a partner at accounting firm PricewaterhouseCoopers, was barred from practicing before the SEC for his involvement in the accounting practices of Tyco Corporation.[103] In a civil fraud lawsuit, the SEC claimed that three former and current PricewaterhouseCoopers accountants had helped to inflate earnings by $59 million, as well as to hide fraud at the Allegheny Health, Education and Research Foundation.[104] Large auditing firms that service multinational corporations periodically produce reports that deal with fraud. In these reports, the auditors warned of the rise in frauds.[105] But, as Professor John Coffee noted, it seems that they did little about fraud in their role as auditors.[106] Among his stories on the recent crash, Roger Lowenstein noted that accounting firms were happy to let the clients choose accounting arrangements that resulted in taking assets (and liabilities) off their balance sheets, as Enron Corporation did [Lowenstein, 65].

The accounting firm KPMG sold tax shelters that were not tested or approved by the Internal Revenue Service (IRS) and involved sham transactions. The firm sheltered itself from scrutiny by other experts and the IRS. It asserted that the shelter was proprietary. Therefore, the buyers of the shelter had to agree not to seek a second opinion of other accountants. In addition, buyers had to agree to hire KPMG to represent them before the IRS. The IRS later disallowed these tax shelters. The clients lost heavily in penalties.[107]

There were instances of accountants who defrauded their clients. In 1996, Donald Bunsis, a former attorney/accountant/financial advisor, pleaded guilty to stealing more than $1.5 million from his clients.[108] In 1995 a verdict was upheld against a lawyer and an accountant who diverted $13.4 million from an estate of a client between 1981 and 1986.[109] In 1992 came news of an accountant in Silver Spring, Maryland, Deborah Prince, who pleaded guilty to stealing $326,679 from a Rockville (Maryland) organization that helps autistic people.[110] In 1997, Thomas E. Karam was indicted for wire fraud and money laundering. He pleaded guilty to wire fraud and was sentenced to two years in prison. He was also required to pay $775,000 in restitution.[111] The *Washington Post* reported that Victor Oliver pleaded guilty to stealing at least $1.5 million from dozens of clients, many of whom were friends.[112]

Some lawyers defrauded their own clients by "padding" their bills. In her 1999 study of lawyers of "elite" firms, Lisa Lerman researched cases involving frauds of "padding the bills and expenses." She found almost no prosecution of such cases before 1989, and 36 such cases during the following 10 years. Of course, this increase could indicate either more incidents or more prosecution. The 16 cases that were studied in more detail involved persons who had privileged background, graduated from elite schools, and worked at a number of large law firms. They were accused of stealing over $100,000 over an average of five years. Collectively, they stole about $16 million from clients. These lawyers were at the height of their careers, serving as managing partners, members of the firms' executive committees, or "rainmakers." The researcher noted that in many cases, "it is clear that their partners knew about and/or participated in the billing fraud."[113] Two lawyers were found guilty of mail fraud. One was disbarred, and one was suspended for three years for padding clients' bills. Another lawyer was found to have breached his contract and committed fraud. Judgment against him amounted to $3,124,414.[114] Put differently, these instances may represent the corruption of private guarantors of trust in the financial sector.

The members of the financial infrastructure, which Americans trusted, have failed to meet the clients' expectations. One example of such failure is the behavior of the investment analysts. Analysts employed by large brokerage firms advised the public to buy securities that these analysts believed to be of little value. Representing themselves as objective professional advisors, they were in fact paid or pressed to sell. Ten Wall Street firms agreed to pay $1.4 billion in fines to settle the charges against them on this score.[115]

Brokers took advantage of their customers' ignorance about the structure of commissions. Commissions paid on mutual funds shares include volume discounts. The commissions on a purchase of a certain number of shares are lower. Just below that cutoff point, the commissions are higher. Customers who were not aware of these cutoff points were sold a number of shares just below these points and paid higher commissions. When the practice was exposed, the brokers had to make "hefty refunds" to the customers.[116] Regulators "accused nearly 450 brokerage firms of overcharging investors for mutual fund purchases," and "10 percent of top mutual fund companies may have been involved in illegal late trading."[117]

The National Association of Securities Dealers (the self-regulatory organization of broker dealers) and the New York State Insurance Department investigated the sale of variable annuities by Prudential Financial Services. These investigations covered "possible forgeries and other improper handling of sales documents," misrepresenting the performance of annuities, and recommending unsuitable investments for customers. Prudential's history involved other scandals. Prudential employees persuaded customers to exchange insurance policies mainly to produce more commissions for the salespersons (settled in 1997). There were "disputes with customers over investments in limited partnerships" (settled in 1993) and violations in connection with the sales of variable life insurance (cited in 1999, fined in 2001).[118]

The weight of the information in this chapter can be disputed. Critics could view it as a hodgepodge of items from various sources. They could say: "This chapter includes many stories and studies based on different evaluation systems. The data is not well tested and may be statistically insignificant. It is impressionistic and could lead to erroneous conclusions." Yet this book is not a study of the methods by which information can point to the present state of affairs, let alone prove the causes of a state of affairs. However, there is enough information to raise concern. Chapter 2 continues the inquiry into the implications of this information.

2

Old and New Concerns

OLD CONCERNS: INVESTOR CONFIDENCE

The recent discoveries of frauds raise old concerns. One serious concern is that investors would lose confidence in the financial system and withdraw from the securities markets. There is a debate on whether the recent discoveries of fraud have affected investors' trust in the markets. Does investor confidence depend on the honesty of corporate and Wall Street leaders? Or does investor confidence relate to the opportunity to make a profit? Trust and the desire to profit need not be linked. They pose two different risks. After all, some investors made enormous profits by trading in the stock of corporations whose financial statements were inflated. These investors just bought and sold at the right time, before the frauds were publicly discovered.

Investor Confidence Is Hard to Gauge with Precision

Different signals of confidence may bring different conclusions. For example, the State Street Investors Confidence Index is based on the fluctuations of stock prices. It showed a rise in investor confidence from December 2002 to December 2003 and a drop from May 2003 to May 2004. The Index is based on a five-year history of investors' attitude to risk. According to State Street, "the index today is somewhat lower than it was, on average, in the late 1990s, but not by much. At shorter horizons, however, changes in stock prices have been associated with shifts in investor confidence." The survey also noted a dramatic fall in 1998 when Russia defaulted on its debts and in 2000 when stock prices fell 13 percent.[1]

In contrast, Professor Robert J. Shiller of Yale University, an authority on investor confidence, found that short-term investor confidence and improved earnings drove the stock prices up from October 2002 to October 2003, but long-term confidence in stock markets has actually deteriorated. In 2001–2002, 60 percent of the wealthy investors who were questioned strongly agreed with the statement that the "stock market is the best investment for long-term holders, who can buy and hold through ups and downs of the market." That number fell to 40 percent in 2003.

Professor Shiller noted: "There is a sour attitude among investors fed by market declines and the sequence of scandals, including the recent investigation of the mutual fund industry. Whatever their opinions about what the stock market will do this year, they just aren't sanguine about it as long-term investment."[2] Therefore, Shiller attributes the rise of investor purchase of stock not so much to confidence in the market but to a rise in market prices.

Perhaps both studies point to the same conclusion, while they give different interpretations and emphasis to the signals they find. Both studies show gains in investor short-term confidence but drops in investor long-term confidence. These studies are supported by other recent reactions of investors. After all, investors could care about profits, as well as about the honesty of their money managers. Investors withdrew from the mutual fund firm Putnam Investments more than $70 billion after the news that its managers benefited themselves at the expense of the investors;[3] while in the first quarter of 2004, investors brought about $6 billion to T. Rowe Price Group, which was not involved in wrongdoings. As compared to the previous year, that was an increase of assets under management of about 50 percent.[4] In the first half of the year, investors also poured about $114 billion into four other funds that were not tainted with fraud: Fidelity Investments, Vanguard Group, and American Funds, and a small boutique fund, Dodge & Cox. This amount almost doubled the money these firms received in the same period the year before. It is about 70 percent of the net investments in mutual funds (about $162 billion) for the first six months of the year 2004.[5]

There are signs of mounting investor anger. There is a rising number of investor arbitration claims against brokers (under the system of the National Association of Securities Dealers [NASD]). Unlike class actions, these claims are usually financed by the investors rather than by the litigation bar. The NASD reported that these claims have risen since 1990 (except for 1996 and 1998). They rose from approximately 3,600 in 1990 to approximately 7,700 in 2002 and 9,000 in 2003.[6]

A view of investors as traders, rather than long-term investors, suggests that investors will trade even in the stocks of corporations suspected of dishonest management, but will discount the stock prices to compensate for the risk. Yet, even if the stock market became a lottery and investors became traders to play the lottery game, investors would withdraw from the game if they discovered that the lottery was rigged to prefer some traders. In such a case, they may realize how low their chances of winning are, and refuse to play. For investors, the integrity of corporate management and the honesty of the brokers, dealers, and underwriters are not only important; they are crucial. They are crucial not only to determining the price the investors would be willing to pay but also whether to invest in the first place. While these investors may be ready to take the risks of market and economy volatility, they are less inclined to take the risk of losing their savings to dishonest management.

I have not found a study that proves this point, but leave this issue to a question. Who would entrust his life savings to a crook?

Trust in analysts waned when it was discovered that their advice was dictated not by their objective analysis but by those who paid them or pressed them. Reliance has shifted to "independent analysis." The *Economist* reported that mutual fund managers no longer rely on outside research analysts but do their own research.[7] Trust has shifted to added verification. As of July 27, 2004, 10 of the largest Wall Street firms that offer research information to clients had to accompany their research with the research of independent analysts.[8] This is a drastic change that requires these firms to verify their analysts' opinions with the opinions of independent analysts.

Corporate top management did not fare well in the market of trusted persons. In October 2003, the *Economist* reported polls finding that top management is "barely more popular than a second-hand car salesman." The few hundred executives who run the large American corporations "are now mistrusted and reviled, just as they were until recently feted and admired." Their tenure has been shortened from nine years in the 1980s to seven years in 2001. The firm of Booz Allen studied 2,500 giant companies all over the globe. Its study showed that in 2002 39 percent of the top executives were replaced for "underachievement." Another explanation for the pressure on management is that investors have become more demanding and are getting involved. "A new corporate leader gets a shorter grace period to prove himself than ever before," the *Economist* notes.[9] The demand may be explained by greed. But it may also denote mistrust of management. To reduce their risk, investors want results in a shorter period, as they would in buying short-term bonds. The old concerns have been raised.

New Concerns: Slipping toward Dishonesty

The recent discoveries of fraud and abuse of trust are raising new concerns, different from the concerns about losing investor trust. The discoveries reveal a slippery slope. Initially, people accept abuse of trust with a sort of resignation. Accepting abuse does not necessarily mean condoning it. It means accepting it the way a sick person accepts a terminal disease. There is nothing to be done but to say: "I know it is wrong. But that is the way things are." Acceptance results in an assumption that dishonesty is rampant, that it is an essential part of human nature, and that dishonesty cannot be changed.

The next step is justification to commit shady acts. Justification goes a bit further than acceptance. It is an attitude that says: "I know it is wrong. But it is not that wrong. There are good reasons for committing the wrong." Justifications lead to the third stage—eliminating the wrong altogether. We simply redefine it out of existence.

Acceptance

A story of a 15-year-old stock manipulator is symbolic. This story may be an isolated and perhaps anomalous case. Yet it is worth telling. In 2000, a 15-year-old boy entered Internet "chat rooms" populated by investors and spread exciting rumors about penny stocks he had bought just a short time before. When interest in the stocks rose and their price climbed, he quickly sold at great profit. The boy traded by using his father's account with the father's blessings, and gained almost a million dollars. The SEC sued the boy, the case was settled, and some money was left for him and his family.[10] The boy "touted" the penny stock after he bought it. Touting is prohibited, especially the touting of penny stock. In 1990, "penny stock swindles" became "the number one" danger of abuse for small investors;[11] and the law was amended to impose tighter restrictions.[12] Penny stock was sold in high-pressure sales tactics, usually by telephone [Loss & Seligman, 8:3885]. The Internet is similar to telemarketing and opened new opportunities for players of the old game. This young man took advantage of these new developments.

The telling point in this story is not what the boy did. The telling point is how the father and the boy's classmates viewed what he did. As *Newsweek* described the event, the father helped his son to manipulate the stock prices, and was proud of his son's accomplishments—making a profit of hundreds of thousands of dollars at such a tender age. The classmates eyed the boy with awe and admiration as he appeared in school each day, carrying his briefcase and acting like a serious securities trader. He became a model of success—someone with a brilliant future.

It is hard to prove that people accept fraud as a "fact of life." Yet even a writer in a small Ventura County newspaper suggested that this view has become accepted. George Sjostrom wrote:

> Fraud has become so widespread that we are in great danger of accepting it as normal, as an ordinary cost of doing business. . . . Sheltered by the rationalization that everyone does it, defrauders feel no moral burden, and are driven only by the belief that their scam will go undetected.[13]

An attorney who specializes in antifraud litigation is quoted as saying: "This is not just a health-care fraud that takes dollars out of the system. This is rank patient abuse. This is as bad as it gets." The article continues: "The real tragedy is not just the proliferation of fraud. The tragedy is that the public seems to have accepted fraud as just another way of doing business."[14] Similarly, if one recognizes as inevitable that it is easy to get personal information, one accepts also as inevitable the fraud that may come with it [Brin, 331–333].

Acceptance of dishonesty has a critical effect on trust. The habit of viewing mistrust as an "aberration" or an "accident" is a major contribution to trust in a social order [Misztal, 107]. That is, rejection of mistrust strengthens trust. The opposite should also be correct. The habit of viewing trust as an "aberration" or an "accident" can be a major contribution to weakening and undermining trust.

How does acceptance develop? Peer pressure can lead to accepting abuse of trust and deception. The pressure can result in tolerating a system uncritically, and submitting one's own opinions to those of the group. If the peers view the system without question, as the "way things are," group members will share this view as well.

Experiments have shown that most people follow the judgment of their peer groups. Solomon Asch conducted a famous experiment, in which a tested individual was confronted with a unanimous judgment of an attendant group. That judgment conflicted with what the tested person saw with his own eyes. The group said that two lines were of equal length. The subject of the test saw clearly that the lines were not of equal length. The results of the experiment showed the power of group pressure. Many tested persons agreed with the group's observation. Even if a tested person continued to disagree with the group, he experienced great distress. In fact, it seemed that the tested person's distress was greater when he resisted the judgment of the group than when he submitted to the judgment of the group against the evidence before his eyes [Ceraso, Gruber, & Rock, 12]. Time and again, it has been shown that people feel constrained to follow the judgment of their peer group. The pressure of "Everyone does it" results in a consensus that it is fine to do it.

While initially peer pressure is limited to the group of peers, it can develop into a cascade. When a cascade occurs, people follow the crowd, mostly of strangers. They follow without questioning rather than relying on their own knowledge and judgment. In fact, they forsake their own convictions, and just "track the pack."[15] Cascades can grow fast today, when so much information is so easily available to the public.

The pressure of authority figures is another factor that contributes to acceptance. If authorities view the system as "the way things are," their followers will tend to share this view as well. In an experiment, Stanley Milgram tested the degree of people's obedience to authority. The subjects of the test were told to administer electric shocks to others, called "learners," by pressing a button if the "learners" made certain mistakes. In fact, no shocks were delivered, but the persons to whom they seemed to be applied were actors, crying in feigned pain and begging for mercy. As the test proceeded, the participants were required to administer "shocks" in increased intensity. If the tested person hesitated, the experimenter told him to do it. Many tested persons obeyed the experimenter, even as the "learners" screamed with pain and pleaded for them to stop [Milgram, 3–5]. The authority's command was powerful.

These experiments suggest that the culture of a peer group can move the members to commit or participate in committing immoral or even illegal acts. Therefore, to the extent that the culture of a group accepts fraud, it is hard for members to break away and oppose it. Building the culture may take time, but when it takes hold, it is hard to change.

Similarly, the signals of persons of authority surrounded with "yes persons" can insulate the members of the group, including its leader, from contrary views of outsiders. The insulation is especially powerful if the group members interact at work as well as socially. Like affinity groups, described in chapter 3, they share and reinforce the group's views of the world. The members' critical independent judgment is subservient to that of the group.

Leadership offers a model of behavior. Dishonest leaders are mimicked. Smart fraudsters who "get away with it" can become a symbol of accomplishment. Deception can become a way to excel in competition. An atmosphere can develop in which "morality," "honesty," and "loyalty" are greeted with open snickers of cynicism or winks of suppressed laughter.

A general acceptance bestows legitimacy. "Legitimate" is not necessarily "legal." Legal is not necessarily legitimate. Legitimacy is a popular consensus that a rule, a decision, or a pattern of behavior should be followed—sometimes because it is right, sometimes because it is expedient, and sometimes simply because it is accepted by many members of the community.

For example, less than a hundred years ago, a child born out of wedlock was held to be "illegitimate." He had no inheritance rights. The child bore the brunt of unacceptable behavior that brought him into the world. Later, the child's status changed. The parents' behavior became far more tolerated. The child became recognized as a person, who should not bear the responsibility for the behavior of the parents. The child's legal status changed, and he acquired inheritance rights [McGovern & Kurtz, 82]. It is hard to say which came first, the social acceptance or the legal consequences. The point here is that when a sufficiently broad consensus and acceptance of a behavior develops, the consensus overcomes the law. If the behavior conflicts with the law, law can become a dead letter, or it is amended to conform to the general acceptable behavior. An acceptable deceptive behavior can overcome the law as well.

Justification

Some frauds and violations on a small scale can be justified as benefits to society. Such violations allow society, and sometimes drive society, to reexamine its rules. Lewis Hyde suggests that "tricksters" contribute to the community. They prevent the community from becoming locked into bad rules by inertia. Because tricksters break the rules, they force society to review its rules and decide which should remain intact and which should be eliminated or changed [Hyde, 70]. This observation is insightful. But it is true only if the number of tricksters is small and if they remain at the fringe of society. If their number grows, and if they infiltrate and creep into the leadership, then at some point they cause not a voluntary review of the rules but a forced revision of the rules in acceptance of the tricksters' ways.

Creative Aggressive Entrepreneurs.   Abuses and deceptions by aggressive entrepreneurs are sometimes justified on the ground that society needs such creators, even if in their experiments and passionate pursuit of innovations they might cross the line. In fact, Enron Corporation had embarked on the new bold experiment to privatize and create a market in energy. The actions of its top management could be justified on this ground. Thus, Professor Douglas Baird did not condone fraud but explained the failure of Enron Corporation by the faulty business plan it had adopted.[16] And yet it is unclear whether innovative, daring businesses that fail should attempt to prolong their agonies and investors' losses by fraud. Entrepreneurs are not justified if they benefited handsomely, and sold their stock before their venture's failure became public, while thousands of investors suffered the losses.

Attacking the Accusers. Another form of justifying abuse of trust attributes wrongful and bad intentions to opponents and accusers. These bad intentions justify unethical behavior as a defense against the "enemies." For example, Gary Johns, who studies organizational behavior, found that when negotiators were encouraged to act unethically, they tended to view their *opponents* as less ethical. Dishonest people will view the others as dishonest, commit dishonest acts first, and justify their behavior as a defense.[17] This approach sows the seeds of fraud as a matter of practice. Fred L. Smith, Jr., president of the Competitive Enterprise Institute in Washington, D.C., wrote in the *Wall Street Journal* that regulators adopt similar tactics. They use "business failures" to increase regulation, presumably for the regulators' own benefit.[18]

"Everyone Does It." This argument provides another defensive justification. "Everybody did this," said Peter Temin, a historian of economics at the Massachusetts Institute of Technology. "The people who got in trouble are those who are most at the edge. Enron didn't get caught. Enron got so far out on the edge that it fell off."[19] Perhaps a corporation should not be an aggressive innovator in fraud but it is fine for a corporation to be a practitioner of acceptable misleading behavior. This argument is not new. In the 1980s, corporate management has taken the position that if "every competitor does it," then one must protect oneself and one's business by doing it too. Otherwise, the competitors will win [Clinard & Yeager, 67]. A prominent sports cyclist expressed his belief that no one who plays by the rules can reach the performance level of someone who has taken steroids. Athletes in Australia were reported to have made similar claims.[20] In a drive to win "no matter how," the mere existence of competition can serve as a justification for stretching and breaking the rules.

The public seems to accept the fact that athletes are using performance-enhancing drugs. The athletes' stories demonstrate the power of an environment that justifies competition without limits. Athletes who took steroids in violation of the prohibition won by deception. When the deception was discovered but not stopped, more athletes began to take drugs in the belief that they could not win otherwise. That is no longer deceptive. Noted the *New York Times:* Taking drugs ended up as an accepted practice by athletes, and perhaps by society.[21] The road to winning by deception is established because the practice teaches a lesson on how to win. It drives to searching for other deceptive means. Competition on talent must include competition for the strongest drugs and a search for other deceptive means of winning. That is how we win!

The Leaders Do It. Fraud is justified by pointing to the leadership. "The leaders do it; why not I?" This is how some students justified cheating in college exams. They emphasized that their behavior was trivial as compared to corporate celebrity scandals and the dishonesty of their leaders' behavior, including "President Clinton, Enron executives and . . . accused plagiarist Doris Kearns Goodwin."[22] "Enron is 'the private sector's Watergate,'" said John Coffee, a Columbia University professor. "Although not all politicians were crooks, Watergate bred a virulent cynicism about government among the public, the press and even some politicians. That cynicism persists 30 years after the White House-blessed burglary of the Democratic National Committee's office."[23] Leadership leaves an impact. The resignation of President Nixon did not erase Watergate memories and lessons and models. Mutual fund manager James Gipson of Clipper Fund said: "I have had a lot of e-mail from shareholders who seem to have gone off the deep end and think all corporate executives are crooks and all accountants are sheep."[24] Of course that is not true. But perception colors the truth, and perception can press to become the reality.

There are compassionate reasons for violating the law. A mother who steals to feed her hungry child has a strong justification for committing the wrong. But the issue is one of degree. Feeding the hungry child is justified by a deeper consensus that the life of the child is more important than someone's property right, even if stealing is generally wrong. Violation of the law can be based on a sense of entitlement. The poor can justify taking other people's property because they feel that they deserve more.

Corporate management accused of misappropriating the shareholders' money can justify its actions by a sense of entitlement based on its greater contributions. Regardless of what the law says, and regardless of whether it is wrong for the managers to take millions from the corporate coffers, management has reasons to compensate itself so richly. Besides, not only is it wrong to withhold from management the compensation, which it deserves for their efforts, but also, if management is not rightly rewarded, management might take its talents and go elsewhere.

Committing Wrong for the Benefit of Others. A wrong can be justified by its results. Writing about Ken Lay, Enron Corporation's president, after he was indicted on July 7, 2004, Holman W. Jenkins, Jr., argued that Lay's behavior helped the investors.[25] Lay's indictment is based mainly on his public announcement of confidence in the company, at the time when he knew that the company was on the verge of bankruptcy. "In theory investors deserve the truth, even if it hurts. Please, can't someone in the economics department figure out a way to measure how many companies lied their way back to solvency, saving their shareholders a total loss?"[26] The idea is that this type of lying benefits the shareholders by preventing a massive sale of the company's shares on the publication of bad news, and presumably inducing shareholders to continue holding and buying newly issued stock of such a company to finance its return to health. Yet the lies induce people to take risks without their knowledge and consent. Besides, in the case of Lay, can't someone in the economics department tell us when Mr. Lay sold his shares to gain millions before his employees could sell their shares at a total loss? The justification is halfhearted, but it demonstrates a move toward justifying a wrong.

Blaming

Blaming others to justify doing wrong is not new. The method is as old as Adam and Eve. When they violated God's prohibition, he blamed her. She blamed the serpent. Fraud is sometimes justified by blaming others: The law is wrong; the government is wrongfully implementing the law; the victims are at fault.

Blaming Government Regulation.   Abusers of trust have blamed the government for the victims' losses. If only the government had not interfered, everything would have worked out fine, they said. Given more time, the enterprises would have become successful. In addition, managers can combine blaming the government with altruistic purposes, such as service to the shareholders. In the story of one of the greatest frauds in this country, Raymond L. Dirks and Leonard Gross described a corporation that was for a while the darling of Wall Street—until it was discovered that this reinsurance company was subsisting on mass forgery of death certificates [Dirks & Gross, 3; Parker, 1998, 65–67]. The management of the company argued that had the government postponed prosecution they would have resolved the company's problems, and saved the stockholders' investments [Parker, 1983, 124]. An Australian con artist had a similar complaint: "The ASC's [Australian Securities Commission] press release said they shut us down because we were destined to fail. Well, they ensured we failed. They wouldn't have a commercial bone in their bodies," he said.[27]

The law was blamed, indirectly justifying or causing the frauds. Jonathan R. Macey and Geoffrey P. Miller blamed the savings-and-loan associations crisis of the 1980s on the regulatory system. "In the early days of the crisis," they wrote, "many believed that fraud, incompetence, and corruption within the banking industry were to blame. But by 1991, it was clear to all that the regulatory system itself was at fault."[28] They are correct. Government regulation made it almost impossible for savings-and-loan associations to remain solvent in a period of double-digit inflation. A depository institution lost the savers' money when the law limited the interest that depository institutions were allowed to pay on deposits and savings accounts. The government itself propped up these associations by relaxing some accounting rules. The rampant fraud of that era reflected an environment in which regulation threatened the existence of financial institutions and offered temptations to fraud, without putting up sufficient barriers to it. Whether this environment justified fraud is another issue. After all, at least at the beginning, savings-and-loan associations received savings money at very low interest but could charge borrowers a much higher interest. There was no legal limit on the interest the savings-and-loan associations (and the banks) could charge the borrowers. Thus, so long as they had deposit and savings money at a limited interest, they could lend at double-digit interest rates to borrowers and collect a very high profit. The legislation became a hindrance only after savers withdrew their money from the savings-and-loan associations. That is when the temptations of the associations to profit in other ways took hold.

A survey of managers in *New York Law Journal* notes similar arguments. The laws, the managers argue, are inefficient and too intrusive. Government regulation is irrelevant and deals with minutiae and "is overly focused on process and procedure."[29] Bureaucrats do not understand business and act too slowly. They hinder American corporations from effectively competing abroad.[30] Besides, government regulation is unnecessary. According to the Cato Institute, a libertarian think tank, regulation is largely unnecessary.[31] The markets sanction the wrongdoers. Honest fiduciaries triumph in their competition with corrupt ones. Matt Ridley agrees. In his opinion, the best environment for balancing selfishness with altruism is the voluntary exchanges among people, without government or legal interference [Ridley, 132–133]. Paradoxically, when the government insisted on passing laws, the managers and lawyers demanded very specific rules. If the lawmakers insist on rules, then specific rules are better than general ones. Specific rules are easier to circumvent.[32]

The arguments of the managers who have been accused of breaking the law in the 1980s were almost identical [Clinard & Yeager, 67–73]. The same language; the same arguments. But the violations of the 1980s aimed at increasing corporate profits (and only indirectly benefiting the managers). In the past 25 years, corporate violations brought direct benefits to management in the form of enormous compensation, such as the compensation of the New York Stock Exchange's CEO.[33]

The attacks on the current law divert attention to other subjects. Business groups blame the laws for the economic downturn and for limiting the emergence of startup companies.[34] The recent Sarbanes-Oxley Act, which converted some financial frauds into criminal offenses, was blamed for slowing the recovery of the stock markets and diluting the quality of corporate boards. The *Wall Street Journal* cited critics who blame state politicians and federal regulators for increasing the financial burdens on corporations.[35] The Act was characterized as a step against capitalism, imposing added expenses, more work, and more hurdles on publicly traded small corporations. Some companies are escaping the public securities markets and their regulators and are "going private," although the reasons for these developments are not necessarily the new regulation.[36] These arguments are supported by theoretical studies, as described in chapter 6, attempting to show that laws exacerbate problems, and that the markets without laws can resolve most problems that may arise. Corporate management and scholars criticized the Sarbanes-Oxley Act as an "overreaction." But George Melloan, in an op-ed piece entitled "Give Thanks for the Resilience of Corporate America," declared that corporate America is sufficiently strong to "overcome these laws."[37]

The *Research Reports* of the American Institute for Economic Research went further. It seemed to suggest that the states would do a better job in regulating the issuance and distribution of securities in national and international markets. In an article titled "Why Have an SEC?" *Research Reports* said: "Few economists now believe that the 1929 stock market crash was an important factor leading to the Great Depression of the 1930s (especially in comparison to the variety of misguided monetary, fiscal, trade, and regulatory policies of the period)." The crash was used as a "convenient scape-goat for the politicians."[38]

The *Research Reports* called for a return to the 1920s, before the establishment of the federal SEC, and scrapping the SEC altogether. In fact, Associated Press reported that a transition team for President Reagan recommended changing the focus of the SEC from enforcement and regulation to encouraging private investment.[39] But the recent approach and the timing of these sharp criticisms are new and quite fresh.

The *Research Reports*' proposal is not realistic. It can bring unanticipated results. It can be more burdensome than the federal regulation, because state regulation is not standardized and is far more intrusive than federal law.[40] Enforcement by state prosecutors can be more aggressive than the federal enforcement, as the recent litigation by the attorney general of New York has shown. Therefore, those who attack the SEC may be wise to think twice before they ask for the return to the laws of the pre-1929 era. The current defiance of particular business leaders may reflect in part the ongoing investigations and court proceedings, which drive to denial. Denial may also reflect the management's perception of public sentiments. If *regulation* is a dirty word, even in the mouths of trusted persons who abused investors' trust, government is perceived as the enemy of successful businesses and shareholders alike.

Blaming Investors. Blaming others, even in part, reduces the guilt, shame, and responsibility of abusers. Blaming the victims establishes a reciprocal arrangement, in which both parties are at fault. This attitude shifts the burden of preventing fraud from the managers to the investors' self-protection and market enforcement. The legal wrong fades away. This attitude may start with "I wronged them. But they had it coming" and then develop into "It is their fault. They had it coming."

In many popular newspaper articles, investors are called "greedy"; they have no one but themselves to blame for their losses. They trusted, and did not verify. They relied too much on others, and not enough on themselves. Investors are called "gullible and greedy"[41] by the *Economist*; "ignorant and greedy" by the editor-in-chief of *On Wall Street*;[42] "lazy," "irresponsible," and "greedy" for demanding more than their fair share of corporate profits by a columnist in the *Cleveland Plain Dealer*.[43] A reader's letter chastised employees who lost their retirement pensions for taking unjustified risks and expecting the 1990s stock prices to continue rising.[44] They should have diversified their holdings, wrote a columnist in the *Honolulu Advertiser*.[45] A chief financial officer, commenting in *CFO.com* on the fall of Enron, advised small investors to follow the famous investor Warren Buffett and never invest in companies whose business the investors do not understand. "Investors wanted unrealistic growth and high returns, management served them to the best of their ability, taking a healthy portion of the returns for themselves along the way. . . . Secondary players are advisors, auditors and the SEC, including Congress."[46] "Greedy" investors were blamed for their stock market losses in the 1990s, because they invested in "risky Internet startups with no earnings."[47] Greedy investors are responsible (together with others) for the decline in the price of "tech" stocks and the weakened telecommunications industry, noted the *Chicago Tribune* and RCR Wireless news.[48]

Investors shared the responsibility of their losses with the managers. In his weekly radio show, the mayor of New York

> condemned as a 'disgrace' the alleged fraudulent accounting by corporate giants . . . [but] went on to say that those who had been buying stocks at multiples that 'never made any sense' should also look at themselves in the mirror. 'They're as responsible, I think, as those who actually committed the crimes of misstating earnings and fudging the numbers,' Mayor Bloomberg charged. [49]

Similarly, Representative Michael N. Castle of Delaware declared that the "blame for the Enron scandal is widely shared by the company's officers, board, auditor, ratings agencies, stock analysts, and even greedy investors." Both management and the investors were interested "'in keeping the stock price high' at whatever cost, he said." "Shareholders have the same interest," except that "they can't do anything about it."[50] It was they who contributed to Enron Corporation's fall (together with management). In sum, investors were blamed in one breath with management for the bubble of the 1990s. They deserved their losses.

Management connected the blame and justification more clearly. Investors not only expected more than they were entitled to but also *forced* corporate managers to feed the market bubble. On December 16, 2003 the *Wall Street Journal* published an article by Bill George, one of the stalwart leaders of American industry, entitled "Wanted: Authentic Leaders." Among his arguments, he noted that the "root cause" of the corporate scandals was the strong pressure to serve the short-term interests of the shareholders. "This mania for making Wall Street's numbers is at the heart of why some CEOs cheat and others have simply mismanaged."[51] In addition, investors are destroying the productivity of management. An article in *Variety* argued that investors who initiate litigation against companies are "distract[ing] management from day-to-day operations."[52]

"Greedy Investors" Are Not So Bad.   The more generous commentators suggested that "greedy investors" should not be blamed for their losses but called them greedy nonetheless. An editorial in the *Toronto Star* noted that losing investors were retired or low-income people and blamed "people who call themselves financial advisors" for the losses. And *Marketing Week* in the United Kingdom argued that investors should not be blamed as greedy or stupid for demanding higher returns in U.K. investment companies.[53]

These blames put the losing investors' imprudence and gullibility on the same level as the management's abuse of trust. Management's greed and investors' greed are at the same level. The leaders' blame was equated with the followers' blame. The managers' responsibility was lowered by the degree of responsibility that the victims were expected to bear. The deceivers and the victims have become participants in a joint venture.

Not all these justifications can be rejected out of hand. There are laws that are too detailed. They not only micromanage business operations unnecessarily but also, as I will discuss later, undermine the spirit of the laws by narrow interpretation. To survive, enterprises may have to meet fraud with brands of fraud of their own. In this section I describe how fraud is justified as protection against harm and how abuse of trust becomes part of everyday life.

Redefining Wrongs

The way to eliminate a wrong is to redefine it. Justifying fraud does not eliminate it. It reduces the responsibility for it. The way to eliminate the wrong is to redefine it.

Redefining Starts with Denial. The ideas of Senator Daniel P. Moynihan in his article "Defining Deviancy Down" are prophetic. He describes the redefinition of deviance by "normalizing" situations that the community can no longer afford to recognize as wrongs—presumably, when the wrongs are too prevalent. "Here we are dealing with the popular psychological notion of 'denial.'" There is no "sense of rage," as Judge Edwin Torres of the New York Supreme Court wrote. That is when "the crime level has been *normalized*."[54] An interesting aspect of the same result is offered by Michael Young: "People with aspirations to power over others are always reinterpreting old customs to their own advantage, trying to shift them so that others will accept their own authority both as a new fact in their society and as properly time-hallowed" [Young, 99]. Reinterpretation creates change. Anchoring the change in the more familiar customary behavior makes the change easier to accept.

Moynihan's article offered an insightful analysis of the pressures today. By defining what is not allowed, we know what is allowed. This definition allows us "to live by shared standards." But the definition does not remain fixed. There is misbehavior that society chooses not to notice and not to control. When prohibited activities become widespread and unenforceable, society cannot "afford to recognize" these activities as violations. At that stage, society redefines the prohibitions and makes the activities legal.

Moynihan wrote:

> The amount of deviant behavior in American society has increased beyond
> the levels the community can "afford to recognize" and . . . accordingly, we
> have been re-defining deviancy so as to exempt much conduct previously

stigmatized, and also quietly raising the "normal" level in categories, where behavior is now abnormal by any earlier standard. This redefining has evoked fierce resistance from defendants of "old" standards, and accounts for much of the present "cultural war" such as proclaimed by many at the 1992 Republican National Convention.[55]

In other words, there comes a point when the wrongs are widespread, and the situation cannot be tolerated. Society is faced with a choice. It can take strict measures to prevent the wrongs. Or it can redefine the wrongs out of existence in the direction of a different culture. In an interview published by the *Harvard Business Review*, Eliot Spitzer, the attorney general of New York, referred to Moynihan's ideas, and said: "There has been an incremental dissipation of standards over time. We grow more comfortable with improper behavior in steps. . . . The real issue we're looking at is conflict of interest—how it starts and how it gets institutionalized."[56]

Moynihan describes three categories of redefinition. The last one is *normalizing*: "the growing acceptance of unprecedented levels of violent crime."[57] In the context of the recent financial scandals, the same category appears. We can repeat Moynihan's words but substitute "abuse of trust and deception" for "violent crime." This would leave us with "*normalizing*: the growing acceptance of unprecedented levels" of abuse of trust and deception.

Redefining starts with denying that an action is wrong, and attacking the law. It is the law that is wrong. This is the way in which some academic writings theorize about corporate governance. By reducing the rights of the shareholders, they increase the power of management. Exalting the enormous capabilities that are necessary to manage large corporations, Professor Steven Bainbridge explains that the shareholders *voluntarily* limited their ability to exercise their votes. Unless such limits were imposed, and unless the management was freed of accountability to shareholders, management would refuse to offer its gigantic talented services. And where would America be then?[58]

In a 2003 article in *Business Lawyer*, Martin Lipton and Steven A. Rosenblum explicitly diverted attention from abuse of trust and deception to question the shareholders' rights. The issue is not honesty, the two renowned corporate lawyers wrote. The issue is how to cater to talented management and induce it to offer its able services. The issue is how to give management the support and the resources and, presumably, the necessary compensation to entice management to accept managerial positions and enable management to perform its functions. Putting the issues in these terms blurs the focus on abuse of trust, diverts the attention to the managers (potential accused), and elevates their status. The issue of honesty becomes a nonissue.

The next step of the authors is to eliminate the wrong altogether. They attack the shareholders' rights as owners of the corporation.[59] That eliminates the very foundation of abuse of trust. If shareholders do not have the rights of the owners, the managers cannot abuse such rights. The shareholders are posited as selfish people who care only for money and profits. The managers are posited as the repositories of the corporate good, the arbitrators among the shareholders and other claimants to the corporate largess; the trustees of the corporation, the economy and the country, and the keepers of global welfare.

Forgotten in this model is the managers' accountability for the claimed increased power. Their possible abuse of this power is swept aside. By attacking and diluting the claim of the shareholders to power, the managers increase their own, and free themselves from accountability. After all, the corporation is a legal entity, not a person who could supervise abuse of trust. The economy and the country are social systems. They can hardly serve as monitors and enforcers of honesty. Management's actions are no longer wrong; they have been legitimized. Their accountability is further limited. Now, if they increase their compensation, only the "corporation, the economy, and the country" can supervise their activities and complain. It is not surprising that this approach mirrors the enormous amounts that corporate managers have collected in the past decade and their sense of entitlement to these amounts. *Business Day* noted that corporate managers express a surprisingly strong feeling that they deserve, and have a right, to whatever money they have taken or considered earned.[60]

Redefinition Can Be Accomplished by Exemptions and Relaxation of the Rules. During the 1990s, legal constraints on business were sometimes relaxed. Many statutes contain avenues of escape by exemptions that Congress and the regulators can offer. For example, Enron Corporation received an exemption from the Investment Company Act of 1940,[61] as well as the Public Utility Holding Company Act of 1935.[62] These exemptions were based on certain assumptions about the business strategy of Enron, as described in the application. Later, Enron changed its basic business strategy and engaged in prohibited activities.

Traditionally, in the United States, business and politics interact through lobbyists and contributions. The 1990s were no exception. Congress exempted energy and minerals commodities from the jurisdiction of the Commodity Futures Trading Commission.[63] As the *Wall Street Journal* reported, Enron Corporation lobbied successfully for this legislation and escaped regulation under that Act.[64] During the investigation of Enron, Senator Fred Thompson said: "The real scandal here may not be what's illegal, but what's permissible."[65]

THE CALMING VOICES: NOT TO WORRY

Just a Few Bad Apples

Time and again, one hears the assertion that the recent revelations of abusive behavior concerned "just a few bad apples." In October 28, 2003, I participated in "Mutual Funds Under Fire," an episode of *On Point* on WBUR public radio.[66] The representative of the mutual funds trade organization asserted that the problems involved just "a few bad apples."

Just a few bad apples, other speakers assert, do not affect the economy or the financial system. Sadly, these statements are inaccurate. As the information in this book demonstrates, the few bad apples have turned out to be too many to ignore. They include too many people from all walks of life and too many horrendously dishonest leaders. Too many investors lost too much money, and too many savers lost too much of their life savings.

In the Market We Trust

Assurance that there is nothing to worry about comes also from the believer in the market as the spontaneous solver of most, if not all, problems. As Michael A. Currier writes, the adherents "put their faith in the market, believing that it can solve problems better than the government."[67] This trust was reintroduced powerfully by Friedrich A. Hayek in support of his objection to government interference in the markets [Hayek, 1:39–43, 2:115–120]. His approach commands a school of thought and a strong following.[68] In the antitrust context, economist Alan A. Fisher and attorney Robert H. Lande said that "the market frequently works more quickly than does federal antitrust enforcement."[69] Matthew Sanderson suggested that if an economic hypothesis of the efficient capital markets were accepted, there would be no need to regulate the securities markets. In his opinion, the theory will become the market reality.[70] The efficient capital markets hypothesis means that the market stock prices represent all the information available in the markets. The price has already absorbed, digested, and adjusted all available information. There is no need for legal requirements to disclosure.

Some of the arguments are revisited in chapter 6, but a thorough discussion on this subject is not necessary to support or refute the message of this book. The question is not merely whether the markets can ultimately resolve these problems but also how and when the hoped-for resolution will come. Being spontaneous, the road to the final solution may be worse than the problem. If you let people drive their cars as they wish, bullies will have their way. The road may be lined with horrendous accidents. If we wait for a solution to the problem of fraud, the spontaneous solution that takes too long may lead to a culture of fraud, at very high cost to America's way of life.

Fraud Is a Natural Cyclical Phenomenon

One argument for calming the concern about the current environment is that the recent experiences are part of the normal state of events. Fraud is cyclical, and the current period is part of the cycle. Fraud rises in good times. Legal prosecutions rise when the good times are over. As Thomas H. Noe and Michael J. Rebello describe, after fraud is discovered, only highly ethical businesses survive. As these businesses reestablish investors' trust, less ethical businesses use the opportunity to masquerade under the same ethical umbrella. Their actions dilute the reputation of businesses for ethical behavior, and the cycle starts all over again.[71] This interpretation suggests that the markets and corporate management can automatically correct weakness in ethical behavior. If this interpretation is correct, then we have nothing to worry about. The markets will take care of the problem, if there is a problem.

Yet, even if this interpretation holds for the market in products, it may not apply with the same force to the market in securities. It is possible that investors would not be able or willing to invest the time and effort necessary to distinguish between the true and honest businesses and the fraudulent ones. Knowledgeable investors might not share their knowledge with other investors. The trades of sophisticated investors may be too opaque to guide unskilled investors. Such unskilled investors may trust all businesses until some businesses fail, for whatever reasons, including illegality. The invisible hand may produce the wrong signals and the wrong results. If deception and abuse of trust become accepted and legitimized, the market will enter a new phase, the phase of deceivers leading the blind. Or it may shrink, as those who were hurt will refuse to engage for fear of being defrauded. Or the price of shares will fall, representing the investors' discount for uncertainty and mistrust.

The danger is not in these scenarios. The danger is not in the existence of a cycle. The danger is that any of these scenarios will become entrenched, because no one would believe in the cycle, even if it arrived. In that case, the base of the cycle will move up. Fraud will fall, but not as low as before. Trust will rise, but not as high as before. Then a new cycle of fraud and falling trust will begin, and the cycle will spiral up for fraud and down for trust. For each step forward in reestablishing trust and honesty, we will move two steps backward by undermining trust and honesty. Of course, this scenario is speculative and cannot be proved. But neither can the precise measure of the cycle theory.

Serious Fraud Is Not New to the United States

America has a history of fraud and abuse of trust. Daniel Drew, born in 1797, a generous and ruthless businessperson, spent his life amassing a fortune by defrauding others, including the money mogul Cornelius Vanderbilt and the public shareholders of Erie Railroad [Drew, 139–154]. The robber barons, such as J. P. Morgan, were not very different from Drew and his kind. Try mentioning fraud on Wall Street and Main Street, and your listeners will perk up and supply names and events on the spot. Individual con artists have prospered in our United States for a century. Even before the rise of the financial markets, con artists would visit communities and persuade the simple folks to part with their money. In the 1920s, an Italian immigrant, Charles Ponzi, drew $9 million of investors' money (or, as he claimed, $15 million) in a fraudulent scheme that carries his name. The scheme is alive and well to this very day; it has merely reappeared in modern versions.

Besides, what seems to be rising fraud today could be merely the result of increased transparency and flow of information. Not only is more information publicly available, but more information can be verified more easily by debates and proofs.[72] To be sure, both true and false information is more available today. While the Internet is a breeding ground for misleading tales, as is described in chapter 6, the Internet is also the home of verifiers who make it their business to check for proof of the truth of important statements by important public officers. Perhaps the greater availability of information can help detect violators and police their deceptions.

Whether the status quo is maintained by heightened transparency remains undetermined. Yet this is not the issue. What is more important is the impression that information leaves, whether true or false. If the impression that everyone is fraudulent is not refuted by information that many are honest, then the impression can affect people's honest behavior. The "herding" effect may result in acceptance of such behavior, since "everyone does it" even though relatively few in fact do it. The warnings against fraud may result in an attitude of distrust, whether justified or not.

In addition, American society has been polarized. The pitch of the debate and the fervor of the contentions have raised incentives to "plant" true and false information and to "snitch," for honest or other motives. As a result of these developments, reporting has risen, but the reports may contain truths, half-truths, and even lies. It is costly to ferret out the truth, and, as I shall show later, it is not easy to determine what truth is. Confusion and uncertainty can rise with the abundance of information, and that may lead to suspicion, mistrust, and an impression that "everyone is not telling the whole truth."

New technology has facilitated new types of frauds, such as the employment of drugs to enhance body performance. Before the use of steroids was publicly known, the users could win by deception, seeming to be better than they truly were. After the frequent misuse of drugs became public knowledge, most competitors continue to take drugs, even though the benefits are no longer great, and even though it is prohibited by the rules. Thus, competition is again on the merit (including the use of steroids), the rule on the books has become less effective, if not a dead letter, and presumably the harmful effects on the competitors have become the acceptable risk of taking part in certain sports. Other technical areas may experience a similar development. They raise opportunities for fraud, then become known, and are incorporated in behavior, regardless of the laws on the books. Yet the "known frauds" remain harmful. They become known and acceptable violations of the law. Unless the law is unjustified, "known frauds" will continue to corrode public trust in the legitimacy of the law.

Even if the frauds of the past are similar in kind, in range, and in relative number to those of the 1990s, the *reaction* of both the leadership and the population to the frauds can differ from the reaction to these frauds in the past. Therefore, the issue is not the nature of the frauds. The issue is how abuse of trust and deception are viewed. As compared to the past, there is greater acceptance of abuse of trust and less condemnation of abuse. There are far more justifications of abuse and less support for the law, the regulators, and the prosecutors of the wrongs. There are many suggestions to legalize the activities that are currently illegal rather than to enforce and strengthen the prohibitions. There is a change in the *attitude* toward dishonesty.

Therefore, the concern is that America is moving toward a different culture: a culture that tolerates and accepts dishonesty as a "fact of life."

Investors' Trust Is Not a Problem

In the past, investors' trust has been lost and regained. In 1977, a partner of the auditing firm PriceWaterhouse wrote that "public confidence in the American corporation is lower than at any time since the Great Depression. In this atmosphere, American business and the accounting profession have been called on the carpet for a kind of zero-based re-justification of just about everything we do" [Clinard & Yeager, 188]. And yet, the markets rebounded. When frauds were revealed, Congress passed stricter laws and sanctions, and regulators enacted tighter rules and increased prosecution of violators. Investors continued to flock to the markets, and America managed to develop a vital economy and a world-renowned financial system. Then things calmed down, life went on; laws, rules, and regulations were relaxed—until the next crisis.

Today, investors are still holding and trading in securities. Besides, selling stocks that declined in price does not necessarily prove loss of trust in the financial system. Even after the market plunge, "the market is still pretty rich by historical standards." In fact, Michael Lewis finds reasons to celebrate scandals, and suggested in the *Los Angeles Business Journal* that business fraud has "instill[ed] greater investor trust in the markets."[73]

And yet, investors could have held on to their stocks, even as they lost trust in the markets. Tax shelters and pension funds, which investors hold in the billions, can be "golden handcuffs" that chain investors to the stock markets. If investors sell their stocks, even at a loss, they may have to pay enormous amounts in taxes. Besides, tax deferral plans can be attractive to investors, even in times of very low returns, the *Wall Street Journal* noted.[74]

Besides, the best judges of investor trust are the corporations and the legislators. They have an interest in "taking the investors' pulse." There is one signal suggesting that corporations feel the need to strengthen investors' trust in them. More successful corporations have begun to pay dividends to stockholders. Unlike creditors (banks and bondholders), shareholders cannot require corporate managers to pay dividends. The managers decide whether to pay. So why have more corporate managers decided to declare dividends, when they did not do so in the recent past?

The managers' reactions demonstrate their own belief that the shareholders are not as trusting as before. By issuing dividends, the managers reduce the cash at their disposal and show a voluntary readiness to limit their own discretion—a sign of integrity. Dividend payments may give shareholders a real or illusory image of being creditors, implying less management discretion. The payments reflect bondholders' benefits: fixed periodic income and lower risk.

The suggestion that managers value equity financing more than debt financing contradicts one of the most illustrious theories of the great finance economists

Merton H. Miller and Franco Modigliani. They asserted that dividend policy is irrelevant to a firm's valuation.[75] They also argued that a firm's capital structure does not affect the market value and the cost of capital to the firm. Barring transaction costs, it does not matter whether corporations finance their operations by issuing equity or debt.[76] So why should corporations pay dividends, and not borrow instead?

The answer is that Miller and Modiglian's theories were based on assumptions that eliminated many aspects of the real markets. Using more realistic assumptions, later theorists disputed their conclusions. Stephen A. Ross argued that signaling may affect the managers' incentives and consequently the firms' capital structure.[77] Sudipto Bhattacharya, Kose John, and Joseph Williams suggested that dividend payments signal to the markets that a firm is in a good financial condition.[78] The dividends offer positive insider information without disclosing the details. Therefore, corporations that sense lower investors' trust pay dividends to show their management's honesty. As John A. Weinberg asserted, "with trust comes an enhanced willingness of investors to provide funds, resulting in reduced funding costs for the business. That is, the behavior of corporate insiders is disciplined by their desire or need to raise funds in financial markets."[79] The assumption is that without proof of honesty, the corporations' cost of capital will rise.

Congress has also reacted to the perceived weakening of the shareholders' trust. After all, political leaders are in touch with their voters-investors. The actions of the legislatures signal the concern that investors are losing trust in the stock market, and the legislators should know. In the recent crisis, congressional reaction was swift and drastic, evidenced by the Sarbanes-Oxley Act.[80] The regulators took aim at deception of analysts, broker dealers, and underwriters.[81] And prosecution of top and middle management is continuing.

This reaction, the story goes, is similar to that of the past. Therefore, there is no basis for worry. After a while, the country continues on its way to greater prosperity. If the past is any indication, America will overcome the scandals and continue to build, develop, and flourish.

No Need to "Overreact"

Kate Berry reported complaints of executives of Southern California public companies about the costs of complying with the Sarbanes-Oxley Act, and called the Act "an overreaction that creates an enormous and unreasonable burden for smaller public companies."[82] Burton G. Malkiel, writing in the *Wall Street Journal*, warns of the danger of regulators' overreaction to the recent financial scandals. Drawing from past government behavior, he wrote, "some abuses are not amenable to a legislative solution."[83] Alan Murray emphasized the warning of the Federal Reserve Board chairman "that the dangers of overreaction to the Enron scandal are large" and declared that "the embrace of the markets over the past 25 years produced one of the greatest periods of prosperity in history; a harsh repudiation of markets would have the opposite effect."[84] Martin Lipton, the New York securities lawyer, wrote that "in our efforts to restore confidence in our markets, we must guard against overregulation and overzealous prosecutions, as these may stifle the recovery of our economy."[85] These are strong arguments against passing prohibitive laws. The signals adopt a negative attitude to law. They aggressively preach the return to "business as usual." Spoken by corporate leaders and the heads of the financial system, they denigrate the law by their very statements, and signal to followers to take a similar attitude.

Little, If Anything, Will Change Anyway

There is also the "hopeless" approach. It results in the same "do little or nothing" argument. Whatever will be done will change nothing anyway. Ken Brown of the *Wall Street Journal* suggested that "despite the bursting of the stock-market bubble, the discrediting of analysts' research and exposure of a slew of accounting tricks that companies use to make their financial figures look better, the earnings-management game is alive and well on Wall Street." Legislation changed little. Professor Lawrence D. Brown said, "'I don't believe there's been a change' since the passage of the Sarbanes-Oxley Act last year and other reforms."[86] Corporate leaders who were charged with grand larceny, use of corporate assets as security for private companies' debts, and obstruction of justice "will put up a good fight in court," the *Economist* noted. They are not likely to be harshly punished.[87]

In sum, there is a strong movement toward accepting today's environment. Everything is fine. Everything is as it should be. Everything is as it was before. Besides, attempts to change the existing structure are bound to fail. So why try?

The Popular Reaction to White-Collar Crime: From Condemnation to Acceptance

White-collar crimes are different from violent crimes. Embezzlement seems less threatening to individuals and to society than assault or robbery. The psychological pain from abuse of trust and the losses from misappropriation of property are less life threatening. In addition, some white-collar crimes are very complex and hard to understand, especially when committed by corporations and other large institutions. These are more easily dismissed. Besides, even though everyone understands that corporations act through people, the people are less prominent. The corporations themselves are "personalized."

These may be some of the reasons for the view that people condemn white-collar crimes less passionately than they condemn violent crimes. In 1939, Edwin H. Sutherland, a famed sociologist and criminologist, wrote a book in which he argued that white-collar criminals are not treated like other criminals. In fact, the procedures used against corporations are different from those used against individuals, and hide the criminality of their actions. The effect, he noted, is to eliminate the stigma of the criminal offenses [Sutherland, 52–53]. In his opinion, one factor in the difference was the weak public reaction to white-collar corporate crime [Sutherland, 56–60].

Sutherland maintained that Americans do not view white-collar criminals as criminals. This position has been strongly repudiated by a number of studies. In 1982, John Braithwaite wrote an article entitled "Challenging Just Deserts: Punishing White-Collar Criminals."[88] Braithwaite reviewed a number of studies going back to 1929 and discovered that, contrary to Sutherland's theory, the American public viewed white-collar crimes quite seriously.[89] Sometimes the public even advocated harsher punishments than the punishments for equivalent street crimes. Indeed, one study found that people wanted to punish a $300 auto repair fraud more harshly than the street theft of the entire auto—a result we can presumably chalk up to the abuse of trust by the auto mechanic.[90] There is less controversy about public attitudes in the post-Watergate era. That period brought a great backlash against abuses of trust and power. Many studies of white-collar crime boomed in that period;[91] and, as Braithwaite shows, the majority of them consistently pointed to strong public sentiment against such crimes.[92]

There are anecdotal stories to the contrary, showing that ordinary people accepted fraud in the past and viewed honesty as naïve and stupid. In 1966, Fred J. Cook, in his book *The Corrupted Land: The Social Morality of Modern America*, described the grief of Douglas Johnson, who found a bag containing $200,000 that fell off an armored car and returned the money. He received from the grateful corporation a $10,000 reward. He got unbelievable abuse from fellow workers, neighbors, and even strangers, who sneered at him and called him "a fool" [Cook, 9, 11]. "Douglas Johnson's experience," wrote Cook, "illustrates a fundamental truth about modern American Society: it is a society in which money has become its own ethic—and so a society in which the morality we practice is virtually the reverse of the morality we preach" [Cook, 13]. He lamented: "A Jay Gould or a Jim Fisk might amass millions, rig the stock market, and engineer the virtual collapse of the national economy; but their deeds did not set a standard the public felt free to ape. Wealth could always command power, but not respect. Today it commands both" [Cook, 13].

This description of a society that has discarded Protestant ethics and substituted for it "borrow, spend, buy, waste, want" is interesting, because this attitude prevails in today's America and is considered good and beneficial. Cook passionately disavowed the "fanaticism of religious bigots to the shibboleths of *free enterprise* and *rugged individualism* and *laissez faire*, the dilutions that prevent our grasping the realities of our time." He continued: "in such a society private greed rules," and he denounced "private profit ethics as *the* goal in the mass society" and called it corruption of ethics [Cook, 331–333]. What Cook called corruption 40 years ago is accepted as a justified goal in society today. Another 1963 book reached a similar conclusion. Scandalous behavior was no longer the domain of "spectacular creatures." It was more generally acceptable. And even though people will not originate frauds, the swindlers' ways have been "sanctified" [Goodman, 4–5].

How should we interpret these statements and stories? Either the writers exaggerated and generalized from too few cases, or they were right, and the America of the 1960s was indeed as they described. If they exaggerated, then today's popular spread of the fraud is even more serious. It shows that the trend described in these books had roots even 40 years ago, and will be harder to uproot. Alternatively, if the writers did not exaggerate, and the America of the 1960s was as they described, then the ideals they represented seem not only to have faded away but also to have been rejected by many members of political, academic, and corporate leadership. And the type of wrongs that they described are far milder than the ones of today [Goodman, 14].

The weight of the evidence suggests that between 1929 and the 1980s, ordinary people condemned white-collar crimes. The recent attitude toward similar crimes is markedly different. Ordinary people, including the young, point to corporate and other white-collar crimes to justify their own deceptions. It is not the nature of the abuse that has changed as much as the attitudes toward the abuse. It is more accepted and justified and, at the extreme, is redefined out of existence.

A New America?

The arguments that all is well in the United States are inconsistent with evidence to the contrary. Blaming the current problems on the investors, the law, the government, and the legislators is questionable. The sharp disagreements about the roots and effects of the recent revelations demonstrate a new twist in America's approach to deception and trust. They present not only debates about the details but disagreements about the very basic meaning and need of honesty and trust in society.

That is the danger. This danger, however, is speculative. As the arguments at the end of this chapter demonstrate, there are explanations for the frauds that we see, and they may lead to the conclusion that nothing needs to change. The new America merely knows more and is wiser today than it was in the past. It sees things as they really are, and no one can "pull the wool over America's eyes." Even assuming that these proofs, positions, and explanations are correct, they do not lead to the conclusion that all will be well in America. That is because America's perceptions and reactions to fraud can change America's behavior.

Defrauded people can reciprocate and retaliate. They can start "paying" for fraud in the same coin, and treat others as their defrauders treated them. They can mimic their abusers in their daily affairs. Today, this possibility looms large and real. This pattern of behavior is more accepted and justified. Too many in America, including institutions and individuals in many areas of life, are becoming too tolerant and too comfortable with deception and abuse of trust.

No one knows whether this trend will continue. But if it does continue unchecked, America may become a society in which trusted people use guile to gain trust and then abuse it in order to maximize their profits. If these patterns of behavior become entrenched within the leadership, its dependents, and its followers, another America will emerge. We may wake up to discover not merely new scandals but a new America, changed beyond recognition. It will be an America shrouded in skepticism, suspicion, and retaliation by fraud against anyone, as a matter of habit. Shady actions at the expense of others will be justified and even admired, so long as they are not detected or punished. Americans will assume that everyone is looking for opportunities to profit from such actions, and this assumption may direct their own actions and competition. They will both look for innovative ways of deceiving each other and develop innovative ways of protection from each other. Trust will become irrelevant and unreal, a figment of an idealist's imagination. Even as a remote possibility, this scenario must be taken seriously.

3

Toward Abuse of Trust and Mistrust

O<small>NE OF THE MAIN THEMES</small> in this book is trust and its opposite or reverse reflection—mistrust. This chapter explores the importance of trusting relationships, their current status, and the direction in which they are moving in American society. After a basic definition I examine trust and its benefits. Next I discuss the paradoxical nature of trust and ways in which people seek to resolve the paradox. Finally, I view modern times that increase the benefits of trust and the dangers of its abuse.

T<small>HE</small> D<small>EFINITION AND</small> I<small>MPORTANCE OF</small> T<small>RUST</small>

In this book, trusting others means "believing that others tell the truth and will keep their promises." Trust is a relationship. That component makes this straightforward definition as complicated as humans and their society.

With few exceptions, trust is essential to economic prosperity. Thousands of people contribute to the sustenance and comfort of each of us, our dress and lodging, transportation and communications, education and entertainment. If we could not rely on the wholesomeness of the food we buy, the expertise of our physicians and lawyers, the honesty of our banks and mutual funds, or, as Sweeney Todd noted, the trustworthiness of the barber with his sharp shaving razor, our lives would be far more primitive. In the words of Alan Greenspan, chairman of the Federal Reserve Board, "trust is at the root of any economic system based on mutually beneficial exchange. In virtually all transactions, we rely on the word of those with whom we do business. Were this not the case, exchange of goods and services could not take place on any reasonable scale."[1] Trust has a crucial role in promoting prosperity. Trust saves time and money. It allows people to believe other persons' statements without checking their truth, and to rely on other persons' promises, without demanding guarantees. It allows people to use the talents of strangers [Fukuyama, 23].

But there may be exceptions. Poor communities, such as the Eskimo community, may have deep trusting relationships.[2] Perhaps, in the hostile natural environment, Eskimo societies would not survive without trust. In contrast, Russell Hardin notes small communities controlled by despotic masters that survive or even prosper on mistrust.[3] He argues that spreading mistrust can be useful, under certain circumstances, for example, to prevent prisoners from forging trust relationships and thus prevent riots and disruptions. Political competitors may spread mistrust of each other to their advantage. Yet these strategies may be dangerous in the long term. For example, when prisoners discover the truth, they may turn in fury against those who separated them by lies. Political competitors may find that spreading untruths about each other is not a healthy strategy to build public trust. Business enterprises may have reached the conclusion that stirring mistrust in competitors is not a good idea. Better to emphasize one's own trustworthiness and the advantages of one's products than become subject to competitors' counterattacks. But Hardin is also correct. Not all cooperation is good. Cooperation among persons for antisocial or cruel purposes, for example, can be bad.[4]

Carol Rose has shown that, in theory, it may be irrational to trust or to be trustworthy. But the theory applies only in short-term situations, and when no emotions or other elements are in play.[5] In other words, the theory applies to hypothetical humans, not real ones, and to hypothetical societies, not real and prosperous ones. These exceptions to the rule that trust is crucial to our lives have not fully convinced American society and its lawmakers. American law protects trust and punishes its abuse.

The Paradoxes of "Trust but Verify," "Rely but Remain Independent"

During the Cold War negotiations with the Soviet Union, the late President Ronald Reagan often borrowed a Russian proverb: "Trust but verify."[6] This statement drew chuckles. It seemed to be a contradiction in terms. After all, the very purpose and value of trust is to *avoid* checking the truth of what trusted persons say and the reliability of their promises. Yet, President Reagan (and Russian folklore) was right. There are reasons for encouraging people to trust each other. There are reasons for encouraging people to protect themselves from each other, and for criticizing those who unreasonably rely on others.

Thus, trust presents a paradox. To survive, individuals must both trust others and protect themselves from others. The cause of this conflicted need to trust and yet verify seems to be rooted in the very nature and existence of humans. Without the support of others, humans cannot survive the dangers of the elements or provide for their needs. But if they rely on others, humans may not survive the danger of other humans' treachery. Wariness and alertness reduce our risks from others. Wariness has an added advantage. It helps discover opportunities that would not be revealed if we fully relied on others. Thus, as we trust, we must also exercise a degree of caution. This leads to a second paradox.

To prosper, individuals and society must specialize. One look at the shopping mall in the United States shows enormous specialization and its blessings. No one person or company can supply all the riches that are offered in that mall. To achieve this result, each person and enterprise must devote its energies and talents to a particular function. To enjoy the fruits of this specialization, individuals and societies must rely and depend on each other for products, services, and knowledge.

But in order to specialize and create, individuals must become independent. Independence means precisely the opposite of relying on others. It means doing things for yourself, thinking for yourself, and deciding for yourself. And yet, only by relying on others for the things we need do we have the time to develop our own expertise (on which others rely). Therefore, the benefits of trusting others are accompanied by risks (and cost of self-protection). The benefits of relying on others are accompanied by the danger of undermining our independence from others.

THE IMBALANCE AND BALANCE BETWEEN TRUST AND VERIFY

The Balance between "Trust" and "Verify" Depends in Part on the Particular Society

Timur Kuran and Cass R. Sunstein note that the society in which we live affects the risk from other people's deception and the acceptable level of trust and mistrust.[7] Years ago, a person who visited a Mediterranean country told me the following story. A father puts his four-year-old son on a high stone wall and says: "Come, jump down. I will catch you." The child hesitates, and the father repeats the promise. After a few more assurances the child jumps, and the father steps aside. The child falls on the hard ground and begins crying. The father kneels lovingly, picks the child up, and says: "This will teach you a lesson not to trust anyone, not even your father!" The implication for the child is broader. If the father is allowed to be untrustworthy, so can the child be untrustworthy. The lesson is: "Do not trust and do not be trustworthy."

A recent essay, "Trust and Trustworthiness among Europeans: South-North Comparison" describes a "Trust Game" that students from different cultures played. The results of the game were that players from the northern cultures discriminated against those from the south not so much for being untrustworthy but for not being trusting. "Southerners are being punished for their own low level of trust (i.e., having a low propensity to contact another player with a generous offer)."[8] This means that the northerners value not only a society of trustworthy people but also a society of trusting people.

In other societies, persons who break their promises are either shunned or cannot be financially successful over the long term. For example, in the United States, reputation for honesty is important to profitable trading on the eBay auction system. Traders are rated by the parties with whom they deal, and the rating is published, thus determining the traders' reputation. Persons with lower reputations offer greater risks to the people with whom they deal. The eBay system operates as an auction. Therefore, those with reduced reputations will sell for less and buy for more. The offers of such persons will attract fewer offers or will cause the offerors to discount the prices for the risk in trading with low-reputation persons. The system provides an incentive to be honest. "A good reputation allows economic agents locked into the relation to cut the transaction costs and overcome limited information, and thus to facilitate efficient contractual relations" [Misztal, 121–39].

The Balance between "Trust" and "Verify" Depends in Part on Costs and Benefits

When the cost of verifying the truth and honesty of the other party is negligible, and the potential losses from the transaction are relatively low, there is no need to trust. In such a case, neither party has to prove its honesty. Each person can verify the facts for himself. The buyer of a newspaper need not trust the seller, because the buyer can verify the nature and price of the paper and check whether the middle section of the Sunday paper is missing. Because the buyer does not have to trust the seller, the seller will not invest in guaranteeing his honesty. The seller does not have to trust the buyer either. The exchange is simultaneous: money for a newspaper. Therefore, neither party must trust the other.

For Small Investors, the Potential Costs of Trusting and of Verifying Corporate Honesty Are Very High

In contrast to newspaper buyers, investors who seek a mutual fund advisor to manage their life savings, must trust the advisor. That is because it is very costly for them to verify the truth of the advisor's stories and the reliability of the advisor's promises to act for the benefit of the investors and not to treat the entrusted money as his own. Small and large investors cannot continuously check the honesty, truth, and reliability of advisors. Investors very rarely have the necessary information, or the qualifications, to judge the advisors. Besides, if investors have to closely control the advisors, they would not have the time to engage in their own activities.

The risk to investors is very high. Trusted persons do not break into investors' homes to take their money; they are offered money and assets voluntarily and even eagerly. Controlling enormous amounts of money could be tempting. There are so many easy-to-hide ways to help oneself to benefits from other people's money. Unless reminded time and again, and unless abuse-preventing mechanisms are in place, trusted persons might forget that entrusted money is not their money. Used to controlling other people's money, they may even begin to feel a sense of ownership and find reasons to justify it. Therefore, investors must rely on guarantors and verifiers in the markets, on the advisors' reputation, and on the law and the government to continuously maintain a high level of advisors' honesty.

The Economic Impact of Failure to Trust or Verify: The Market for Lemons

Verifying information and honesty has economic effects. Trusting persons may choose to pay for information about the honesty of the persons with whom they deal, or to pay for verifying the truth and reliability of their promises. Alternatively, trusting people can factor the risk of abuse of trust into the price of the item they buy. The higher the buyers' risk, the lower the price will be. In many such cases, and especially when the market is competitive, trusted persons will supply and guarantee the truth of their information and their reliability in order to gain a higher price. And if providing the information and guarantees is too costly, other guarantors may intercede, including the government. Or, for lack of trust, the parties may not interact at all, no transactions will take place, and the market will fail, as George A. Akerlof explained in his famous article "The Market for 'Lemons,'" which will be discussed in other parts of this book.[9] Thus, Robert Prentice concludes that if investors cannot distinguish between true and false information, for example, in corporate financial statements, they will tend to reduce the offered price for all corporate shares, both true and false, or not invest at all.[10]

Imbalance between Trust and Verify—Gullibility, and Vulnerability to Deception

The word *trusting* is usually reserved to reasonable trusting. Unreasonable trusting is called by another name. It is called *gullibility*. Trust draws sympathy. Gullibility draws little sympathy. In business relationships, people expect a measure of reciprocity, playing by the market rules and the dictates of an exchange. Deceivers intentionally take without giving, or without giving back enough, as expected. Perhaps gullibility in business relationships is condemned for a similar reason. Gullible persons unknowingly and unreasonably give too much, or give without receiving enough, as expected.

Investors, who should know better, will be called gullible if they are drawn to the promise of large profits and invest even if they see signals that the investments are too good to be true. These investors are like the person who believes that the Brooklyn Bridge is for sale. Their belief is closer to faith.

Imbalance between Trust and Verify—Faith, and Vulnerability to Deception

Like trust, faith is a belief. But, as the Merriam-Webster Dictionary tells us, unlike trust, *faith* is a "firm belief in something for which there is no proof" [*Merriam-Webster's Collegiate Dictionary*, 418]. I would add that faith is a belief for which no proof is sought. It is an unquestioning belief. It is trust without the need for verification. A person can say to the other: "I have faith in you." That would mean belief without "ifs" or "buts" or doubts. Usually the word *faith* is reserved to a belief in something that cannot be proved, such as that the human race will overcome its treacherous tendencies. Mostly, the word *faith* is used to describe belief in God.

Faith supports unlimited trust and reliance. People need to belong to a society of others, and religion is one way in which they congregate for mutual support. Religious impulse evolved early on in society. Religious groups may survive better than groups that are less cohesively organized. Religion includes many aspects of group experiences, equality of membership, and satisfaction of other social needs [Wilson, 5, 47–61]. A religious bond can exist even among strangers. Thus, religion is strong emotional and social glue. Religion does not inculcate in the group members the negative need for protection from each other. That is because there is no drive to be protected from the God in whom the members believe. After all, one cannot protect oneself from God's wrath. This unquestioning shared faith is transferred to members of the group. There is less need for protection against group members and fellow worshipers.

The shared faith and trust in each other makes such groups vulnerable to deception. They "trust" but do not "verify." The problem arises when some individuals in the group create a "sting operation" that defrauds the others. As Wilson notes, like other such situations, when there is opportunity to abuse and no protections, someone may try to abuse. Churches provide white-collar criminals with vulnerable groups of potential victims. The business sense and independent judgment of the congregations' members are dulled by their reliance on others. A large number of criminals use a church and appear under its mantle to persuade the victims. Jim and Tammy Bakker, a television evangelist couple, raised over $66 million to build a development in which the buyers were promised a lifetime shared vacation place and religious activities. But only 52 percent of this amount was used for this purpose. The rest of the money was spent for operating expenses and financing the lavish lifestyle of the Bakkers and their entourage [Tidwell, 74]. Among such charlatans were managers of church plans for the poor, such as Alice Faye Redd, who hosted many fundraisers for the church.[11] A charity can fall prey to fraud. In the largest charity fraud in history, charities lost $350 million.[12] Thus, religion can make its adherents vulnerable to fraud.

Affinity Groups and Vulnerability to Deception

Like religious groups, affinity groups are vulnerable to fraud, for similar reasons. Members share values and tastes, and, most important, often trust each other. When a fellow employee introduces an investment, the other employees are not inclined to investigate closely. In Australia, the *South Australia Advertiser* reports, a large group of police officers invested in a fraudulent scheme, and up to 200 police agents, including the wife of an Australian federal police commissioner, lost their investments.[13] They trusted too much and verified too little.

The Balance between "Rely" and "Remain Independent" Is More Personal Than a Cost-Benefit Analysis of "Trust but Verify"

Reliance depends on the needs and values of the parties and the society in which they live. For example, children must rely on others more than knowledgeable, healthy, and wealthy adults must. But whether to rely or maintain independence depends greatly on social attitudes. As a society, Americans present an enigma.

The perception is that Americans value and prefer independence. Yet Lawrence E. Mitchell argues that the American theme of independence and self-sufficiency is a myth [Mitchell, 10–28]. Americans attempt to maintain their independence while depending heavily on others by relying on institutions and systems. This solution is crucial; and that can explain the danger that American society is facing today.

An effective way to increase trust is to establish trustworthy institutions and reliable systems. In spite of the risks, Americans are trusting people. They are proud of their independence and their ability to protect themselves from deception by others. Thus, we trust and rely on others, but we also seek independence and rely on ourselves.

If you were to ask most Americans, you would likely find that they rely on their financial system perhaps more than they rely on their brokers, advisors, and investment bankers. You would also find that they trust the law perhaps more than they trust the lawyers, judges, and regulators. Americans have long felt confident in and admired the corporate system perhaps more than they trusted corporate management. Today, their trust in management is wavering, but it seems that their trust in corporations and financial institutions and the legal system is still intact, even as it is being doubted more than before.

Trust in institutions is also linked to modern times. "While in the past routine was connected to tradition and rituals . . . in modern societies [it is] integrated into the system of institutions"[Misztal, 169]. Trust in institutions, systems, and ideas is impersonal, unattached to any particular individual. After all, a system is a concept, or an expected pattern of behavior, within an organization or in society. A system can be inanimate, like the solar system, which is believed to behave in a certain way. A system (even a chaotic system) may reflect a more predictable and less fickle pattern than the behavior of particular individuals. A system also signifies a consensus, or at least a significant following. Perhaps because Americans value individual freedom and independence, they trust their systems with something close to passion. This impersonal relationship allows them to "herd" by their own free will, without subjugation. This attitude may be one reason why Americans are so attracted to the invisible hand of the market system, its signals and its promises.

Besides, it is efficient to trust institutions. Checking out the other parties to a relationship is costly. Throughout life, most people form personal, long-term relationships with not more than a couple of hundred people, 500 at most. Because the number of institutions is smaller than the number of individuals, it is less costly to check out institutions before trusting them. In addition, trustworthiness is easier to verify if it is limited to a particular context. Impersonal trust in business relationships is similarly "tailored" to a context. For example, a bank verifies the borrowers' creditworthiness but little else. This limited context allows a bank to develop an efficient system to verify the creditworthiness of customers (or employ more persons to do just that).

While people can personally rely on a small number of businesses and few employees, trusting large institutions can expand reliance on thousands of employees, even if the employees are unknown and even if they change over time. While it is impossible to develop personal relationships with so many, it is possible to verify the honesty of the institutions that support their employees' honesty. Thus, trust in corporations with hundreds of thousands of employees, managers, and contracting parties, is efficient for the customers, for the institutions, and for the economy as a whole. Americans are the masters of efficient organizations. No wonder they trust their own creations.

Americans' trust in institutions is not complete, nor is it blind. Perhaps the American experience involving serious frauds has introduced demand for guarantees, not only of individuals but also of institutions. America is covered with layers of private-sector guarantors of trust. Some guarantors are in turn insured by the government or by institutions that are supervised by the government.

Driver's licenses are the prevalent form of identification. They are backed by the government. But on the Internet, credit cards have evolved into the most used form of identification—more than driver's licenses. That is perhaps because the picture in the driver's license cannot help to identify the sender online. In addition, banks have historically guaranteed transactions among strangers, for example by letters of credit.[14] And even though the banks issue the credit cards and not the government, the government strictly regulates the banks and ensures their reliability. Bank promises and obligations are covered by a number of guarantors. Their deposits are insured for up to $100,000 by the Federal Deposit Insurance Corporation. They are regulated by the Federal Reserve Board. State banks are regulated by their state agencies, and federal banks are further regulated by the Office of the Comptroller.[15] Their rise as guarantors of payment and identity in Internet transactions is logical and efficient. It is based on trust in the banks as institutions.

Private Sector Guarantors of Trust

The American private sector is populated with many guarantors, such as lawyers, accountants, advisers, commercial and investment bankers, rating agencies, credit card issuers, and Internet "verifiers" such as Verisign and eTrust. All provide services to reduce the cost and risk of trusting, and all allow people to rely on others.

Organizations That Vouch for Members

An efficient way to strengthen trust is to create organizations that check out and guarantee their members' trustworthiness. Physicians, lawyers, accountants, investment bankers, and broker dealers belong to such organizations. These organizations regulate their members not only for the protection of their clients but also for the protection of their own reputations. The organization of the broker dealers, the NASD, doubles the effect of its members' honesty with the backing of SEC's regulation. Organizations such as the bar associations are also regulated by state regulators and sometimes by the courts. Physicians and pharmacists have a self-regulatory system backed by government regulation.[16] These organizations are not entirely public service oriented. They serve the interests of their members as well. The American Bar Association is the guardian of the lawyers' turf. It imposes high entry costs that serve to keep down the number of lawyers (although the number of lawyers is high as compared to the number in other countries).[17] The American Bar Association offers members continuing education and networking. It created the American Bar Foundation, which supports research that is relevant to lawyers. Other professional organizations serve as the guardians of their members' financial interests. Whether the objectives of establishing trustworthiness are subsumed in the self-interested objectives can be debated.

Why don't banks and insurance companies organize to self-regulate? They need to establish a high level of trust, yet they don't need self-regulation or private guarantors. That is because the government strictly regulates them, and their obligations are backed by insurance funds that are controlled by the government [Malloy, 1:1.2–.3, .69–.70]. Another explanation for the absence of self-regulatory organizations of banks and insurance companies is that their members are too diverse in practice and size. Therefore, they must be regulated in different ways. By implication, however, it's the need for a guaranty of trust that primarily drives the creation of self-regulating organizations.

Trust Can Be Established by Indirect Evidence

Networks and reputations establish trust. For example, the parents of a newborn infant ask friends to recommend a reliable pediatrician. People seek opinions of friends about lawyers. Reputation for ability and honesty is established over time, not necessarily by direct contact but often through a network of clients and patients. Reputation can be established by newspaper articles written by or about a person. Rating agencies establish the reputation of corporate debt. By inviting parties to rate the reliability of those with whom they deal, eBay has established a system of reputation for individuals. Public polls have the same effect. As I shall show, when recommendations are paid for, or when the recommending parties have no expertise or personal experience in the matter, reputation may be laced with deception.[18]

TODAY'S CHANGING ENVIRONMENT

In modern society, mobility and communications have increased the opportunities of dealing with strangers. These opportunities bring enormous benefits and greater dangers. In small, stationary communities, people trusted mainly those they knew long and well. Their opportunities to benefit were also limited to the members of the community. Strangers had to earn the trust of the community they passed through or joined. These communities were not immune from fraud, however. Con artists occasionally visited and sold "snake oil" and medicines laced with whisky to eager buyers. There were towns described in Wild West stories that could be very open to strangers. Yet none compare to the opportunities and frauds of today.

Today's cell phones, television, and especially the Internet have created a habit of trusting "virtual people." Mobility and quick interactions among people blur the difference between friends and casual acquaintances. In the networking mentality of business circles, people often confuse exchanging business cards with "time-tested relationships" [Walsh, 122]. People often assume that sharing the same occupation means sharing the same level of trustworthiness. These assumptions can be wrong. But it is too costly to check every person that one meets in conferences and business engagements. Yet many opportunities are lost in avoiding meeting people also.

Thus, as profitable opportunities from interacting with strangers have increased, people have been risking deception and abuse of trust. Even if they verify the other party's identity (when communicating by telephone, fax and on the Internet), the available information can be false. If they could not establish the honesty of the other party, people attempt to verify the other party's statements and promises, and that increases costs.

The Shift from Trusting to Verifying; from Reliance to Independence

In the past three decades, the government and private-sector leaders, law, and the markets have urged trusting people to rely on themselves. The law has lowered the cost of verification. For example, the law requires trusted persons in securities transactions to provide investors or clients with relevant information. Medical personnel and hospitals offer patients information. But once they receive the information, the burden is shifted to the trusting persons—the patients. They receive cheaper means of verification rather than evidence of trustworthiness. The shift to verification is likely to reduce trust; the shift to independence is likely to reduce reliance. As the following chapters show, the shift to verifying and independence does not necessarily reflect a cost-benefit analysis. Rather, it seems to follow an ideology; a belief that human nature is self-centered, selfish, and prone to dishonesty and that the markets will protect people from each other's harm by helping them to protect themselves.

The developments during the past three decades threaten people's trust in institutions. The stories unfolding in the news, the courts, and Congress raise the question: Can we trust the corporations, the institutions, the guarantors of trust, and the financial system as a whole?

4

Toward Deception

DECEPTION AND TRUTH

In this book, not only trust but also truth and deception involve relationships. Like trust, truth and deceptions are complex, precisely because they involve humans and their society. Groups tend to adopt one system by which the members define and measure truth, and each group can have its own, and different, system of truth.

Truth depends on the "truth system" in which the information is communicated. A truth system is a set of principles that defines truth, and the information that proves what is true. A reader may say: "It is not true that America is moving toward dishonesty. You have not shown it. You have it all wrong." That is because the reader has adopted for this issue a "truth system" that rejects the information this book offers and demands more or different proof. Another reader may accept the evidence in this book and hold it to be true. The two hypothetical readers disagree about the principles that define truth and the information that proves what is true. Suppose I tell a story in humor. If a person does not know that the facts I described are meant as a joke, my truth is distorted. The reverse is also true. If the facts are true and are taken as a joke, my truth is distorted. If a person shows much suffering on the theater stage, but the spectator does not know that the sufferer is an actor, the truth in one truth system is distorted. But if the sufferer is not acting, and the spectators think he is, the different truth system subverts the meaning of what the spectators see as truth.

However, when a lie blatantly contradicts one system of truth, it signals to the reader that the system of truth in which the lie is told is different from the first one [Hyde, 70]. Readers know that the poetic description of clouds as sheep floating in the sky is true in the system of poetic truth, even if it is untrue in our everyday truth system. Pablo Picasso's paintings do not lie. Viewers recognize that his painting of a woman's face does not mirror the face of any woman in the viewers' truth system. Therefore, the painting does not deceive the viewer. It declares another system of truth—that is, the system of the painter.

Practical jokes, acting, and games need not deceive. Americans are willing to laugh at themselves, and some feel quite good about making fun of others. P. T. Barnum was a practical joker and a great American entertainer. His family and the village in which he was reared relished a good practical joke and retold it for years. He was known for the saying: "There is a sucker born every minute." R. J. Brown, on the website "History Buff," expressed doubts whether Barnum even said it, and suggests that Barnum's competitor said it.[1] After all, Barnum was not about to humiliate and offend his vast audiences. But he did play jokes on them, and they loved him for it. They loved his museum, his fake mermaid, and his circus. He knew how to draw attention, to build expectations, and to whip up curiosity to a frenzied pitch. This was a significant part of the pleasure he gave.

Barnum manipulated, but he did not deceive. Like theatergoers, Barnum's audience knew that they were about to play the "marks" and paid to be tricked in his museums [Werner, 56–64]. The truth system of the activities was entertainment. He took their money in exchange for fun. In contrast, the investing public expects another kind of truth from the sellers of securities, because investments are not usually considered entertainment and are expected to bring returns.

Honest liars tell the truth about their lying. The system in which they deliver their information, such as the stage, or the film, or the circus, puts the spectators on notice that they are witnessing deceivers, not true-acting persons. Deceivers send the opposite message—that the spectators are witnessing true-acting persons, not deceivers.

Deception Depends Not Only on the Falsity (Nontruth) of the Message but Also on the Party Who Received It

"A liar seeks to accomplish his purpose by creating a false belief in his interlocutor, and so he may be said to do harm by touching the mind, as an assailant does harm by laying hands on his victim's body" [Trebilcock, 103–104]. "Deceit and violence— these are the two forms of deliberate assault on human beings" [Bok, 19]. But deception is different from physical abuse. So long as the other party knows the falsehood, he or she is not deceived. And if the information is ambiguous, some people may be misled while others may not. There is a difference between deceiving an uneducated and uninformed party, who is conditioned to intellectual obedience and cannot easily uncover the truth, and deceiving an educated and informed person with an inquiring mind who is able to distinguish true from the false. The first is like a blind man, who cannot protect himself, and the second is like a person who can see, who can protect himself.

Still, this kind of nondeception is very different from the kind of deceptive messages that actors send from the stage. When a person feigns illness and suffering to gain sympathy, for example, his friends are not deceived if they know that he is not ill. And yet, the person is a liar. Unlike the true actor on the stage, this person "acts" in our truth system, which requires that the person who acts "sickly" be truly sick. It is this type of deception that is linked to abuse of trust. Even if we know the truth, we also know that such a person does not tell the truth. He is not likely to be trusted.

Fraud affects not only the deceived but also the deceiver. Some people may enjoy manipulating others, and some may look for the benefits that come from their deception. Some people continuously plan deceptions and manipulation. They lack or lose the sense of "right" and the discomfort and shame that honest people feel when they defraud. Such deceivers affect themselves and their colleagues, their children, their spouses, and their friends. When their circle shares the foggy view of honesty and deception and values the fruits of such behavior highly, this behavior spreads an attitude of accepting or justifying deception.

THE FOG OF DECEPTION

Human communication can mislead. Communication is a complex composite of signals, "not just a transfer of information like two fax machines connected by a wire. . . . It is a series of alternating displays of behavior by sensitive, scheming, second-guessing social animals." Communications by words are not perfect. Genuine communications can attempt to deliver the meaning that speakers intend to share with their listeners [Trebilcock, 116]. But these messages can be misunderstood. Misleading messages can be believed. A clear, bright line is hard to discover.

Some of the most intentionally misleading statements are found in the corporate disclosures of the 1990s. Corporations expressed concerns for the shareholders while at the same time they delivered misleading "revenue growth" that was achieved by "secretly offering huge discounts" to get rid of "dead inventory" and by inflating profits [Lowenstein, 61]. IBM had a practice of bunching single sales with administrative expenses, which gave the impression that these were costs. When asked about this practice, an IBM representative answered that its accounting was "within the letter of accepted industry practice" and "fully compliant with regulatory standards" [Lowenstein, 61]. To measure the growth of these misstatements, Roger Lowenstein notes that the number of "companies that were forced to restate earnings because of accounting errors rose from a handful a year in the early '80s to more than 150 a year by the late '90s" [Lowenstein, 62]. According to the Wall Street Journal, that number grew to 323 in 2003.[2] Intentional or not, their statements were misleading.

Silence can mislead. The notorious Charles Ponzi was a master of deception by silent signals. As Ponzi tells the story in his autobiography, he opened a demand deposit account in a Boston bank. He deposited a very large sum of money in the account, and made no withdrawals for about six months. This inaction led the bank's officials to assume that the account was "dormant"—that is, that the money would remain in the account over the long term. Therefore, they invested the amount in long-term obligations that brought a higher return. One day, Ponzi appeared at the bank and offered to buy controlling shares of the bank. The officials, who viewed this Italian immigrant with disdain, refused. Ponzi then took out his checkbook and demanded his money. But the bank did not have the cash; that amount was locked in an investment. The officials had no choice. They sold him a sufficient number of shares to give him control of the bank.

Ponzi did not deceive by words or by positive actions. His right to withdraw the money was unquestioned. The officials should have known better than to view a demand deposit as a long-term deposit, even if it was inactive. They should have made arrangements to cover the risk of a demand. But Ponzi signaled them through inaction [Ponzi, 99]. And they took the bait.

On the corporate level, Halliburton Corporation changed its accounting rules in 1998 for 18 months. The results of the change were to reduce losses or increase the dollar amount of revenues. The corporation settled with the SEC. It did not admit blame. The lawyer of one of the accused officers said in the Wall Street Journal: "We believe the commission is using a rather novel theory of disclosure, which is not supported by the precedent of the time. . . . There were no investors that were mis-led and no investor loss and no personal benefit to the executives of Halliburton."[3] What was missing? The missing information was the fact that the company changed the accounting rules for its financial statements, and that as a result of the new ac-counting rules, the numbers in the financial statements had changed. The silence in that sense was misleading, even when the executives of the company did not benefit from the (higher) numbers. However, changing the rules without disclosing the change and its impact may have indeed been the way things were done, and the company may have followed the "usual practice."

Names can mislead. Deception by name was practiced during the market bubble of the late 1990s. Securities "analysts," wearing the mantle of objective stock evalu-ators, were paid or pressured to recommend stocks that they considered worthless. They became salespersons. That was deemed illegal deception. As reported in the Wall Street Journal in May 2002, Merrill Lynch, the giant broker dealer organiza-tion, among others, agreed to pay a large fine for failing to control the analysts.[4]

But what was the analysts' deception in the first place? Why should analysts be singled out to be more informing than other sellers? Why should they disclose the sources of their fees and benefits? The answer is that the costs of checking securities and the amounts involved in investments are high, as compared, for example, to the cost of checking groceries and the amounts of money involved in buying food. There-fore, the buyers of the securities, even if securities and food are both called "com-modities," have different expectations. The name "analysts" and the traditional position of analysts signaled that analysts were professionals, expected to give ob-jective and disinterested expert opinions. So long as the customers do not know about the analysts' subservience to the issuers of the securities, the analysts should disclose to the customers the analysts' positions as salespersons. Otherwise, the analysts' si-lence is deceptive. But when it is publicly known that analysts have strong incen-tives to sell, they need not disclose their different incentives, because their silence on this point is no longer deceptive.

Why did the analysts fail to disclose their true function as salespersons? They did so for precisely the reason that rendered their behavior deceptive. They wanted to seem objective and trustworthy professionals. They wanted their clients to trust them more than the clients would trust salespersons. Had the buyers known the real pressures on the analysts and incentives that they were receiving, the opinions of the analysts would not be as effective. Hence the deception.

Actions can mislead. Facts can seem true but may give entirely false information. In the late 1990s, Tyco Corporation "crossed an ethical line, ordering dealers for one of its subsidiaries to venture into drug-infested slums and sign up any customer with a pulse, without regard to his ability to make payments. 'Tyco kept pushing. They wanted numbers,'" one manager said. They did not care if the buyers failed to pay later [Lowenstein, 74]. Thus, the installment sales to buyers who could pay only the first installment or two and could not possibly pay the full price counted as sales, and gave the impression of legitimate sales, which they were not.

The timing of true information can mislead. The *New York Times* reported that Warnaco Corporation capitalized the costs of opening stores over 18 months instead of the typical 12 months. This change helped the corporation to artificially inflate its earnings.[5] America Online used another accounting practice that was described as "legal" but "'financially aggressive.'" As the *Washington Post* noted, the corporation spread its expenses over a long period and took an immediate large charge against its earnings "to get the bad news out of the way in one big chunk."[6] In addition, by timing their disclosure of true numbers, publicly held companies manipulated the investors and analysts. As the *Wall Street Journal* described, companies waited until after the market closed to announce higher earnings than the analysts' unenthusiastic predictions. The next day, the marketplace overreacted, and the price of the stock rose significantly.[7] Professor Claire A. Hill examined companies that "window dressed" their financial statements by using accounting techniques to create an appearance of increased or "smoothed" earnings or reduced debt.[8] These companies were not lying outright. Their accounting techniques were usually disclosed in the fine print. But they nonetheless gave deceptive impressions, by spinning true facts. They produced impressions that misled most people, except the real experts.

THERE ARE LIES THAT DO NO HARM OR DO NOT DECEIVE

Deception can smooth social relationships. There are lies that are acceptable. These lies can ease social tensions for the public good [Bok, 174–191]. Deceivers need not necessarily hurt others. The truth may hurt more. Justifiably and by custom, sometimes people show friendship and even love when they feel neither. They give compliments that they believe or know are untrue; sympathize and admire when they inwardly criticize. Deceivers can be driven by a need to be liked, by conforming to norms of behavior, or by compassion. Deception can help avoid open conflicts. For some people, concealment helps retain excitement even in the closest relationships. "Little mysteries give intimacy its thrill" [McNeill, 241]. True, not all people prefer fake compliments, love, or the thrill of a mystery. Regardless, the point is that society does not condemn lies that stay within the acceptable bounds of social relationships.

Deception can be a legal and socially acceptable game, provided the players play by the rules. Poker players may, and indeed are expected to, keep their own cards secret, misinform the other players on what cards they really hold, and try to discover what the other parties' cards hold. But discovery is limited to the information that each player sends by facial or other signals (e.g., the number of cards a player asks to change). Hiding and discovering information depend on the players' skills. And all the players have the same information that each player sends. But if a player receives secret signals about the cards that the other players hold, he breaks the rule. He is deceitful and is condemned. A similar rule applies to lotteries. It does not matter what rules the lottery schemes adopt. What matters is that the lotteries are bound by a scheme, and that the scheme is being followed without exceptions. A lottery that announced one rule for picking a winner but in fact used another rule would be deceptive, even if the results of the lottery were the same in both cases.

SLIDING INTO DECEPTION: PYRAMID SCHEMES

Some deceptions are difficult to uncover because they are so similar to legitimate activities. Pyramid schemes are of this sort. They mirror the sale of products and services or franchising of businesses but are neither. The "investors" in these schemes are not true investors; most of them are looking for work. They are not true salespersons either; they sell neither products nor services. They are deceived, and deceive as well.

A pyramid scheme combines two usual and legitimate transactions to create an unusual sales force of a third, illegal kind. The scheme consists of two deals. The buyers—for example, of precious metals—pay part of the price in cash. They remain owing, say, 80 percent of the price. The rest of the price they can pay in commissions for selling precious metals. The buyers to whom they sell the metals also have the choice. They can pay the full price or cover it by selling more precious metals, and give their buyers the same choice, and so on.

Each seller receives part of the price of the precious metals that he sold, as commission (in cash or to cover the amount he owes on the precious metals that he bought). The rest of the price is paid to the person who recruited him. That person, in turn, retains part of the payment and pays the rest to the person, who recruited him. The money keeps climbing up the transaction chain until it reaches the only person who did not pay anything—the promoter of the scheme. The scheme is named after this feature—"a pyramid."

Enterprises can build pyramid distributions. Some manufacturers and service providers press all employees, from top to bottom, to sell the products or services.

The employees receive a percentage of the price of the goods they sell, and pass the rest on to their superiors. The superiors collect these earnings and in exchange support the employees-salespersons with services, information, and direction. In such a distribution system, the pyramid is relatively flat. A true sales-system cannot sustain more than five levels of markup on the cost of production. Above that, the price would become too high, and the products could not be sold.[9] In contrast, the number of levels in illegal pyramid schemes, that sell no product, is as high as the number of recruited victims. Although the illegal scheme involves a product, the product is unique, and often very expensive, and nearly impossible to sell. Investors turned salespersons discover that selling the "right to sell" is far more lucrative, and they follow the more profitable route. The legal pyramid-type scheme serves to sell products or services. The buyers are the consumers. The illegal pyramid scheme serves to "market" marketing. Most buyers are future distributors.

The case of David and Martha Crowe. The story of David and Martha Crowe was told in an episode of *America's Most Wanted*, "Capture Archives";[10] and in the case against the corporation through which they operated, that is, *United States v. Gold Unlimited.*[11] The couple founded a number of corporations, all offering more or less the same "Gold Matching Program." For a down payment of $200, participants could receive $800 in gold. The enticing part of the offer was that the buyers could earn the rest of the price, that is, $600, by selling the program to others. Every sale to others brought a stream of income to the recruiters.

Participants who paid $200 and recruited two investors into the program became a moneymaking "cell." As one court described it, the cells were

> much like cells in hierarchical organizations, with the original participant at the top and with two branches diverging from the center, each branch containing three recruits. For every group of three that joined the matching program, the original participant received a $300 commission toward the purchase of the laid-away gold. After recruiting two groups (six individuals), the original participant could take the gold or roll over the $600 credit into a new recruitment arrangement that offered a higher ceiling on commissions (conditioned on enrolling more participants, of course).

When their last caper that lasted four years ended, the Crowes left a large number of devastated investor groups. As of March 1995, 96,000 participants had paid $43,000,000 to the company through which the Crowes operated. The company paid participants $25,000,000 in commissions. Its profits from the sales of 12,628 gold coins produced $552,620.[12] The rest of the money was gone.

Where Is the Deception?

Pyramid schemes may be illegal, as may the distribution of unregistered securities.[13] They are illegal as fraudulent practices and were outlawed by the Federal Trade Commission as "nothing more than an elaborate chain letter device"; the buyers "are bound to be disappointed."[14] Investors buy "sure losses." Presumably, no one would pay to surely lose. But it's not that simple. Pyramid schemes typically benefit the early recruits, as Debra A. Valentine said in the case of *United States v. Gold Unlimited*.[15] That's part of the schemes' strength and attraction. Besides, lotteries, gambling, and entertainment can be legal, even though the players are often "disappointed" and even if they are "sure losers." Therefore, the prohibitions on pyramid schemes can be considered "paternalistic," protecting people from their own folly.

Are the schemes contrary to public policy? After all, they offer no social benefits. They produce nothing. Sell nothing. Buy nothing. They offer no pleasure or entertainment. Yet lotteries and gambling have similar features. Gambling may be viewed as entertainment, in which case it produces value for the gamblers. But lotteries offer no social benefits to the players and are not clearly entertainment. How do these differ from pyramid schemes that "redistribute wealth"? The difference is deception.

Pyramid schemes are "wealth distribution" by guile and gullibility. Compare the investors in the schemes to the buyers of lottery tickets. Few buyers view the tickets as "investment." Neither do they work for their prizes. They gamble. Pyramid schemes are sold as investments; but they are not. The "investors" rarely have money to invest. Promoters are drawing the victims by advertising in newspapers' "help wanted" sections. These advertisements imply job offers. The people who respond to the ads need work. But once they contact the promoters, they are drawn into buying "participations" in the scheme as a way of earning much more by selling.[16] In addition, the buyers of lottery tickets know that the chances of winning are very small, even if they cannot calculate the odds precisely. The buyers of the pyramid scams do not know the true picture, because they do not know whether they stand near the head of the pyramid or at the base. The schemes are therefore sold by deceit.

Most perniciously, pyramid schemes corrupt the victims. The schemes fan greed ("look at the number of dollars; get more"). There is something enticing and challenging in the image of the pyramid: "Oh! To climb to the top!" The schemes tempt the victims to cajole, induce, or defraud in order to recruit others. The victims are desperate to recoup the money they paid for the "investment." They approach family, fellow employees, and friends and induce them to "invest" and market. When the later recruits lose, close relationships may be marred for life, damaged by anger and suspicion.[17] The human cost of these schemes is high.

SLIDING INTO DECEPTION: ADVERTISING AND MARKETING

Advertising and the Market

Exchange in its various forms is indispensable to social interaction. In fact, not only humans but also primates have innate rules regarding exchange, reciprocity, tolerance for some deception in interaction, and drawing a line on how much deception is acceptable. Eugene Linden showed that primates in captivity learn to sell and bargain [Linden, 50–51, 70–72]. Primates can evaluate the demand of the "market," that is, zookeepers and spectators. They can negotiate and barter. My daughter, who worked with primates, described the behavior of chimpanzees. If an item falls into their cage and they are asked to return it, they learn to demand rewards, such as juice. But if they sense that the item in their cage is valuable (e.g., something that is dangerous to the animal, which the zookeeper wishes to retrieve quickly), they will demand not juice, which is their commonplace drink, but grapes, which they prefer and receive infrequently.

Advertising reflects demand and supply. When demand exceeds supply, sellers could limit their advertising to information about the availability of the products for sale. In some cases, the sellers do not bother to advertise at all. The buyers are waiting at the door. When I visited East Berlin in the 1960s, I saw no advertising, but a long line of people waiting at the shop for a ration of sausages. West Berlin was awash with advertising.

Abundance and competition press for aggressive advertising. After identifying the market for a particular product and the demand for it, the advertiser attempts to draw the buyers to his product. The advertiser can highlight what public users want and crave. That craving may have little to do with the product. The "Marlboro Man" macho image had little to do with smoking. The beautiful woman in the car has little to do with the car. But the cigarette and the car are now wrapped with these images.

The formula is to identify a market for a product, identify a "mass desire" of people, and then "channel that desire to a particular product." "Mass desire," the private desires that are shared by many consumers, is what makes advertising work [Schwartz, ix, 3–4]. Thus, the advertiser must relate the product to the desire. To the extent that the buyers are unaware of this connection (or lack of connection), the buyers are influenced by a combination of desiring the product and preferring the particular brand because it satisfies unrelated wants. The buyers may be manipulated but are hardly deceived. The connection between the (irrelevant) wishes and the product is not hidden. The Marlboro Man is on his horse, galloping over the plains.

There is another way to advertise, as William Bernbach taught two decades ago. He was a master who created the "We Try Harder" advertisement for the Avis car rentalcompany. He also came up with the name for a German car—the "Beetle"— in an era of large chrome-covered cars. The images that he built are linked not to the latent desires of the buyers but to the advertised product.[18] One can bring attention to the product by linking it to an innovative description or by linking it to latent desires. Recognizing the range of truth and falsity, Bernbach said: "All of us who professionally use the mass media are the shapers of society. We can vulgarize that society. We can brutalize it. Or we can help lift it onto a higher level."[19] How correct he was!

Suppose the salesperson exaggerates in his praise of his merchandise. The customer is not necessarily deceived; he expects the salesperson to exaggerate a little. In addition, the customer may know the truth about the deceptive information that he receives. At the other extreme is a less watchful and more gullible customer who is unreasonably trusting. Such a customer loses the protection of social sympathy and sometimes the protection of the law as well. The customer must balance his trust with some measure of verification. If he can easily check an item he is interested in buying, a customer should not expect the salesperson to describe the item with meticulous accuracy.

The balance between trust and verify depends on many factors. How often did the customer interact with the salesperson? If he has had a long-term relationship with the salesperson, he may trust more and seek less verification. What is the value of the items that the customer buys? If it is very expensive jewelry, it might be reasonable for him to seek an independent expert, unless the customer is an expert or knows and trusts the seller. The balance between "trust" and "verify" and "rely" and "remain independent" is a moving target. In recent years, advertising and marketing have pushed toward the need for more verification.

The Use of Celebrities

Some companies use celebrities to sell their goods to targeted groups. The celebrities are not salespersons but the adored leaders of a group or a pop culture. For example, a television commercial for caffeine-free coffee used an actor who played the role of a doctor on a television series, recommending the coffee to people. The commercial was successful and played on the respect given to doctors [Cialdini, 220].

There is some deception here if people can reasonably assume facts that differ from the truth. There may be no deception if, in the particular culture, buyers understand that the purpose of employing celebrities is to draw attention, no more. It is common knowledge that actresses at the Oscar festivities act as "shills" by wearing fabulous jewels on loan and beautiful gowns, perhaps as gifts. It is also known that some celebrities are richly compensated for endorsing products. No deception there. But "shills" may mislead if the buyers assume that the celebrities bought the items, and if people rely on the celebrities' judgment as to quality or future use of these items. So if a golf champion carries a certain kind of golf clubs, potential buyers may assume that he uses this kind of club. If he does not, the appearance with these clubs may send a deceptive message. So long as most people do not know about the use of "shills," their use can be judged as deceptive. Once the information is widespread, it is no longer deceptive. It simply means that the corporations use celebrities to sell by drawing attention to their products.

Wrapping Advertising in Misleading Appearances

There are situations in which advertising has been wrapped in misleading appearances. For example, an insurance company sends uninsured persons a "pink slip" or a "final notice" that is in fact an invitation to buy insurance. A registrar of domain names sends a "final notice" implying that the person who received the notice may lose his domain name unless he subscribes, when in fact the subscriber's name is registered with another registrar. A notice from a newspaper distributor entitled "Your Account Is Overdue" warns to have the subscription canceled, even though the recipient never subscribed to the paper and owed it nothing. Some people might mistakenly send the "overdue" subscription amounts. A bank sends a credit card with a $1000 credit limit, and a few months later sends a notice of late payment of $35 for managing this account. When the recipient, who has not used the card or the credit, refuses to pay, he is told that he must pay because he did not reject the card. A gardener who treats a lawn one season manages, without special authority, to treat the lawn the next season, and sends a bill, together with a threat of using a collection agency. When told that he was not asked to provide the service, he shows agreement forms that were never signed, which specify an annual service unless terminated. These are anecdotal and new situations.[20]

"Objective" Surveys and Polls

Advertisers have used "objective surveys," which are not entirely objective. A story in the *Wall Street Journal* told of Coca-Cola officials who ordered an objective survey of a new drink. The teenagers who were tested were offered the drink but also received a free lunch as part of the evaluation exercise. The teenagers liked the drink.[21] How objective was the survey? How misleading was the result? Are the results important to an adventurous customer who would like to try the drink anyway?

The disturbing aspect of this exercise is what it says about the people who prepared the survey and their ways of thinking. The information is presented as objective but is edging closer to an induced result. This trend could lead customers to worry not only about trusting the advertising (they do not) but also about trusting the producers of the advertised products. This foggy deception may induce competitors to follow the same innovative advertising technique and may induce customers to react with greater mistrust. Rather than rely on the "objective studies," they may wait for more evidence. Or they may offer lower prices for the products, reflecting their uncertainty about the quality of the product.[22] Consumers may mistrust and discount the price not only of the publishers of the "surveys" but also of the products of other surveys as well. Customers would do so if they found it difficult to distinguish the fake from the real advertising, unless they know and trust the manufacturers. The price of all such products may first rise, and ultimately fall, and their markets may shrink.

Polls, like "objective surveys," may not be objective. Pollsters have interests that conflict with objectivity. They are paid by the parties that are interested in specific results of the polls. How reliable are their polls? What if some polltakers agree to change the results of their research after they presented the result to the clients? How can the public distinguish between those who made changes and those who published the results regardless of the clients' desires? What seems to be an objective poll may not be objective.

Besides, "objective polls" may be the wrong term. Polls are far from a precise science. Their results depend on the choice of the people asked, the ways the questions are phrased, the questions that are omitted, the weight given to the answers, and much more. *Financial Adviser* reported a review of a poll by the Financial Services Authority, a U.K. regulator. The review found that the data was manipulated to reach the desired results.[23] Since polls are not precise, they hover in a gray area. If they are designed to predict a future outcome—the results of an election, for example—the polltakers are unlikely to influence the result. But if the polls are used as a selling device, then they may predict correctly, at least for the first wave of purchases. That is because the poll itself creates the results of its prediction by inducing the customers to buy.

Puffing and Other Techniques

Salespersons use known and effective psychological techniques of persuasion. Douglas Rushkoff describes in detail how salespersons may "puff" and exaggerate the virtues of their merchandise and services [Rushkoff, 6, 13, 33–35, 37–38]. Professor Avner Offer has elaborated on the salespersons' tendency to give gifts, a behavior that the buyers are expected to reciprocate by buying. Gifts may help reduce the buyers' inclination to return overpriced items [Offer, 211]. Salespersons attempt to forge friendships with customers to gain their trust. Some salespersons are conditioned to use these techniques, and some are just overenthusiastic about what they sell. In most cases, salespersons' behavior is not deceitful. They are expected to behave this way and therefore do not deceive the buyers. But if a negotiator of the deal is a *representative of the buyer*, gifts to the representative have a different meaning.

Suppose corporate top management decides to make a public offering of the corporation's stock. The times are good. Investors are clamoring for shares. The corporation needs financing. Top management makes its plans known. A number of underwriters knock on its door and vie for the underwriting business. The underwriters do not approach the corporation's shareholders, because shareholders are not authorized to choose the underwriter. The underwriters concentrate on management. The corporations extract payments from the underwriters to play. The underwriters promise management to buy more services from the corporations. The corporation, in turn, may use the underwriter payments to increase corporate revenues. The parties "squeeze" and extract payments from each other, averting their attention from their shareholders' interests.[24] Underwriters who vied for the business of selling municipal bonds begin to "pay to play." They make political donations to the elected officials who are in charge of picking the underwriters of the municipal bonds. The contributions influence the government officials. They might lean toward those underwriters who paid the most and contributed the most. The interests of the shareholders and citizens are not served as well as they should be. It took government intervention to attack this practice. Paul Maco, the director of the Office of Municipal Securities at the SEC, under Chairman Arthur Levitt, launched the campaign, and was fairly successful.[25]

Gifts can lead to conflicting interest. The gray area can begin with a bottle of wine at Christmas, evolve into a trip to Bermuda with the family, and end with the dot-com IPO stock that brings millions within a few weeks. The gifts of stock that corporate management received and the donations that elected officials collected were not publicized. The impression was that their choice of the underwriters was objective and disinterested. In fact, the choice was self-interested. It was deceptive and a breach of trust.

SLIDING INTO DECEPTION: DATA MINING AND PRIVACY INVASIONS

Culling Information

The cameras in large stores watch and record the actions, reactions, and expressions of shopping customers as they walk throughout the stores. Unobtrusively, changes are made in the stores to meet customers' needs or affect their wishes and buying habits. For example, it seems that, upon entering the supermarkets, most customers turn to the right. Hence, expensive items are displayed on the right of the stores' entrances. It was observed that many customers cease to examine a product when someone brushes against them. Therefore, aisles have been widened, allowing customers to avoid contact with others who pass by. Shoppers put more grocery items on the cashier's moving belt if the belt is wider. Therefore, the belts were widened. Some of these changes make customers more comfortable. Others help induce customers to buy more, pay more, or choose more of the items that the stores' owners wish to sell [Rushkoff, 103–107].

If the customers are not warned and not aware of these changes, and if customers would consider the changes important, then the changes are deceptive. But how many buyers do not know that they are being watched and measured to become targets of advertising? Besides, what is the harm of being watched?

Supermarket owners are entitled to protect their stores from pilfering, and some customers may welcome select advertising that results from the information that was collected. Would it really make a difference if the customers were aware of the use of their personal habits? If there is a conflict between the sellers' "mining" of customer personal information and the desire of some customers to protect their personal information from being mined, market forces can resolve it. Customers will show displeasure by going elsewhere. The situation of the banks is different. Banks that disclose customer information are required by law to notify the customers and allow them to opt out.[26] That is because banks have available far more detailed personal information on borrowers and depositors than do supermarkets on their customers. Ask a depositor or a borrower, and the answer is likely to be that they choose confidentiality. "It is no one's business how much money I own or owe."

The arguments on this score may be dead. It may well be that mining personal information is no longer deceptive. In his book *The Transparent Society*, David Brin shows that America is already a transparent society [Brin, 331–333]. There are pros and cons to personal transparency. There are protections against its abuse. So perhaps most people have given up the fight and accepted their loss of privacy. And even those who continue to fight for privacy are no longer deceived.

DECEPTION ACCOMPANIES WRONGS

Deception and abuse of trust are intertwined. In business relations, trust is abused when people are induced to hand over their property by deception, and when trusted persons misuse their power over other people's money. Deception often appears as the aftereffect of other wrongs or crimes. For example, as reported in *Forbes,* Martha Stewart was accused of attempts to cover up her alleged violations of the securities laws. These laws prohibit trading securities on the basis of insider information that was not available to the general public.[27] Similarly, the Justice Department accused the accounting firm of Arthur Andersen of "shredding" thousands of documents related to the Enron Corporation. It seems that the documents were shredded to cover up the firm's support of Enron's accounting irregularities.[28] Whether they committed the crimes or not, people may not lie to investigators, destroy evidence, and commit perjury when testifying in court. These deceptions undermine the enforcement of the law.

In addition, some wrongs lead to other deceptions. For example, embezzlers cannot declare their ill-gotten gains to the authorities, even if they wished to pay taxes. They are driven to falsify the accounting books and hide the cash in order to avoid reporting to the tax authorities. Tax evasion and deception thus become the prosecutors' tools when they cannot reach and prove the graver crimes. For example, Al Capone, who fostered gambling and prostitution on Chicago, corrupted the city's political machine and police, and ordered the murder of dozens of competitors, was convicted of tax evasion and sent to prison for five years. It was nearly impossible to prove the murders and widespread corruption that he introduced in Chicago. Tax evasion and his attempts to hide it were more possible to prove. His downfall was the purchase of a mansion in Florida. His declared income simply did not match the price for the mansion, and he failed to erase the trail that led to his ownership.[29]

In sum, we do not live by the rules of absolute truth and ironclad, guaranteed performance of promises under all circumstances. In fact, there is no consensus on what truth is. Even if there were a consensus, it is often hard to distinguish the fraudulent from the legitimate. Good intentions do not provide a clear test either. And much depends not only on the deceivers but also on those who deal with them, on the signals that the parties send and receive, and on their interpretation of these signals. Much depends on the assumptions that people make when dealing with each other and on their expectations. That, in turn, depends on the society in which we live.

THE CONSEQUENCES OF ABUSE OF TRUST TO SOCIETY

Abuse of trust and deception interact and feed on each other. Like a virus, they contaminate the social body. Abuses lead to mistrust and may ricochet with more of the same from each side of the relationship. The consequences touch the abusers, the abused, and the society in which both live. The abused may withdraw from interaction, or pay less, or protect themselves in various ways and impose costs on others that may revert back to them. And they may reciprocate and treat their abusers the way they were treated. But they may also get used to the treatment and behave toward others the way they were treated, or worse. As this behavior spreads, rising costs follow.

The Economic Costs

A 2002 report by the Association of Certified Fraud Examiners estimates the annual cost of occupational fraud in the United States at $600 billion.[30] These costs, however, do not reflect the losses from abuse of trust to other types of institutions. Calculate just the overstated earnings, frauds, and fines and settlements discussed in chapter 1, and you reach over $140 billion. In 2002 the General Accounting Office studied the restatements of corporate financial statements between January 1997 and March 2002. It found that during that period investors lost "billions of dollars in market capitalizations." On the average, from a day before to a day after the restatements stocks lost 10 percent of their value; from two months before to two months after restatements stocks lost 18 percent of their value.[31]

The precise number of frauds and their cost is unknown. The reluctance to report distinguishes fraud and abuse of trust from physical and violent crimes. We may not know the identity of thieves, robbers, and murderers, but we have a fairly accurate idea of the number of these crimes. Most victims will report the crimes and their losses. But in the case of financial frauds, the amounts of losses can be ascertained mainly from the reports of bankruptcy cases, and far less by the victims' reporting. The fraudulent companies are not likely to advertise their violations. Success is more likely to be publicized.

The disclosed numbers are mostly relative to previous years; they signal a rise of fraud.[32] KPMG's *International Fraud Report* of April 1996, already noted, emphasizes this point. It notes that "fraud is big business internationally. Reported losses are in excess of US$1 billion and no country is immune to the depredations of the fraudster." The report assumes that the $1 billion is the "tip of the international fraud iceberg" and that the losses are higher, in light of the limited sample and reluctance of the participants to provide detailed information.[33]

Researchers Patricia M. Dechow, Richard G. Sloan, and Amy P. Sweeney noted the rising cost of capital for firms that were caught engaging in financial fraud. They wrote: "Our results are consistent with the firms experiencing a significant increase in their costs of capital following the revelation that their earnings have been overstated."[34] Robert Prentice agreed, and extended this conclusion to firms that were found to have committed financial frauds in general.[35] Issuers with a reputation for honesty have lower long-term capital costs. Companies seemed to agree. They reacted to the possible loss of reputation. Between 1982 and 1989, 72 percent of the companies that were found by the SEC to have had accounting irregularities fired or forced resignations of their top management.[36]

The Cost of Self-Protection

Abuse of trust and deception lead to the victims' self-protection. Having discovered that they have been deceived, some people and companies seek ways to protect themselves. For example, insurance companies sought the help of technology to uncover fraudulent claims. The Los Alamos Lab has devised computers and software that dredge information and point to patterns of possible deceptive claims. These protections are costly.[37] Physicians, who have been subject to malpractice suits at an increasing rate and higher insurance costs, are looking for such protection as well. On April 19, 2004, the *National Law Journal* reported that physicians are beginning to use technology and databases to identify (and blacklist) patients who have had a history or are in the habit of suing physicians for malpractice. This movement not only protects physicians from malpractice suits but also excludes patients who have a legitimate claim from healthcare services in the future. There are physicians that refuse to treat litigation lawyers. Perhaps in the future they might refuse to treat any lawyer.[38]

To be sure, these actions may offer an opportunity to other physicians to serve the blacklisted persons. In such a case, market pressures will take care of this trend. Otherwise, society will bear a cost when part of the population is excluded from receiving important specialized services. Besides, these costs are not likely to stop with the physicians' retaliation. If blacklisting becomes prevalent, it is likely to trigger a regulatory reaction and some prohibition on discrimination. Where did this vicious circle start? As will be discussed in chapter 6, the image of physicians as trusted professionals in the public service has paled in the light of their focus on money and insurance costs. And with the change came the bitter medicine of predatory practices, from which they try to protect themselves. If they exceed the legitimate limits of protection, they may find themselves exposed to legal duties. This vicious circle brings financial and social costs.

Self-protection has appeared in other areas. The *ADP Advisor* notes that companies that are recruiting new workers employ special firms to verify the facts stated in applicants' resumes.[39] These services are not free. The costs are transferred to the clients or the shareholders—and ultimately to the system. In the final round, the costs also rest on job applicants. Conditioned by the misleading statements in resumes, the companies' interviewers adopt the attitude of care, suspicion, and perhaps initial mistrust.

Theo Francis of the *Wall Street Journal* has described how the recent spate of corporate scandals has raised the cost of directors-and-officers insurance, although the rise may have slowed, reflecting the pressures for more cautious and assertive boards of directors.[40] It is likely to slow down or reverse with more evidence that the boards are doing a better job of keeping excesses of management in check. All these guarantees have a price.

People who are invited to sit on corporate boards have become more cautious. "In Era of Fraud, Board Prospects Probe for Dirt" reads a headline in the *Wall Street Journal.*

> Not long ago, a friendly lunch with the chief executive would suffice to persuade a potential director to come aboard. But in this post-Enron era of heightened legal risks, and expanded duties and expectations for board members, candidates do a lot more homework before they take a seat—or decline the offer. . . . [One person] probed [the company] for nearly six months before he went on the board.

Some candidates ask to sit in on board meetings before they accept the position. The reaction of the executives varies. Some approve of the candidate's probing and would "cool" their enthusiasm if he did not probe; some disapprove of candidates who "asked too much, and would cool their enthusiasm the other way, selecting the ones that asked the least."[41] They are angry at being mistrusted. Thus, in an environment of mistrust, people demand from each other proof of truthfulness and guarantees that promises would be fulfilled. Demand for assurances denotes mistrust and may poison relationships. In addition, the guarantees cost.

A Suspicion-Discount: The Market for Lemons. In chapter 3 I discussed the insights of Nobel Prize–winner George A. Akerlof.[42] Akerlof suggested that the advantages of the informed party to a potential bargain could end up in its loss. In fact, the advantages could even end in undermining the market. The difference in the information between a seller and buyer is translated into dollars and cents. The less informed buyer would discount the price of the commodity. The market for used cars could collapse for lack of trust in the dealer, and for the high cost of verifying the condition of a used car.[43] Thus, even if the dealer did not abuse his trust, unless he establishes his trustworthiness or provides an independent evidence of the value of the car, the dealer will be offered less than he knows the car is worth. The seller must convince the buyer either to "trust" or to "verify."

The law can play a significant role in reducing the information gap among the parties, and in preventing the more informed party from using its advantageous position. In Massachusetts, for example, the law addressed the problem by requiring used car dealers to replace unreliable cars that they had sold or refund their price.[44] The assurance of the truth helps the honest dealer collect the price that reflects the worth of the car, and reduces the chances of misrepresentation by a dishonest dealer. He cannot hide its faults without breaking the law. Law can lower the losses from a market for lemons, but losses may still exist.

A Cascade of Dishonesty in Competition. Abuse of trust and deception can undermine the social value of competition. In business transactions, as in sports, American society encourages competition for a number of reasons. One reason is that competition motivates competitors to "push the envelope." Competition increases the pool of people with skills and persistence toward better results. This drive enriches society as a whole.

Competition by deception reduces a serious effort to win on the merits. If one competitor cheats and wins, others may refrain from further interaction. Or they may adopt cheating. Or they may seek better ways to cheat and win. In such cases, winning will depend not only on skills and quality products but also on creative deception. Attention is shifted from performing better to searching for more potent fraud. That trend may result in a habit of deceit. It may create a new breed of competitors who do not care how they win, so long as they win. When deception is discovered, the actors devote their energies to creating more original and effective deceptions. The main loser in this trend is society, as the pool of talented persons dwindles and the pool of talented swindlers grows.

Toward a Culture of Deception

In a number of businesses, hidden manipulation and persuasion by "soft" deceit make it harder to separate the more precise truth from its embellishments. They make it harder to separate the manipulation of human desires from information about products for sale. On the other extreme, lies can be known. If everyone knows that the information is false, then no one is deceived. In between, there is a range of possibilities, and the dividing line is unclear. Besides, in most cases, deception benefits the deceivers only if it remains unknown to the deceived. Therefore, once the truth is revealed, deceivers must create another lie in order to benefit. In addition, the benefits from deception must be hidden not only from the authorities but also from their competitors. Competitors might either "snitch" or copy the innovation.[45] In both cases, the value of the deception is gone.

If people often discover lies in their business dealings, they will begin to take them for granted and accept deception and abuse of trust as the "way things are." They will assume that everyone else is dishonest, including those with whom they did not deal. This assumption can become ingrained to form patterns of expectations and behavior that harden into a societal habit. Such a habit is difficult to uproot. "Basic assumptions," wrote Edgar H. Schein, "tend to be those we neither confront nor debate and hence are extremely difficult to change." Questioning our basic assumptions is also difficult for psychological reasons. The questioning invokes anxieties because it "destabiliz[es] our cognitive and interpersonal world" [Schein, 21–22]. These assumptions distort our judgment. "Rather than tolerating such anxiety levels we tend to want to perceive the events around us as congruent with our assumptions, even if that means distorting, denying, projecting, or in other ways falsifying to ourselves what may be going on around us." For example: "If we assume, on the basis of past experience or education, that other people will take advantage of us whenever they have an opportunity, we expect to be taken advantage of and then interpret the behavior of others in a way that coincides with those expectations."

Assumptions can distort the true reality. Cynical managers may not perceive how devoted the workforce really is. Idealistic managers may not perceive how incompetent the workforce really is [Schein, 23–24].

Repetition reinforces underlying assumptions as to behavior. "The binding force of custom [which in this book is called culture] is continuously recreated by cyclical behavior. Members of a group interacting together again and again in the same fashion generate not only solidarity with each other but also solidarity on behalf of the recurrent behavior itself" [Young, 100]. Solidarity need not be positive. People could be bound together by mistrust and even hatred as they are by love and trust. If people in society abuse each other's trust and expect others to do the same to them, most people will interact in accordance with these expectations; in addition, their actions will strengthen and reinforce dishonesty.

5

Toward a Different American Culture

THE PRECEDING CHAPTERS signal more than isolated cases. They show a trend that can lead to a change in American culture—a change that is in the making. The idea of culture is central to this book. It is the key to understanding the trend and, if undesirable, how to control it.

WHAT IS CULTURE?

Culture has many definitions. The *Merriam-Webster Dictionary* includes in the definition of culture "the customary beliefs, social forms, and material traits of a racial, religious, or social group" and "the set of shared attitudes, values, goals, and practices that characterizes a company or corporation."[1] A culture within organizations is

> [a] pattern of shared basic assumptions that the group learned as it solved its problems of external adaptation and internal integration, that has worked well enough to be considered valid, and therefore to be taught to new members as the correct way to perceive, think, and feel in relation to those problems" [Schein, 12]. Culture implies "some level of *structural stability* in the group." It is "not only shared but deep and stable." [Schein, 10–11]

In a diverse society, culture is less stable or uniform or shared. But at a more general level, it exists and affects the assumptions that people make about their own and other people's behavior. Social habits are formed by "many people joining together to do the same thing repeatedly at the same time on different occasions" [Schein, 95].

In this book, *culture* follows the dictionary definitions, with emphasis on accepting and complying with "the way things are done," emphasizing that culture is society's habits. It is what people do without much analysis and debate. It is what people assume "is, and will always be." Once people form habits, people "go on automatic" [Young, 80–81]. To take an extreme example, our culture rejects killing one's competitors, but the culture of the Mafia may accept competition by these means as a way of life. In our culture, people assume that contracts can be enforced in the courts of law, but in parts of Sicily, contract performance is mainly enforced and guaranteed by the Mafia [Gambetta, 1].

"Things as they are done" include motivation, habits of the mind, and patterns of action. "Motivation, like action, may also be habitual: I take my purpose for granted without necessarily having the means settled. Largely automatic habits take us out of time into timelessness." Customs and social habits are "the whole body of habits of mind which belongs to a particular society" [Young, 142]. The habit of the mind is illustrated in the story of a man who met another on the street and exclaimed: "Mr. Rabinowitz! How you have changed. Your hair used to be brown and it is now completely white. You were clean shaven and now you have a beard. And your eyes used to be brown and now they are black. And you also lost height." And the other man responds: "I am not Rabinowitz." To which the first man exclaims: "What! You have changed your name as well?!" The man's unshakeable assumption is that the other person is Rabinowitz. He interprets every fact to fit the assumption, even though the overwhelming evidence points to the contrary.

Culture shares with morality a prominent feature. Both involve what people will do or not do even if there are no police around. The *Economist* describes corporate culture in the same way. Corporate culture "determines how people behave *when they are not being watched.*"[2] Mark D. West explored and compared the practice of people of returning lost property in Japan and the United States. In the year 2002, people in Tokyo turned in about $23 million, which they found in the streets, subways, and public places. About 72 percent of the money was then returned to claimants through lost-and-found centers. This is part of the Japanese culture. As West shows, this culture is the product of many social pressures. At any rate, generally, people do not take and keep what does not belong to them.[3]

Sociologists have been excluding "habit" from their vocabulary for some time, writes Charles Camic. Yet great sociologists of the past have emphasized social habits and recognized their powerful force in society. Camic discusses Emile Durkheim's description of social habit.

> Primitive peoples, in [Durkheim's] judgment, live to a large extent by the "force of habit" under the "yoke of habit" . . . for "when things go on happening in the same way, habit . . . suffice[s] for conduct" and moral behavior itself is easily transformed "into habit mechanically carried out."[4]

Culture Is a Societal Habit

Like habits, culture saves attention, of which humans have a limited capacity. Culture economizes on memory. Like habits, culture is "a memory unconsciously edited for belief" [Young, 84–85]. Habit reduces the tension of weighing pros and cons before making a decision. Intensive consideration of every decision can freeze persons into inaction. Thus, like habits, culture offers stability and predictability. The habit of trust "is a protective mechanism relying on everyday routines, stable reputations and tacit memories, which together push out of modern life fear and uncertainty as well as moral problems" [Misztal, 102].

Culture, like habits, is built on, and grows by repetition. Culture creates uniform expectations of the future. Summarizing Hume's thoughts, Michael Young writes: "The repetition of experience by dint of repetition alone, creates habits of thought about cause and effect. What has always happened, we are impelled to think, will continue to happen" [Young, 97]. But habits need not be fully automatic. Just as a seasoned driver drives to a great extent automatically, his attention becomes focused on signals of danger, or when he comes close to his destination. These ideas apply to the theme of this book as well.

"Habits are not usually chosen with any deliberation; they just grow, like wild flowers, rather than cultivated ones. They would not do this so readily and constantly without a series of overlapping advantages which assure that their growth will not be stopped" [Young, 82]. A culture of dishonesty and mistrust may move in the same way. It is a "creeping" movement, built on small repeated changes that offer short-term advantages. This may be the reason why habits, including social habits, take a long time to form. And that is why they take a long time to redirect. It takes an effort to change habits. If people do things a certain way without much consideration and thought, they have to focus on the way they act before they can change it. That requires attention, and effort. That induces tension, confusion, and sometimes resentment.

One of the reasons for the difficulties in merging two corporations is the difference in their culture [Frankel (2005)]. The relationships between the employees and top management, the flow of information, the competition among people of the same rank, and whether they are pitted against each other to win or whether they are expected to cooperate and increase the general welfare and how they are rewarded may differ. And such different cultures are hard to reconcile and difficult to meld.[5] Culture is both affected by and affects the personalities of the people who compose it [Young, 99]. That too is hard to reconcile and change.

Durkheim was of the same opinion. He wrote: "It is always a laborious operation to pull out the roots of habits that time has fixed and organized in us."[6] As Camic explained, Durkheim's idea was that "by its very nature, human action, whether individual or collective, oscillates between two poles, that of consciousness or reflection on the one side, and that of habit on the other side, with the latter pole being the stronger."[7]

In modern societies, it has become crucial to trust abstract systems, like "business as usual" [Giddens, 120, 147]. However, if trust is eroded or misplaced by a habit and culture of mistrust, the feeling of comfort does not disappear completely. It is simply that one knows what to expect and one acts accordingly and routinely, to protect one's self. Thus, if a balance between "trust" and "verify" or "mistrust" becomes part of the culture, we may be almost as comfortable as before, even if over the long term the change devastates our safety and prosperity.

Culture embodies history but does not necessarily remain historical. Culture is similar to an aging person as time goes by. He is not another person, but neither is he the same person he was even yesterday. As time goes by, repeated events and behaviors that represent the culture are not necessarily identical. They are absorbed in memory, and adjust to new constraints and opportunities.

> Habitus, the product of history, produces individual and collective practices, and hence history, in accordance with the schemes engendered by history. The system of dispositions—a past which survives in the present and tends to perpetuate itself into the future by making itself present in practices structured according to its principles, an internal law relaying the continuously exercise of the law of external necessities . . . —is the principle of the continuity and regularity which [objective observation] discerns in the social world without being able to give them a rational basis. [Bourdieu, 82]

CULTURE OF RECIPROCITY AND BY RECIPROCITY: THE PASSIVE MAJORITY

Accepting and legitimating certain behavior can create a culture, if a sufficient number of people act in the same way and if others expect them to act in that way. A theory of reciprocity suggests that most people will contribute to the pool of public goods (the commons) if they believe that other people will do the same. People will not contribute to the pool of public goods if they believe that others will not contribute. The "public" need not be a specific community, or known people, writes Aaron-Andrew P. Bruhl.[8]

This theory has been tested in experiments and supported by events. In a "public goods game," each participant received an amount of money. Each person could either keep the money or contribute to a common fund. The fund will grow and then be distributed equally to everyone, both to those who contributed and to those who did not. This game presented a dilemma for the players. As Bruhl notes:

> The socially optimal outcome is for each person to contribute all of his endowment to the public good, but it is in each individual's interest to keep his tokens and free ride on the contributions (if any) of the other players. These games are typically anonymous, so that participants need not fear sanctions outside the laboratory.[9]

The game posed a conflict between short-term and long-term approaches and between selfishness and commitment to the communities. It presented an issue of trust. If the culture of the community is based on trust, people will believe that they will receive their share, and that over the long term, their share will be larger than if they free ride on the contributions. But if they believe that the others are free riders, people will attempt to be the first free riders and take as much as they can right away.

The experiments showed that what governs people's behavior is not the evidence of reality but belief. As Bruhl noted,

> Contrary to the conventional theory's implication that citizens will vie to be a lucky free rider whenever a public good can be produced with less than universal cooperation, evidence shows that citizens' dislike of making redundant contributions is less important than their desire to avoid making futile contributions. In other words, they certainly don't want to contribute when too few others are contributing, but they don't much bother with seeking out opportunities to free ride when contribution is the norm.[10]

The same results were observed outside the laboratory.

> A recent study of tax compliance . . . found that sending taxpayers a letter telling them that the overwhelming majority of citizens pay all of their taxes was more effective in promoting compliance than a letter telling them that their returns were especially likely to be audited. . . . The perceived level of tax compliance is the most important factor in an individual's decision.

A similar conclusion was reached in a study of the reactions to required desegregation of school children. Opposition was fed by other people's opposition.[11] Thus, people will restrain themselves when they see that others do so, and will not restrain themselves when others do not.

Does people's behavior change if they are the majority? Experiments relating to people's cruelty and inhumanity toward each other show that if good and benevolent people view cruel abuse *without reacting,* they help support the abuse. By analogy, we may speculate that if honest and good people view abuse of trust and do nothing about it, they help spread abuse by their very inaction.

In an experiment conducted in 1971 by Philip Zimbardo at Stanford University, college students were placed in a "prison" and divided into "prisoners" and "guards."[12] The experiment, which was planned to last for two weeks, was terminated after six days when the guards increasingly "[took] pleasure in cruelty" toward the student "prisoners." Yet only about a third of the student guards behaved like that. The rest did not.

An important lesson from this experiment is that the majority of the students, who did not take part in the torture of their colleagues, easily *accepted the new moral order.* The "good guards"' passive behavior was necessary for the establishment of the new order. These "good guards" never interfered in any way, Zimbardo told Congress. The bad guards terrorized. But the good guards maintained the atmosphere of the prison.[13] "While a few bad apples might spoil the barrel," Zimbardo wrote, "a vinegar barrel will *always* transform sweet cucumbers into sour pickles."[14] Few crooks do not turn the whole society into a society of crooks. But a sufficient number of crooks with leadership and determination may do just that.

Culture Can Transform into Rules of Conduct

Our actions trigger supports for new actions, each feeding on the next "like a train bringing along its own rails" [Bourdieu, 79]. Social habit takes long to form. A long-time habit is more entrenched than a new one. When certain ways are "in accordance with the nature of things, [they] are repeated more often and become habits; then the habits, as they acquire force, are transformed into rules of conduct.[15] Max Weber expressed a similar idea. "Customs are frequently transformed into binding norms, [since] the mere fact of the regular recurrence of certain events, somehow confers on them the dignity of [what one ought to do]."[16]

This is an important transformation, from how things *are* done to how things *ought* to be done. "What were originally plain habits of conduct owing to psychological disposition . . . come later to be experienced as binding; then, [when many people behave the same way] it comes to be incorporated [in] 'expectations' as to the meaningfully corresponding conduct of others."[17] Therefore, repeated acceptance and justification of dishonesty can lead to habits of dishonesty. Habits of dishonesty can make their appearance as rules of conduct—dishonesty in its ultimate social power.

The longer America proceeds toward abuse of trust, the longer people remain passive (accepting) and do not act to stop abuse, and the longer people become less aware of their acceptance of dishonesty, the longer it will take to redirect these tendencies. The power of familiarity is enormous. The power of "Everyone does it" is oppressive. The power of habit and culture can be coercive.

The process is familiar. Acceptance of some fraud becomes the foundation for more and more audacious fraud. First, there is shock at the conspicuous new form of abuse. Then there is curiosity. (How did they do it?) Then there is a grudging admiration. (They were very wrong, but they got what they wanted, at least for a while.) And then the doubt. (Is this the way to go? Why not?) Then comes conviction. (This is the way to go.) Finally, there is coercion. (There is no other way to go.) The rise of a habit of behavior is in part a description of this environment. The new environment is accompanied by justification. Then comes evidence: Whatever *is* must be good. For example, if people are selfish, selfishness must be good. Even what looks unselfish is in truth selfish. Whatever is practiced by the leaders and by many followers and called dishonest is dishonest no longer, because it is practiced by the leaders and by many.

Regardless of when the move toward dishonesty started, it seems that America is going in that direction. If this is not the way to go, then it is not too soon to stop moving on automatic pilot, and regain full awareness. How is each person acting? What are each person's views as "normal"? Where are we as a society? And where are we going?

PART II

*Rising Opportunities and
Temptations and Falling Barriers
to Abuse of Trust and Deception*

6

Rising Opportunities and Temptations

WHAT KIND OF AN ENVIRONMENT supports abuse of trust and deception? Is there anything new or unique in this supportive environment in recent times? This chapter examines the role of money in American society and the drive for "more." If it is uncontrolled, and is combined with unbridled competition, the desire for more may lead to greed and financial fraud. Greed and financial fraud are not new. And neither are the cycles of fraud and rebuilding of trust that have visited America periodically. What is new, however, is the change in the balance between the pressure to gain, which may lead to fraud, and the personal and institutional barriers on dishonesty, which prevent fraud from rising.

In the past three decades, pressures and opportunities for quick gains have risen. This rise was combined with lower and weakened counterpressures to prevent gains by deceit and abuse of trust. There is a danger that this transformed balance in the environment will produce antisocial habits and patterns of behavior—a culture that is not easily reversed.

The *International Fraud Report* of KPMG noted the same change in culture and values. "A consensus among regions [of surveyed entities] indicates that the *two major factors affecting the level of fraud are society's weakening values and economic pressures.*" I interpret "economic pressures" to mean opportunities for greater gain and fierce competition. PricewaterhouseCoopers' report made similar observations. The roots of fraud, it said, included pressures to gain capital market access, to show performance, to obtain financing, and to meet legal, marketing, and personal concerns.[1]

THE ROLE OF CULTURE

We live within a social framework. We take many things for granted because they are part of our culture. There are basic underlying assumptions in culture, writes Edgar H. Schein. They are "easy to observe and very difficult to decipher." They are "unconscious, taken for granted beliefs, perceptions, thoughts, and feelings (ultimate source of values and action)." These basic assumptions emerge when "a solution to a problem works repeatedly." That solution then is "taken for granted" [Schein, 17, 21].

> What was once a hypothesis, supported only by a hunch or a value, comes gradually to be treated as a reality. We come to believe that nature really works this way . . . In a capitalistic country it is inconceivable that one might design a company to operate consistently at a financial loss. [Schein, 21–22]

This last observation is generally accurate. But there are businesses that are designed for continued loss with the expectations of supplemental resources from charity or the government. There are businesses designed fraudulently, like Ponzi schemes, which operate without any revenue except the money raised from new investors. But these are at the fringe of the mainstream in American society.

Personal ambitions and the social structure play a major role in the pressures of the environment. A social environment can drive people's desires. People's view of their place and the place of others in society determines the ways they act and live [de Botton, 32–34]. This observation is generally accurate. But history is peppered with exceptions, from Spartacus, who led the rebellion of the slaves in Rome, to the peasants' revolts throughout the fourteenth century in France and England. The main point, however, is that these events tugged the social order at the fringes. It took other powerful pressures such as the French Revolution, and the Civil War in these United States, to change the social structure.

In a structured society, each person knows his place. In feudal times, people did not expect their place in society to change. Generally, a serf never considered the possibility of becoming a squire, even when the serf rebelled against taxes. Most people were accepting. Some were even proud of their positions. One example is the expression "the big house" or "upstairs and downstairs." "Upstairs" was where the masters lived, and "downstairs" was where the servants worked and sometimes lived. The physical boundary signaled fairly clearly the identity of each group and its place in the social order.

But in a more flexible social order that offers the individuals the opportunity to better their lot, acceptance and certainty give way to a drive: envy and continuous dissatisfaction. Social mobility and the idea of equality avoid the horrible uprisings and bloody revolutions that visited the "fixed" society. But they come at a price. Alexis de Tocqueville noted in 1835 that in a society of established and impregnable classes, there were no expectations of crossing the boundaries. Inequality, being the order of things, did not degrade. With the notion of equality, expectations and opportunities for better living by everyone, came envy and discontent and a feeling of degradation [de Botton, 32–34]. Erzo F. P. Luttmer found that for people whose enjoyment depends on relative consumption, "higher earnings of neighbors are associated with lower levels of self-reported happiness."[2]

One example of status competition is the demands of top corporate management for compensation. During the 1990s, the status of top management was linked to the dollars they received. However, during that period, people could still argue that higher salaries, bonuses, stock options, loans, paid obligations to stay on the job, and alike were linked to performance. The shareholders became rich, and the managers—richer.

But when the market price of shares crashed, the compensation of the top management did not crash. According to Equilar, Inc., a corporation that deals with executive compensation, from 2002 to 2003 the salaries of CEOs of the companies on the Standard & Poor's 500 index rose 1.6 percent. Bonuses, which account for a larger portion than the salaries of take-home pay, rose even more, by 18.9 percent. Altogether, the rise in cash compensation amounted to about 10 percent.

While there was a considerable reduction in the value of stock options that were granted during the period, the value of actual (restricted) stock grants has risen rapidly to take the place of stock options. Thirty-seven percent of Standard & Poor's 500 CEOs received restricted stock grants in 2003, up from 32 percent in 2002, and there was a 31.8 percent increase in the size of the median grant. There's also an increase in so-called long-term incentive plans, which seem to be payments or stock allocations that are more clearly tied to performance. The main metric used for payouts is "total shareholder return": a combination of share price increase, dividends paid, and earnings per share. There were other incentives, including revenue and earnings before interest, taxes, depreciation, and amortization (EBITDA).[3] Thus, performance fell, if measured by the stock prices. Yet compensation of top management rose. One explanation is that managers demand high *relative* salaries. When compensation is linked to status and prestige, and only partially to performance, executives demand "more than someone else" to feel better.

A related explanation for the "runaway compensation at the top," not only in business but also in sports and entertainment, is the shift of American society to a "winner-take-all" system. One of the side effects of this system is "the amplifying effect of social context," that is, the strong tendency of people to compare themselves to others, and their salaries to the salaries of others. That is to make sure that they are the best and gain the most [Frank & Cook, 45–60].

The flip side of the claim to equality is the resentment of inequality, even justified inequality. One example is Quentin Letts's story in the *Wall Street Journal*.[4] Pressed by a secretary for a promotion, Prince Charles wrote a note to an aide, which said in part:

> What is it that makes everyone seem to think they are qualified to do things far beyond their technical capabilities? . . . It is a consequence of a child-centered system which admits no failure and tells people they can all be pop stars, high court judges, brilliant TV personalities . . . without ever putting in the necessary effort or having natural abilities.

This memo raised an uproar in the British media. The prince was accused of snobbery, a "Don't Get above Yourself" attitude.

Resentment of inequality has many effects. It feeds the belief that people can become what they want to become, and fills them with hope and energy to try. It may also feed an unrealistic belief that people are equal in capacity and lead to disappointment and resentment.

FROM THE REIGNING DOLLAR TO THE INSATIABLE DRIVE FOR MORE

People seek power to satisfy their needs and to be free of other people's controls. In feudal times, power came by a number of routes, such as birthright, land ownership, knighthood, military rank and valor on the battlefield, place in the church hierarchy, or an office granted by the sovereign. These positions were sources of income. Knighthood could bestow the right to tax the population for the use of salt or wine. Some of the positions bestowed the right to other people's services, such as services in wartime and tilling the fields in peacetime. In the United States and in many democratic countries, money is usually sufficient to attain power. One can accumulate money regardless of birthright, valor, or piety. Money can equalize and empower. Money can become power.

It is not surprising that the United States has been singled out as the land of unlimited opportunities. In the United States, even the very poor believe that they can become rich, regardless of their present state. While America has remained the land of opportunity for wealth and for power, the way to capture the opportunity has been changing. Hard work is not necessarily the only or the best way to riches. When people see that others have amassed a fortune in a shorter time, people attempt to imitate what these others have done and follow the shorter routes.

Controlling Other People's Money

Controlling the use of other people's money is almost as good as owning the money. Sometimes it is even better. Control of other people's money brings many of the owner's benefits but bears little or none of the owner's risks. Controlling the money that belongs to many small investors is better than controlling the money of a few owners. This control creates a new power that none of the individual small owners possesses alone—being in charge of more money than any one individual owner owns. And when money becomes a symbol of success rather than a means of satisfying one's needs, more is always better.

The Drive for More: For Good and Evil

The drive for *more* has positive and negative aspects. After all, it is good for people to seek a better life. Lack of the desire for money is not necessarily socially good. In contrast to Western culture, for example, the "karma" attitude in India leaves millions near starvation. They believe that life is but a speck in eternity through which one is floating. "In the East, where the notion of *karma* is general and by no means confined to Buddhist circles, this can result in extreme political *laissez-faire*"

[Snelling, 57–59]. Millions of people make little effort to change the old ways in order to produce more food and gain better living conditions.

People can become richer by gaining more money or by curbing their appetites. Modern Western societies have whetted people's appetites. And since these societies are based on equality, the feeling of being rich depends on a comparison with others (to whom one seeks to be equal). Higher incomes may still impoverish, if there are no limits to expectations, and the gap with others continues to be the same or even grow. One can amass more money and feel poorer, depending on how much money other people have [de Botton, 42–43].

The "level of economic need" is determined by custom. The "patterns of use" are determined by habit.[5] The quest for money and for more money can be or become a matter of culture, accepted by people as the predominant "natural" quest. It becomes an underlying assumption leading to a social habit.

Economics explains rich people's desire for more. As people become wealthier, their desire for more does not diminish. In fact, the desired amount of money increases. "As individuals get wealthier, each dollar is less important."[6] The more we have of something, the less we value it. The more money we have, the more money we need in order to value it. For someone who has $100, $50 is much. For someone who has $1 million, $50 is far less. And yet one could view unrestrained desire for more money, regardless of how much one has, as greed—a hunger that cannot be satisfied.

Greed Is an Insatiable Craving for More

Greed, the insatiable craving for more, can result from weak self-esteem and envy [Golomb, 12–13]. In its extreme form, it has been characterized as a narcissistic personality disorder. According to the current edition of the *Diagnostic and Statistical Manual of Mental Disorders*, the disorder includes: "a grandiose sense of self-importance"; preoccupation "with fantasies of unlimited success, power, brilliance, [or] beauty"; "unreasonable expectations of especially favorable treatment," and "tak[ing] advantage of others to achieve his or her ends" [American Psychiatric Association, 717].

Although few people are free of all the traits associated with narcissism, it is only when all these traits are combined that they can result in a disorder.

> We are said to live in the age of narcissism. Few of us are entirely free of its traits. It is in our label, "the Me Generation," and shows up in popular expressions such as "What's in it for me?" and "taking care of number one." Those who are philosophically inclined might ask which comes first, the narcissism of the individual or that of the society in which he is formed. There probably is a point at which the ills of a society and the neuroses of individuals living within it feed into a common stream. If society worships such external things as how you appear to others, your status, power, and money, a person may acquire the belief that what she keeps inside, her emotions and

the deeds that only she knows about, do not count. Yet the only real and last-
ing sense of self-worth that a person can have is the feeling of and for her
essential self, the sense of being real, of doing what possibly she alone thinks
appropriate. Having an appreciation of the subjective intangible is what we
mean when we say that someone has "character." [Golomb, 19–20]

In the 1980s, "corporate deviance" was driven by the strong desire to increase corporate profits [Clinard & Yeager, 46–48]. There is nothing wrong with the desire to
profit. All for-profit corporations should aim at profit; this objective is beneficial to
the economy and the country's population. Indirectly, the shareholders' gain benefits
corporate management as well. There is nothing wrong with management's desire for
achievement, recognition, and rewards either. Therefore, it is not the profit motive or
the quest for prestige that constitutes greed. *It is the insatiable desire for profits that knows
no limits. It is this uncontrollable drive that leads to corporate deviance.*

There is strong evidence that one trigger to the corruption of corporate management in the 1990s was the enormous compensation that management collects,
whether earned or not. The compensation that corporate managers started collecting during the last decade of the twentieth century triggered envy and status building that drove to greed—the hunger without limits.

CORPORATE GREED

The Bubble Years

The demands of corporate managers for higher compensation rose during the stock
market bubble years. It was easy to justify these demands as performance that was
manifested by rising stock prices. In addition, the managers' demands were linked
to the pay packages of other executives. The managers group at the top is sufficiently
small. The amounts that others were collecting were no secret. If a top manager
perceived himself to be better than another, he demanded more than what others
were paid. Monetary rewards became linked to a hierarchy.

Never before did CEOs and other members of top management collect in pay,
bonuses, and exercised stock options $50 million or more in one year! That is pre-
cisely when the controls of abuse of trust were weakened. The online magazine *PM*
reported that "during the periods for which their companies are being investigated,
CEOs took in the following amounts in bonuses, stock sales and company loans: . . .
Enron—$184 million (1997–2001) . . . WorldCom—$45 million (1999–2002) . . . Tyco
International—$332 million (1999–2001) . . . Global Crossing—$123 million in stock
sales alone (2001)." *Money* magazine reported in 2002 that "CEOs now make 500
times what the average worker does."[7]

"Corporate greed exploded beyond anything that could have been imagined in
1990," said Paul Volcker, a former chairman of the Federal Reserve Board. "Tradi-

tional norms didn't exist. You had this whole culture where the only sign of worth was how much money you made."[8] In the opinion of CNN's Lou Dobbs,

> it's going to take corporate America much longer to earn back the nation's trust than it took to lose it. . . . I am a conservative, and it's difficult for me to say this, but this is a time when we simply have to have more regulation . . . more oversight and we surely have to have more character in the boardroom and in the executive suites of corporate America. . . . The culture of greed that grew up through the late 90's overwhelmed corporate America. And the culture has to be ripped up.[9]

Bill George, a highly respected CEO, wrote:

> My generation of CEOs, like many of today's business students, embarked on our careers with a mixture of ambition and idealism. But something happened along the way. We began listening to the wrong people: Wall Street analysts, media pundits, economists, compensation consultants, public relations staffs, hedge funds, fellow CEOs—all the players in what I call the Game.
>
> That Game has stopped today's chief executives from focusing their energies on their company's customers, employees, and—ironically, since the Game is supposed to be all about them—shareholders. That's right. The biggest losers of the shareholder-value movement have been the shareholders themselves.[10]

Lawyers, we should note, took advantage of the same opportunities and some succumbed to similar temptations. In May 2004, *American Lawyer* called the past 25 years "a golden age of growth" for law firms and noted that between 1987 and 2003, "revenues at the top 100 firms quintupled to $38 billion, while profits quadrupled to $13.5 billion."[11]

In 2004–2005, corporate compensation has not fallen by much, and the quest for higher compensation does not seem to be any weaker. "There have been improvements, but pay for performance is still not the standard practice everywhere," wrote Louis Lavelle in *Business Week* in April 2005.[12] A new item has been added to executive compensation. The package includes not only stock options but also corporate stock. The difference between stock options and stock is significant. Stock options can become worthless, if the market price of the stock is lower than the price at which the holder of the option is entitled to buy the stock. Thus, if an option holder can buy stock at $10 when the market price is $20, the option is worth $10. But if the price drops to $5, the option is worth nothing. It is cheaper to buy the stock directly in the market. In contrast, if the stock is allocated when the price is $10, and the price falls to $5, the executive can still sell the stock at $5. In any event, and regardless of the form of compensation, the system of evaluating the compensation does not seem to have changed. Managers still attempt to outdo each other in compensation. According to the *Wall Street Journal* companies have been paying their CEOs the expenses for maintaining a second home in places that the CEOs visit in connection with their work. Time-Warner has paid its CEO $400–plus a month for his apartment in Los Angeles in addition to his $9.5 million salary and bonus. Walt Disney paid its CEO $10,000 a month to cover part of his New York apartment expenses, in addition to his compensation of $8.5 million, and Viacom's vice-president has received $105,000 for a New York apartment's expenses in addition to a compensation package of $19.8 million. In some cases companies could have paid far less to cover the expenses of their CEOs' actual stay in high-quality hotels. In others the CEOs regularly worked in two places each month and a home was the better choice. These payments to the CEOs are tax-free; the second home perk is viewed as the CEOs' business expense.[13]

Where Stock Options Can Lead

The theory of stock options was logical. But people do not always act logically when they have much power and little accountability. The logical idea helped produce greed and corruption. The creators of theories do not necessarily intend the use (or abuse) of their theories. It is doubtful that Karl Marx envisioned Joseph Stalin and Mao Zedong and the way they used his theory. Clearly Michael C. Jensen and William H. Meckling, who designed and advocated the award of stock options to corporate managers, did not envision, let alone intend, the excesses of some corporate top management that became a virus of corruption.

These economists theorized that by providing managers with stock options, the managers' interests will be more aligned with the interests of the shareholders. It turns out that this theory did not work. First, managers did not take the risk that shareholders do. They took the upside benefit but far less of the downside loss. Second, managers borrowed corporate money in order to buy the stock when they exercised their stock options. Few shareholders have money available to invest in a large number of corporate shares. Third, the managers had begun to focus on share prices, and started to realize that the rewards of a rising stock market can be enormous as compared to salaries. And finally, these managers had the power to manipulate the corporations' financial statements and affect the prices. In an interview at the *New Yorker*, Michael Jensen admitted his distress about a theory that went wrong.[14]

Managers blame the pressures of "greedy" shareholders for their own manipulation, and for the managers' focus on short-term share prices. But no public shareholder had as much power to force the managers to manipulate the stock prices and focus on short-term prices as the managers had themselves. The opportunities were there, the amounts were astronomical, many managers could not withstand the temptations, and there were weak or no barriers and no strong gatekeepers to stop them. It is interesting that some management supporters argue for a new view of managers' power. They argue that managers represent not only the shareholders but also all stakeholders involved in the corporate enterprise, as well as the financial system and the country's economy as a whole.[15] Forgotten are the justifications for the rich and enriching stock option—the idea that such stock options will align the managers' interests with those of the shareholders!

Overpaid Managers?

Should managers be paid so much? Corporate managers express a surprisingly strong sense of entitlement for whatever money they have collected, noted *Business Day*.[16] Why should managers not earn as much as famous movie stars, brilliant writers, and superb athletes? There are reasons why they should not. Top managers and CEOs are different [Bebchuk & Fried, 20–21]. Sports figures and stars act alone and earn alone. No one can take their place. They cannot use "shadow" performers. Even with helpers, they are the main, if not the only, source of the revenue. In addition, some performers, like sports figures and models, can perform only for a limited time. They are entitled to their profits.

Chief executive officers manage other people's actions and marshal other people's talents and production. Management is indeed a talent in and of itself. But CEOs cannot assert a claim to any specific product of their management, nor can they appropriate the production of their corporations as their own. They share the corporations' successes or failures with many others. Besides, the main productive assets of sports figures are their talents and their bodies, which belong to them. At least in part the CEOs' productive assets are other people's money and other people's labor. The money is not theirs. The labor is not theirs. As highly as their abilities have been exalted lately, it is harder to value managers' services and the link between their contributions and the success of their corporations. Because an athlete's performance is clearly tied to his or her efforts, it is easier to pick a star athlete. Because the corporation's success is not directly linked to the CEO's efforts, it is far more difficult to identify a star CEO. The corporation's success may have been achieved in spite of him or her.

Lost Team Effort

The pressure for more profits can undermine the team effort in corporations. It can cause a shift from a joint effort of management and employees to management's pressure on the employees. Corporate employees are assigned profit objectives, accompanied by an implicit or explicit threat of layoffs. If these objectives are not realistic, employees' anxiety drives them to cut corners or "pad" their reports, or try to take credit for other employees' production, in order to show that they met their quotas. Driven management and hard-pressed employees provide a model for each other, creating a culture of a frenzied drive for more, with less concern about how it is achieved.

In the 1963 case of *Graham v. Allis-Chalmers Manufacturing Co.*,[17] the salespersons were required to annually increase profits by 20 percent. The corporate structure was quite decentralized. The same salespersons were authorized to determine the market price of the products they sold. Not surprisingly, the salespersons sought relief by price-fixing arrangements with the salespersons of competing organizations. In 1996, more than 30 years later, the same scenario repeated itself. In the case *In re Caremark International Inc. Derivative Litigation*,[18] the company, engaged in the sale of medical products, was highly decentralized. The salespersons were authorized to offer physicians incentives for referrals. The salespersons utilized their freedom to pay bribes and hide the payments by fake consulting and other types of contracts. When Medicare began to tighten and enforce its rules, the company's board gingerly kept as close as possible to the line. It seems that little attention was paid to the employees' incentives. The employees continued the practices, and the company ended up paying a significant fine. Only then did the board prohibit all such inducements to physicians and centralize the control over this practice. The problem is not that profits are bad. The problem is that the pressure and temptations to produce them *at an ever-increasing, unrealistic higher rate* have become uncontrolled and uncontrollable.

Mutual "Hard Bargains" among Managers

Greed seems to have changed corporate business practices. During the heyday of the stock market bubble, Wall Street and Main Street bargained to squeeze as much as they could from each other. For example, underwriters engaged in fierce competition for lucrative business. For awarding this lucrative underwriting business, corporate managers pressed underwriters to increase the services that the corporations sold to the underwriters. In fact, as the *Wall Street Journal* described the relationship, underwriters had to "pay to play," and they reciprocated by charging high underwriting fees.[19] There seem to be no limits on both sides of the bargain.

Underwriters and brokers pressed advisors who manage mutual funds for a share of the advisors' fees instead of the traditional commissions (or perhaps in addition to commissions). Advisors were hard pressed to oblige. Funds that offer redeemable shares must replenish their assests. Otherwise, their expenses will rise, and their advisors' fees will fall because the fees are measured as a percentage of the assets under management [Frankel & Schwing, 2:12-70–12-71]. There seem to be no limits on both sides of the bargain.

THE SHIFT FROM PRODUCING TO SELLING

Pyramid schemes have appeared within productive enterprises. The past 25 years have seen the rise of the value and rewards for selling as compared to producing. One result of this trend is a conflict between sales and production. For some products, increased sales requires creating the customers' need. "Built-in obsolescence" in cars, linking advertising to the consumers' ego, and many other methods can create an addictive need. Thus, the manufacturer designs products aimed to attract buyers not only with their quality and duration but also by the pleasure of buying more. Traditionally, sales have been important within productive units, and "rainmakers" have been rewarded more than others. But in recent years, some enterprises have adopted the sales motive as part of the whole organizational system. They have created in-house pyramid sales schemes.

As noted before, pyramid schemes are deceptive because they are similar to legitimate sales of goods, and yet they are fundamentally different. Classic pyramid schemes have no socially redeeming features of either sales or investment, since they offer nothing but "selling the right to sell." The structure of pyramid schemes has been seeping into productive enterprises as an incentive to sell. In such productive enterprises, pyramids are not illegal, so long as the enterprises and their employee-salespersons offer and sell products to consumers.

The rise of in-house pyramids may be due to the combined effect of ferocious competition, unimaginable financial rewards of success, and more emphasis on personal initiative as a model of behavior. However, pyramid sales structures can shift the attention of all employees, including the productive personnel, from production to sales and advertising. Every productive employee, including the higher echelon, is pressed to sell as well as produce. Compensation depends on how much money the lower echelon "workers" bring. Members of all echelons become competitors, often undermining each other's efforts by attempting to capture each other's clients, and taking steps to guard against the raids of their colleagues.[20] The shift from production to sales sets up conflicts among the employees and could result in reduced product quality.

The move to pyramid schemes poses dangers. If one member of the enterprise begins to sell stories rather than the products and is rewarded by the results, others may follow as a matter of "self-protection" in the competitive mode. When a sufficient number of members take this route, the firm turns into a classic pyramid scheme, selling little or nothing.

A similar kind of sales structure and accompanying pressure can appear in professional organizations. For example, one accounting firm began to require the partners to meet revenue quotas. It also changed the fee structure, charging clients a percentage of the tax savings that the firm provided the clients rather than on an hourly basis. One could argue that this measure of fees is more in line with the clients' interests. But that is not necessarily so. A peek into the internal working of the firm is offered in a *Wall Street Journal* story. In an e-mail in February 2000, a senior partner in the KPMG accounting firm told colleagues that the company should put off for five months all non-revenue-producing activities: "'We are dealing with ruthless execution—hand to hand combat—blocking and tackling.' Whatever the mixed metaphor, let's just do it." This tax partner joined the sales side.[21] Service to existing clients took second place to sales to new clients. While he represented himself as a professional that puts service to the clients first, he was not.

THE SHIFT FROM STOCK MARKET EFFICIENCY TO MARKET BUBBLE

We need not evaluate the economic benefits and costs of stock market bubbles. This inquiry focuses on a bubble-trading system that increases pressures and opportunities to become very rich very quickly. Without counterlimitations, underwriters, brokers, and trading investors feed the bubble. Without limitations, they may feed the bubble by deceptive means.

Bubbles Reflect a Spirit of Deception and Greed

As its name suggests, a stock market bubble represents not merely rising prices but prices that rise on air rather than substance. The less weight they carry, the higher they rise. When they rise high enough, they meet the cold air and burst, leaving nothing. When stock prices rise, investors can unwittingly contribute to creation of a bubble by increasing demand that is not backed by substance. Analysts, brokers, underwriters, and issuers and sellers of securities add fuel to the fire of desire and whet the investors' appetite for securities. Market mechanisms make it easier to raise prices without paying dividends or interest, and can entice sales without true and reliable information. For example, demand for derivatives can be raised to a frenzy by deceptive financial statements and an aggressive sales force, leading to a public cascade [Partnoy, 225].

Bubbles as Ponzi schemes. Society benefits from securities trades by enabling corporations to raise capital, producing additional information and analysis about the issuers, and offering liquidity for investors. These features reduce the cost of capital to the issuers, and enable small investors to participate in the economic prosperity of the country.

But stock market bubbles are a different species of stock market. They produce no new knowledge, no needed liquidity, nor anything new. They usually produce more shares backed by little if any products. "Most price bubbles start with initial good news." In the famed tulip mania, for example, growers developed interesting tulips for which collectors were ready to pay very high prices. The railroad boom started with the excitement about a new form of transportation. This may be one of the reasons for the start of the dot-com mania [Shleifer, 169–174]. The second stage in a stock market mania is the production and increased supply of the desirable assets (the tulips), as well as the supply of claims to these assets (the securities). Unsold securities can be packaged into a fund that offers its "new" securities. Thus, securities can grow not only on the basis of real underlying assets but also on the basis of other securities that represent few or no assets. And in both cases, the mania drives the securities' value well above the value of the underlying assets. The broker dealers and underwriters, their friends, and favored customers buy the stock early, to be sold shortly thereafter, when it "ripens" to a higher price. In a bubble, regardless of whether the assets increase, the price of the shares does not represent anything close to the present value of the issuing corporation's enterprises. For example, the aggregate stock of NetEase.com was valued at one time at over $2 billion. In the 12-month period before that, sales amounted to $27 million.[22]

When a true bubble develops, as it did in the case of the dot-coms during the 1990s, the market begins to lose its distinctive character and mirrors a Ponzi process. Shares do not necessarily represent value or promise any hope of ever gaining value. Investors do not require information or research the nature of the issuers, and do not expect to gain from the purported value of the underlying assets. They expect to gain from rising prices representing the demand of other investors for the shares. Investors buy the shares in order to "flip" and resell them.

Many buyers in the dot-com debacle were not investors but traders, who bought the securities for the purpose of quickly selling them to others at a higher price.[23] The underwriters allotted the dot-com shares to preferred customers as valuable gifts.[24] The underwriters may not have planned a conspiracy to manipulate the markets; they simply created a hype in which brokers, sellers, and buyers joined.

Not everyone agrees with this description. Not everyone agrees on the relationship between the bubble of the 1990s and the abuses that were recently discovered. The explanation may be buried in a trend that was making its way to the bubble for many years. David Wessel wrote in the *Wall Street Journal:*

> Why is so much corporate venality surfacing now? Is there more of it, or is more attention being paid? Did a few executives lose their ethical moorings in the exuberance of the 1990s? Or did a few notorious offenders break rules that many others merely bent? Is the entire system of corporate governance and regulation flawed? Or was the system abused by a few cleverly diabolical executives who deserve, as Treasury Secretary Paul O'Neill puts it, "to hang . . . from the very highest branches?"
>
> The answer, put simply is: *A stock-market bubble magnified changes in business mores and brought trends that had been building for years to a climax.*[25]

The point here is not whether bubbles are good or bad for the economy or for the financial system. The point here is that the bubble brought out pressures, expectations, and deteriorating public morals that may have been festering for years. Without the counterbalance of barriers, these pressures burst into abuse of trust.

THE PROCESS OF FRAUD

The Creeping Fraud within an Organization

The initial steps of the crimes, such as in Enron Corporation, are usually not large-scale. Rather these are small steps, followed by others, one at a time. There can be an entry in the books to cover a small deficit or a small shady payment, or the private use of corporate funds in a "gray area" situation, or a well reasoned limited conflict of interest. With no detection or adverse reaction, and with strong support for self-interest and weak pressures for self-limitation, the steps are repeated more frequently, and the system is refined. New tricks are developed "correcting and fine-tuning" prices. "Aggressive and innovative" accounting is introduced [Swartz & Watkins, 88]. As these patterns are built, so are the justifications and legal protections. The practices may extend from an individual to a tightly closed group of peers that share the same objectives and attitudes.

Then other industry members of the network may envy the successful results they notice, discover the system, and imitate the process. The virus of deception thus spreads, accompanied by brazen justifications. With legal wrappings produced by competing lawyers and accountants, and a supportive or passive board of directors, caught up in "creative accounting" that produces an incredible rise in reported income, the actors slide into embezzlement, and the corporation ends in bankruptcy.

The same process can occur on the personal level. Patrick Schiltz, a law-school dean, described a hypothetical young overworked first-year associate in a law firm. How would this young man start cheating by "padding" his time sheet? At the end of a reporting period he misses a small number of chargeable hours. He adds the hours and promises himself to "pay back" the work later. As time goes by, he acquires the habit of adding hours as a matter of course. At the beginning of this practice he promises himself to cover these missing working hours. But then he stops paying back the "time loans," but continues the padding. At the beginning, the associate may rationalize the fraudulent practice, but later he ceases to do that [Callahan, 39]. If he discovers that other associates are padding as well, he feels less ashamed and guilty. He has slid from acceptance into a habit. He continues padding, but does not worry or even think about it anymore.

The Revolving Door of Top Management—Private and Public Sectors

Conflict of interest developed within the group of top government officials that had the power to allocate millions to private sector corporations. That conflict reached a climax. As the *New York Times* reported in June 29, 2004, "[f]or years, the revolving door between the Pentagon and military contractors has spun without much notice in Washington. But the multiple roles played by top Pentagon and government officials . . . who have joined the ranks of military contractors as executives, board members and lobbyists, are now coming under closer scrutiny after a top Air Force official negotiated a lucrative job contract with the Boeing Company while still overseeing Boeing business."[26] The Project on Government Oversight noted that "288 top government officials since 1997 have taken positions at the 20 largest military contractors at levels high enough so that they were disclosed in federal regulatory filings." "The infusion . . . at Lockheed, Boeing, Northrop Grumman and Raytheon makes it difficult 'to determine where the government stops and private sector begins.'" Drawing the line is all the more difficult when the government pays the private sector with public money. And yet, the proposal to insert an ethics requirement into the Pentagon's expenditure bill for 2005 continues to meet strong objections.[27]

The problem is not that top government officials leave for the private sector. The problem is not that the "revolving door" goes in the opposite direction as well, as private sector corporate management joins the Pentagon. The problem is that public officials negotiate their future positions in the private sector *when they are still in the government, and have the power to determine which firm in the private sector will gain an enormous sum of public money.* The officials violated their trust because the power they exercised did not belong to them. It was given for a limited purpose—to represent the interests of the government. The power could not be used for their benefit or for the benefit of others. It could be used only for the purpose for which it was given. It does not matter that the government was not injured by the contracts these officials signed. It does not matter that the officials may have chosen the best contractors for the jobs. The officials abused their trust by misappropriating for their own benefit the power that did not belong to them.

That is where legitimate arrangements can slide into conflicts of interest and in some, perhaps unique, cases, into corruption.[28] As the *Los Angeles Times* reported on June 13, 2004, Darleen Druyun, who controlled a $30 billion a year procurement budget of the military pleaded guilty to a federal charge of conspiracy to obstruct justice. She tried to conceal the fact that she brokered a $250,000 a year executive position with Boeing Corporation when she signed off on a $20 billion contract for Boeing on behalf of the Air Force.[29] In principle, the idea of a revolving door is not a bad one. But without barriers to conflicts of interest, corruption sneaks in as the doors revolve.

The Rising Conflicts of Interest in Mutual Funds

Market timing in mutual funds shows how conflicts of interest can spread. Market timing is unique to mutual funds because of their structure. Shareholders of these funds do not sell their shares in the market when they want their money back. They tender their shares to the funds and receive a pro rata share of the value of the fund's portfolio; they redeem their shares. In this respect mutual funds are similar to banks. You pay the fund for a share, and when you want out, you get from the fund the value of the share. To be fair to all shareholders, the price of shares, whether to buy or redeem, must be equal to the pro rata value of the whole portfolio. If a shareholder redeems and takes out more than the value, the shares of the other investors are diluted. If a shareholder buys for less than the value, the shares of the other investors are diluted. The legal system is intended to ensure that the value of the shares for buying and redeeming is as economically correct as possible, and to prevent insiders from manipulating the price for themselves and their favorites. The system is designed in such a way that the buyers and redeemers of mutual fund shares do not know the precise price at which their orders will be executed. The *price will be determined after the "buy" or "redeem" orders are tendered* [Frankel & Schwing, ch. 26]. This self-limiting arrangement also commands trust.

The redemption arrangement raises another problem. Even though the shareholders have the right to redeem their shares, when some shareholders buy and redeem frequently they impose transaction costs on the long-term investors, and make it difficult for the portfolio managers to plan and follow their investment strategies.

The issue of quick and frequent "turn over" has existed for many years. But in this case the interests of fund managers and of long-term investors were close. Fund managers want to retain and increase the assets under management and to discourage redemption. After all, their fees depend on the size of the assets in the funds. In addition fund managers wanted to produce the best performance for their funds. The regulators left the issues to the market. Each fund complex found a way of reducing the problems. However, the market bubble increased the investors' profits from frequent purchases and redemptions. Investors who could circumvent the legal limitations on preference among shareholders and on insider information could reap hefty profits, especially if the other shareholders did not engage in the same practice. That is when some fund managers were offered high compensation to prefer select investors and allow them to increase the buying and trading. Soon they crossed the line and violated express prohibitions of the law. And too many managers took the compensation. In addition, there were unregulated entities that were put in a position to change the timing of the orders and give insider information to preferred investors for compensation. They, too, took the compensation from investors who sought preferences.

The complaint of Eliot Spitzer, the attorney general of New York, describes how the corruption has spread.[30] A manager of Canary Hedge Fund contacted the managers of funds under the Bank of America's umbrella and sought a preferred status and permission to "market time." In exchange for the preferred status, the hedge fund manager promised to leave millions of dollars in Bank of America funds over the long term. That meant increased fees for the bank. The bank managers agreed. Canary profited handsomely. The bank profited handsomely. The other mutual fund shareholders lost. The value of their shares was diluted. Canary's manager contacted other mutual fund managers and offered deals for a similar preferred status. Other traders followed in Canary's footsteps; other managers of mutual funds followed the first mutual fund management's footsteps. Some fund managers adopted the same technique personally or through a software service provider, such as Security Trust Company. In the end, dozens of fund complexes joined this lucrative practice at the expense of their shareholders.

So long as this type of buying and redeeming conflicted with the interests of the portfolio managers, the managers took steps to reduce the problem by limiting or preventing the practice entirely. The self-interest of honest managers, who sought the best performance for their funds (and higher fees for themselves), took care to reduce this problem. But if someone offered them a better deal, some managers began to make a cost benefit analysis. They found that whatever they lost from market timing in fees was compensated handsomely for allowing the preference. There are managers who rejected the offers. Their service to their shareholders came first. But others accepted the pay and allowed the preferences. Market timing mushroomed, and spilled over to clear violations of the law.

The example of market timing shows that cheating can start small and grow, if it is not nipped in the bud. It shows that a gray area can be left to market actors so long as they have the right incentives. The spread of market timing during the 1990s demonstrates the environment in which it could flourish. This is the environment in which pressures, opportunities, and higher dollar amounts to gain from abuse of trust become stronger, and the barriers to abuse of trust become weaker.

THE INTERNET: NEW MEDIUM FOR OLD FRAUDS

More Opportunities; Fewer Barriers

The Internet is a wonderful technological innovation that, among other things, allows strangers to interact all around the world. It has, however, changed the balance between opportunities to defraud and barriers to fraud. It shifted the costs of interaction between trusting and trusted persons. It is far easier to send fraudulent messages and far more costly to distinguish the true from the false and identify the senders.

"Barbara House" e-mailed to me a message on June 3, 2004, regarding "Important Information About Your House." The e-mail read:

> I wanted you to know that we have received and reviewed your mortgage application. We are happy to let you know that it has been approved. But first, to ensure the best results, we'll need some more information. Please fill up the final details we need to complete the process. . . . We look forward to hearing from you.

At the end of the message is a line and underneath the words: "not interested." The same day I received another e-mail from "Abigail Self": "Responding back to your email." It read: "I am sorry that it took so long to review your application but you were finally approved with a 3% fixed ra.te [*sic*]. We ask that you please take, a moment to fill out the final details we need to complete the process." Then was the line and underneath the words: "not interested." The same person may have sent these messages under different names.

I did not seek a mortgage. These messages could have been advertisements by lenders. The last sentence leads me to suspect that the purpose of the senders was to verify that I exist. My e-mail address would then carry a higher price. Had I offered more information, it could be used for other ventures, including unlawful use, such as identity theft. And perhaps, if I truly needed a loan, the loan shark would have bought my address. Had I opened the attachments, my computer may have been contaminated, and years of work would have been erased. I could have also damaged the computers of others.

There are many fraudulent and dangerous messages on the Internet. The sender may live in a culture that admires the power of destruction. Verifying the honesty of the sender is enormously costly. What I can do is erase these messages. But these daily messages create for me an environment that teaches suspicion and warns me to be on my guard. To be sure, I take a risk when I buy through the Internet. But as I get used to the risk, and continue to use the Internet and my e-mail, I become less trusting and more accepting of fraud: "This is life."

New Tricks

The Internet has created boundless opportunities to deceive. It is hard to protect copyrighted materials from being sold freely. It is hard to protect brand names from being used on fake products and offered for very little. In an article entitled "Psst, Wanna Buy a Cheap Bracelet?" the *Economist* describes the attempts of Tiffany to protect its brand name from fake products that carried its name and were sold through eBay. Tiffany bought cheap "Tiffany" jewelry through eBay and found that 73 percent of it was fake jewelry. It blocked 19,000 transactions but could not prevent the continuous stream of sales. It is now suing eBay for its losses.[31] Apart from the interesting issue of who is responsible for facilitating these sales, it is clear that such fake products can now be sold more easily and better protected from detection. No longer must the seller be cornering possible buyers in a dark alley. It is also hard to distinguish this seller from the legitimate seller of estate items that may be offered at very low prices. There are great opportunities for these kinds of fraud on the Internet, and far weaker barriers to prevent them.

7

The Shift to Weaker Morality, Weaker Law, and Stronger Market Discipline

Barriers to Abuse of Trust and Fraud

While opportunities to abuse trust and the drive for *more* have been rising, the barriers against dishonest behavior have been falling. There are many barriers to dishonesty, but among the main barriers are three. One is moral behavior, where trusted persons exercise self-control over temptations. The second is self-protection, where trusting people protect themselves with the help of market sanctions against abuse of trust. Market sanctions represent mostly self-protection of many people, each acting in his or her own interest. The third barrier to abuse of trust is the law. Morality reflects mainly the "trust" component in "trust but verify." One can trust people who exercise self-control in face of temptations. Self-protection and the markets reflect mainly the "but verify" component in "trust but verify." One must verify the other person's statements and promises. The law reflects and supports both the "trust" component and the self-protection "verify" component. Some rules are designed to put barriers to temptations. These rules are addressed to trusted persons. Some rules require trusted people to disclose true information. These rules are addressed to the recipients of the information, and they are expected to decide for themselves whether and how to engage in business with the disclosing parties. And some rules go further and withdraw legal protection from people who do not protect themselves from the fraud of others, even though they can do so.

Barriers to dishonesty are not free. They cost. Morality puts the burden on the trusted persons to withstand temptation. Law shifts the burden to the government and taxpayers to prevent trusted persons from succumbing to temptation. And the markets transfer the burden to the other parties to the relationships; they should protect themselves from trusted persons who cannot withstand temptation. However, by themselves, none of these barriers to abuse of trust has been effective. Morality alone is not strong enough to enforce honesty. Markets alone do not achieve the goal either. And law on its own has not succeeded in imposing truth and trustworthiness. Each mechanism has supported the other and has drawn on the other for support. Together, they form a whole—a "diversified" package. The relative weight of the components in the package changes with the nature of the relationship among people and with the environment. As their balance changes, the costs that they impose change as well. But so do the deterrent and preventive effects of the barriers. The issue is not merely how much the barriers cost but also how much harm they prevent.

The Dramatic Shift from Morality and the Law to the Markets

In the past few decades, the balance among morality, law, and self-protection in the markets has changed. Morality and the law have weakened. The burden of preventing fraud has been shifting from the trusted parties, such as management, physicians, and lawyers, to the trusting persons, that is, investors, patients, and clients. The law has shifted the focus from regulating trusted persons to providing trusting persons with information with which they are expected to protect themselves against abuse by trusted persons. This chapter discusses morality, the law, and the markets, and the support they derive from each other. I start by examining each mechanism, and then focus on the shift that has occurred between them and the consequences of the shifts.

MORALITY AS SELF-LIMITATION

What Is Morality?

The idea of morality is complex and open to many interpretations and debates. For the purpose of this book, however, people are moral people if they control their temptations to do the wrong thing, and are inclined to do the right thing. The "wrong and right things" are narrowly defined to include a few principles. Moral persons do not abuse the trust that is vested in them and do not deceive. They refrain from misleading others intentionally or negligently, for their own benefit. Moral persons need not give, but they do not *take what they do not own* without the owners' permission. And, most important, they should behave in this manner *even if there are no police around*, that is, even when they are likely to "get away with it."

Moral people impose the rules of honesty on themselves [Hoffman, 123]. If people are *forced* to act according to the same rules, they are not moral. At least one reason for the distinction is that moral persons relieve society from the burden of enforcing its rules. For moral persons, a reward for doing the right thing is not only in the actual right behavior but ultimate power—the power of control: "No one tells me what to do." And even more important, the reward is the power of self-control: "I am the master of myself, and can control my weaknesses in the face of great temptations." From this point of view, rewards or punishments to do the right thing do not empower but signify the opposite. A person who is motivated by rewards or punishments submits to the control of others who can manipulate him by benefits and disadvantages. It is those others who decide how he would act, and have the tools to motivate him [Hoffman, 123]. This distinction is not lost on trusting persons. Therefore, they would trust those who impose limiting rules on themselves more than they would trust those who are forced to follow rules imposed by others.

On the other side of this coin are persons who may claim to be moral but follow their own standards and own rules of morality. This attitude may lead trusting people to trust them less. The self-restraining morality according to one's moral standards is not self-restraining at all. If people reserve to themselves the right to define the temptations that they will withstand, there may be no real temptations. An aspect of moral behavior is self-negation in relation to others, and often for the benefit of others. And if people masqueraded as moral people according to their own rules, they could design rules for their own benefit and comfort, at the expense of those who trust them.

Educating Moral People, and the "Selfish Gene"

Learning moral behavior usually starts at an early age. Parents continuously tell children "not to." Children are admonished not to play with fire, not to hit the little brother, not to torture the cat. Most parents teach their children not to take what does not belong to them, to share their toys with other children, and to tell the truth. Just as important, children are taught to exercise self-restraint even if the parents are not around. Children are thus rewarded for policing themselves. Their self-interest is not dormant, however. What they learn is not necessarily self-sacrifice. What they learn is to avoid antisocial behavior. They learn self-limitation.

Because acting morally is necessarily a habit, morality should be instilled by education at an early age.[1] "Certain components of morality [are] inherently matters of habit: to become attached to collective ideals, 'one must have developed the habits of acting and thinking in common; to assure regularity, it is only necessary that habits be strongly founded.'"[2] We must create "a general disposition of the mind and the will": "a *habitus* of moral being."[3]

For hundreds of years, philosophers, theologians, and scientists have debated the question of whether humans are born good and evil, selfish and unselfish, or whether they develop these tendencies depending on their environment. Researchers have found that people have a "selfish gene" that strives to ensure survival. Yet the "selfish gene" is compatible with moral sentiments [Ridley, 39–40]. Rarely will the individual survive without a society; rarely will society survive if its members are intent only on taking, and each member must continuously protect himself from others.

It is unclear whether all people have sadistic inclinations. Zimbardo's experiments may point both ways. On the one hand, the "guards" were sadistic. On the other hand, only a minority of the subjects of the experiments acted cruelly, even under pressure. After all, most of the subjects—the persons who participated in the experiment—did not take the opportunity to hurt or humiliate others. Most people probably fall in the middle.

In an article entitled "What Makes You Who You Are," Matt Ridley offers an interesting story of the new scientific development on this subject. As animal and human genes were discovered and analyzed, scientists found a remarkable answer to the riddle. They found *flexible genes* that can change with their environment.

> In this new view, genes allow the human mind to learn, remember, imi-
> tate, imprint language, absorb culture and express instincts. Genes are not
> puppet masters or blueprints, nor are they just the carriers of heredity. They
> are active during life; they switch one another on and off; they respond to the
> environment. They may direct the construction of the body and brain in the
> womb, but then almost at once, in response to experience, they set about
> dismantling and rebuilding what they have made. They are both the cause
> and the consequence of our actions.[4]

Society is oscillating in a similar manner. The innate tendencies to self-interest and self-protection are also balanced in marketplace transactions. Adam Smith taught us that morality is important to the maintenance of markets. Society cannot survive if it is composed of people who are always ready to injure one another [Smith, 189–190]. Society may not be able to survive if people are unable to rely on each other. Recent research suggests that Darwin's theory consisted of two parts. One was indeed the survival of the fittest and the strongest. The other, however, was love of other people. The two parts could and should be melded [Loye, 15–22].

The balance between individualism and commitment to the group is demonstrated in a fascinating example of a species of primitive amoebas. As the amoebas emerge from a spore, they begin to feed on the bacteria around them. Then the amoebas divide.

> At this rate it does not take long for them to eat all the bacteria on the agar
> surface—usually about two days. Next comes the magic. After a few hours of
> starvation, these totally independent cells stream into aggregation, each of
> which now acts as an organized multicellular organism. It can crawl towards
> light, orient in the heat gradients, and show an organized unity in various
> other ways. It looks like a small translucent slug. . . . It has clear front and
> hind ends and its body is sheathed in a very delicate coating. . . . After a pe-
> riod of migration . . . the slug stops, points up into the air, and slowly trans-
> forms itself into a fruiting body consisting of tapered stalk [Bonner, 1]

Then the organism splits, and some cells die while others are released and become spores. This living being reflects the duality of human individual and social existence.

The Psychological Supports of Morality

There are self-inflicted and built-in psychological punishments for violating the norms that people feel morally compelled to follow. The norms may be rules of behavior that people have been taught to follow or the rules that the culture of the community has imposed on its members. Whatever their source, when people violate these rules, called "internalized norms," the violators feel psychological pain, even if the violations bring them benefits [Axelrod, 57]. These powerful internal directives distinguish moral people, who follow the norms under internal threats of pain, from others, who follow the norms under external threats of pain.

Shame, guilt and empathy are emotions that humans have developed. These emotions help human beings to reject the temptations to hurt others and demonstrate their reliability to others. Shame and guilt can control the drive to cheat, even if it is "rational" to do so, and even if the cheaters have a good chance of "getting away with it" [Ridley, 134].

How does empathy protect humans from each other? It enables most humans to identify with others, to imagine others' feelings, and sometimes to actually feel the pain and joy of others. To avoid experiencing the victims' pain, people who can feel empathy tend to avoid hurting others. That is why the ability or inability to empathize is considered in sentencing and paroling offenders.[5] The absence of empathy signifies weak self-limiting barriers to injuring others, and the likelihood of repeating these injuries.

Empathy is linked to caring for others and to justice [Hoffman, 228–229]. A bond of empathy can be felt even to people we do not know personally. When we can imagine ourselves as the victims, we more easily demand justice to right a wrong. Thus, empathetic people may go further and give in order to relieve the pain of others. That is why many Americans contribute to feed the hungry in faraway lands. They feel empathy with the hungry.

We would chuckle at the story of the mother who says to her child: "Eat your lunch. Think of all the hungry people in Africa." Rationally, how would someone eating in America alleviate starvation in Africa? In fact, eating the lunch may make a person a bit ashamed at having food when others are hungry. Or did the mother mean: "You are lucky to have food. Others do not have it. So eat." Or the mother could evoke hunger in the child by raising the child's empathy and identity with the hungry. Perhaps the words trigger the child's memory of an incident when he was hungry. Then the child feels like the hungry people in Africa. This last explanation suggests that the mother is raising pangs of hunger in the child as well as the satisfaction of eating when the child identifies with the hungry people in Africa. The chuckle may be explained by the combined empathy for suffering and self-interest of satisfaction.

Empathy can ricochet back from the victims. There is evidence that *showing* remorse and admitting guilt can sooth the victims' anger. For example, the *Wall Street Journal* recently reported on an anesthesiologist who by mistake caused the patient's heart to stop and almost brought about her death. Instead of defending himself against a potential lawsuit, he wrote a letter of apology to the patient and visited her and her husband. He told them he was very sorry, and they believed him.[6] The patient did not sue. As she described her reaction: The doctor was "a real person. . . .

He made an effort to seek me out and say he was sorry I suffered."[7] Empathy helped bind her self-interest with the interest of the doctor. She could imagine, and felt, his anguish. In light of this and similar experiences, hospitals, doctors, and insurers are changing their attitude, and allow doctors to apologize for mistakes, notwithstanding the legal risks.[8]

Shame, guilt, and empathy are not identical with trustworthiness. People can be honest yet lack shame, guilt, and empathy. The law does not require people to experience these feelings. It is not a breach of a duty for corporate management to be insensitive to the pain of others. In fact, lack of empathy can be justified and approved when it might hinder helping others. Physicians and lawyers must control their empathy lest they become dysfunctional by suffering too much. This limitation is understood and accepted.

And yet generally, when people lack these feelings, it is easier for them to harm others. That may include harm in legal and honest ways, as Scrooge did. It may include harm in illegal and dishonest ways as well. But these feelings are linked to honesty and trust because they help people to control their drive to hurt others. Therefore, people who show that they feel shame, guilt, and empathy demonstrate their reliability to others, and are more likely to be trusted.

Even if lack of empathy does not violate the law, it may violate social norms, and be punished by social sanctions. For example, the president of American Airlines negotiated with the corporation's unions a 15 percent cut in the employees' salary. As he was conducting the negotiations, he was "packing and securing" the severance fees and benefits for the corporation's top executives. He attempted to ensure their pensions if American Airlines declared bankruptcy. But he did not disclose these facts to the union negotiators. It may well be that, financially, the management's pension increase of about $100 million was irrelevant to the negotiations. That $100 million may have been insignificant as compared to 15 percent of the employees' salaries, which were slated for reduction. Legally, he may have had the right to withhold the information on the pension arrangements until after the deal with the employees was closed. But this president (and perhaps his advisors) failed to recognize an implicit deception in his silence about the contradictory arrangements. The impression was that he failed to empathize (and identify) with the union members. It seems that he did not feel as one of the employees; and he did not feel for the employees. This was not a legal deception or a breach of any legal duty. But the social sanction followed. The negotiations with the union were poisoned with mistrust, and he had to resign.

Feelings of guilt, shame, and empathy are personal. They may be ingrained in some people more than in others. The depth of these feelings, and especially the desire to avoid inflicting pain on others, are influenced by the attitude of peers and the culture of the communities in which people live. In a culture that undervalues guilt, shame, and empathy, people can be under pressure to share passively in cruelty to others. A national survey of the culture of student hazing, conducted by Alfred

University, demonstrates how such cruelty to others can be practiced.[9] And even if people do not feel hard pressed to join in cruelty to others, and even if these people are the majority, they may still remain passive. They may feel sufficient shame and guilt not to participate in the behavior. But they may still watch cruelty without condemning it or attempting to prevent it. The experiments of Phillip Zimbardo illustrate the point.[10] In those experiments, the majority of the students watched abusive cruelty by students to other students. The majority did not join in the abuse. But the majority also avoided interfering to prevent the cruelty, even though the cruel abusers were in the minority.[11]

It is likely that the same practices apply to abuse of trust and deception. Honest people may be driven to dishonest actions if caught in the frenzy of the crowd. But even those who remain honest may not be driven to condemn fraud or attempt to prevent it. These aspects of honesty depend not merely on the personal tendencies of each member of the community but on the culture of the community as a whole.

TOWARD REDUCING EMPATHY, GUILT, AND SHAME

Intellectualizing

There are ways in which people reduce empathy and "protect themselves from such a weakness." One way is by "intellectualizing" and viewing humans as numbers. As reported in the *Chicago Tribune* and *Chicago Sun-Times*,[12] when Motorola fired about 60,000 employees, it lowered its costs short-term and achieved higher earnings. Management increased its own compensation. Employees can be viewed in terms of expense and income, as $50,000 persons, $30,000 persons, or $100,000 persons—net. When cast in these terms, the employees no longer "feel" like separate units but rather as an indistinguishable part of the expense side and income side of the financial statements [Lynn & Snyder, ch. 28]. Shareholders and bondholders can be aggregated into the right-hand side of the balance sheet. A common denominator, the dollar that represents them, makes them fungible. With this perspective, it is difficult to empathize with each of them or even to empathize with them as a group. Generally, numbers don't raise feelings of identity. It is easier to "deceive and abuse the trust" of numbers. In addition, discussing people in technical terms can help reduce empathy. Words like "downsizing an enterprise" blur the reality of anxious and suffering people who lose their livelihoods. Thus, language and image can lower empathy even in people who naturally possess it.

Blaming Others

Sensitive people can seek to escape the pain they feel for others by blame. For example, close friends may wish to escape the hospital room of a patient whom they love. It is too painful for them to see the patient and feel his discomfort. They may blame the hospital for not making the patient more comfortable as a pretext for leaving the room by [Stotland et al., 73] Other protections are not as benign. When people have done wrong, they can blame others to alleviate the pain of guilt and shame. Managers and financial actors are blaming the victimized investors, thus establishing a new guilt relationship, in which both parties are at fault.

Denial and Normalizing the Wrongs

Some violators protect themselves from the pain of guilt and shame by denial. White-collar offenders are "highly resistant to negative interpretations of their actions, [and] they rationalize their crimes even after conviction and display a remarkable inability to accept the moral implications of their convictions. . . . In rejecting negative labeling, . . . they also reject or manage the accompanying emotions."[13] Armed with this deep conviction, they avoid the internal conflicts and feelings of guilt and shame that usually accompany recognition that one's actions are wrong. Dr. Neal Shover and Glenn S. Coffey noted in their study of telemarketing con artists that they share a "strong culture of denial," according to the *Knoxville (Tennessee) News-Sentinel*. They typically dispute the very criminality of their behavior. They did not accept the authorities' definition of wrong. The telemarketers refused to admit that they were criminals even after they were convicted. Most "rejected the words 'criminal' and 'crime' as being applicable to them and their activities."[14]

SELF-LIMITATION VERSUS SELF-INTEREST

In humans, the drive to take and the pressure not to take (or even give) go hand in hand. Both are part of our nature, and both can be cultivated from an early age [Ridley, 132–141]. Just as self-interest is crucial to survival, so is altruistic behavior necessary for survival [Schulman, ch. 36]. An article published by Nava Ashraf, Iris Bohnet, and Nikita Piankov described an experiment. They found that only about a third of the examined individuals who gave money in trust expected to make money from giving. The other two-thirds got satisfaction from the mere giving, or a "warm glow," as the writers described it.[15] Therefore, giving "pays," not necessarily in the monetary sense. If feeling good about giving and being honest is self-interested, then we are self-interested.

One can interpret all human actions as totally self-interested. The argument would be that self-interest is the exclusive guide to behavior. It motivates every action and excludes consideration of the interests of others, including moral fairness. The argument would be that the motivation for being good to others is to be good to ourselves. The self is the beginning and end. What determines giving is a cost-benefit analysis—that is, an assessment of whether the benefit of giving is greater than the loss of giving.

Yet Matt Ridley notes that "moral motives are as primary, powerful, and emotionally intense as our aggressive and acquisitive ones; . . . concern for others emerges *spontaneously* in very young children (unconnected with any developmental stages)" [Ridley, 38–40]. We want to do good for ourselves. But we also want to do good for others, our community, our dear ones, and people whom we do not know. We want to give without thinking of the benefits that we derive from the giving. In fact, sometimes people may sacrifice rather than benefit, although it is unclear whether this attitude is widespread. Often, however, giving and taking are balanced. When the pressure to take seems stronger, many societies keep the balance between the self and its limitation by imposing a taboo on taking without giving back enough [Ridley, 38–40].

Alan Greenspan, chairman of the Federal Reserve Board, expressed this attitude. In the 1999 commencement speech at Duke University he said:

> At the risk of sounding a bit uncool, I say to the graduating class of 1999 that your success . . . and the success of our country, is going to depend on the integrity and other qualities of character that you . . . will continue to develop. . . . It is decidedly not true that "nice guys finish last." . . . I do not deny that many appear to have succeeded in a material way by cutting corners and manipulating associates. But material success is possible in this world and far more satisfying when it comes without exploiting others.[16]

To paraphrase the statement: The cost of honesty is not very high. Honesty is not altruism. You can reap rewards by self-limitations. It pays to be honest.

Michael Shermer offered a similar view. Leaders, he wrote in *Fortune* magazine, should indeed be selfish and ambitious. But true leaders link their selfishness to the broader view of society and the cosmos:

> Good leaders have a vision for the larger society. . . . [Some of these leaders are] young and rich, and they have these grand visions for colonizing Mars and creating a new society somewhere. They aren't in it to make money, retire, and play golf. You want a visionary leader who is selfish enough to really want to be successful because that is what will drive the company, but also someone who goes beyond that to think about how to improve society.[17]

After all, a world that consists exclusively of the "self" is but a speck, as compared to the cosmos, of which the self can become a part. The selfish drive of a true leader is to become part of something far greater than the mere "self."

The Changing Balance among Morality, Law, and the Markets

In the past few decades, the balance among morality, law, and the markets has shifted. Morality and the law have lost to the markets. There are arguments for "privatizing" morality, as two important legal scholars have made the case forcefully [Kaplow & Shavell, 10–11]. Although these scholars do not necessarily subscribe to the markets as the only lens through which the world can be seen, a movement to privatize morality can reduce its authority and uniformity. Morality can become a purely private matter. Each person should have the right to determine the balance between self-limitation, as compared to self-interest of his conduct. Public policy and the law should have nothing to do with morality. Perhaps the consensus of many persons should guide moral behavior. But how can you determine the guidance and who should declare it, if not some central authority?

Strong self-interest and the freedom to choose when and how to withstand temptation weaken the habit of moral self-limitation. Instead of automatically withstanding temptation as a matter of habit, people would make a cost-benefit analysis of whether self-limitation would serve them well. As John Berryhill wrote:

> The prevailing vision of the US these days is "I got mine, now you get yours." We do not have a society on our hands here. It is simply a free-for-all to grab what you can, and those best at grabbing are the most laudable citizens. The notion of supporting this country through, for example, the payment of taxes is unpatriotic. Patriotism is what those other people's children do in far away countries, so long as the rest of us aren't asked to pay for it.

Law, Morality, and Trust

Law does not fully support morality. It deprives moral people of an advantage, as Gerardo Guerra wrote. Law relegates moral people to the same category as others who must be forced to act honestly. To be sure, moral people can show in other ways that they are intrinsically honest. But they can no longer point to the fact that they are *voluntarily* honest, as compared to those who must be *forced* to be honest.[18] The magazine *CIO* reported that IBM "has beaten its competitors to market with a startlingly new strategy for selling technology: the truth."[19] If legal rules require the same policy, the strategy may not be as startling.

In addition, when fraud and deception are discovered within a group, stricter rules are imposed to prevent wrongful behavior by enterprises that failed to obey the law. But legal rules must deal equally with members of defined groups. Therefore, all similar enterprises are caught in the net of the rule, including those that behaved legally. The new stricter rules can impose unwarranted costs on the moral enterprises. Thus, corporations and financial institutions that acted lawfully are caught in the same net with the wrongdoers and pay the price that only the wrongdoers should have paid.

Legal action and inaction can stimulate immoral actions by recognizing some immoral acts as legal;[20] or by allowing legal violations to go unpunished. In the financial area, if the public is aware that the regulators tolerate illegal activities, the regulators' inaction can send a worse signal than no law at all. A "dead letter" rule promotes disrespect for other legal rules as well. Weak or no enforcement signals to the public that breaking the law is not "really very wrong." Therefore, there is a relationship between what individual market actors do and the rules of the markets and morality. Morals and laws shape each other. [Kaplow & Shavell, 62].

Law Can Help Maintain Morality by Trusted Persons

Even though law deprives moral people of the advantage of acting voluntarily in an honest way, law rewards all honest people (whether moral or not) by helping them to establish a reputation for honesty. It declares that those who act in accordance with the rules are honest, and helps establish a reputation for honesty. Sometimes it is hardly possible to prove negative facts. Establishing a reputation for honesty among strangers is not easy. Building a reputation takes time; offering guarantees, such as insurance, takes money. The law reduces these burdens.

Many of the traditional rules governing people who hold other people's money are of the "not to" category, infused with approval of those who withstand temptations. The famous case of *Meinhard v. Salmon* demonstrates the link of law to the morality of trusted people. The case involved a managing partner and a "silent partner" who initially financed the deal. A few months before the end of the twenty-year partnership term, the managing partner obtained a business opportunity, which he received at least in part as a result of his managerial position. He took the opportunity to the exclusion of his silent partner. The silent partner did not lose any money. He lost the opportunity to make more money. One would call him greedy. Nonetheless, the court entitled the silent partner to the information about the profitable opportunity. Justice Cardozo wrote:

> Many forms of conduct permissible in a workaday world for those acting at arm's length are forbidden to those bound by fiduciary ties. A trustee is held to something stricter than the morals of the market place. Not honesty alone, but the punctilio of honor the most sensitive, is then the standard of behavior. . . . Only thus has the level of conduct for fiduciaries been kept at a level higher than that trodden by the crowd.[21]

Justice Cardozo stereotypes fiduciaries (trusted persons) in a masterful way. He announces as a matter of fact that fiduciaries behave morally. He builds up their reputation as honest persons. But he also notifies the whole world and the fiduciaries that fiduciaries *should* behave as they are described. This statement backs up the commitment of the law to moral behavior. It induces fiduciaries to internalize their obligations and moral self-limitations. In Justice Cardozo's book, law and morality interact and support one another.

Justice Cardozo does not suggest that market transactions need not involve trust. In fact, verifying the other party's statements and promises is often necessary in market contract relationships. Verification is especially necessary when the parties have different levels of information. George Akerlof's market for lemons is relevant here. When a dealer and a potential buyer negotiate the price of a used car, the dealer knows far more about the history and flaws of the car than the buyer knows. Considering the uncertainties, the inability to trust the dealer whom he does not know and to verify the facts, the buyer will offer a lower price for the car than the seller is willing to accept. In such a case, the market for used cars will collapse.[22] The legal rules help maintain such a market. The rules prohibit the car dealers from hiding facts that are costly to discover (e.g., changing the number of miles that the car was driven). If the "market of lemons" theory is correct, then the law helps reduce the buyers' uncertainty about the dealer's honesty. Thus, law helps the dealer collect a higher price reflecting the worth of the car. Not more; but also not less.

The disclosure requirements under the securities laws are based on the same assumptions. If a potential buyer of a used car cannot discover secrets of the car's past and its potential future, a buyer of a share in an ongoing business is even more in the dark. It is far harder to know and evaluate the business. The federal laws do not require issuers to offer their securities at a fair price, as some state laws of the past have commanded. Rather, the federal securities laws require the issuers to provide potential investors with true and detailed information.[23] These laws reduce for potential investors the cost of verifying the issuers' statements and promises. The information reduces the investors' uncertainty and risk and enables the issuers to collect a price, which better reflects the worth of the business. Not more; but also not less.

In addition to prohibitions, there is a type of rule that resembles moral self-limitation. One example is the law that aims at preventing preference in pricing mutual fund shares. The law does not prohibit such preference. It provides that the price of mutual funds shares that are bought or redeemed will be the price *after the orders have been placed.* This type of rule eliminates hard-to-discover preferences. Another example is the rules governing teachers' grading at Boston University Law School and other schools. Except in a relatively small class, the exam papers are marked by numbers. This system eliminates even instinctive likes and dislikes that teacher might have toward students. After the "blind" grading, the teachers receive the students' names, and the teachers may make small adjustments in light of the students' performance in class. Otherwise, a grade cannot be changed except by a formal vote of the whole faculty. This self-limiting system relieves teachers of temptation and of students' pressures. The rule does not prohibit preference. It practically eliminates the possibility of preference. This is the kind of rule that inspires trust.

Psychological Effect of the Law in Maintaining Honesty

Law has a special psychological effect on people's behavior. In general, people respond instinctively to the expectations of others. If they are trusted, most people usually feel compelled to be trustworthy. But if the same people are shown mistrust and suspicion, they are more likely to take offense and become less trustworthy. This is why it is more difficult to ask a friend rather than a stranger to prove the truth of what he says or promises to do. You do not maintain friendship by doubting a friend's words and promises [Barber, 11–14]. An experiment conducted by Maurice E. Schweitzer sought to determine the relationship between monitoring, which signals lack of trust or suspicion, and a certain trusted behavior. The experiment showed that the trusted or honest behavior increased with frequent monitoring. That is not hard to understand. The higher probability of being caught prevented dishonest behavior. The people who expected to be monitored were more honest than others during the periods that they were monitored. But the overall trustworthy behavior of these people decreased. This result suggests that as monitoring signified lack of trust, they lived down to the expectation by being less trustworthy.

The judgment of the monitors is interesting. The monitors trusted less the people who knew that they are being monitored. The monitoring parties trusted more the people who did not know that they were watched. This reaction suggests that a person who acts honestly without suspicion that the police are around is more trustworthy. The presence of police makes it harder to distinguish a moral trustworthy person from a dishonest person. Both will act honestly. But only a moral honest person will act honestly when police are not around.[24]

A demand for proof as protection against abuse of trust affects both the trusted persons and the other parties to the relationship—the trusting persons. If a person is continuously suspected, he or she develops a habit of being less trustworthy. If a person continuously demands proof and guarantees, the very pattern of asking for verification may breed a habit of suspicion and mistrust. However, the parties need not develop this pattern of behavior when the responsibility and blame for demanding verification can be shifted to others.

Law can play the role of that third party. Law can encourage or even require a party to question and investigate a trusted person without giving offense, and without creating a habit of mistrust. When parents tell their teenage children not to drive after drinking alcohol, they help the children ward off the pressure of their friends, who might dare the children to drive after drinking. The children could blame the parents for this "unreasonable" rule. "What can I do? My father said that if I drive after drinking he will ground me for a month."[25] If an authority rather than the trusting party demands proof, the trusted person is not offended and continues to feel trusted. When the trusting party is forced to ask for verification, it can ask for proof without suspicion and skepticism. It simply obeys the order of someone else. In business relationships, law serves the role of a "parent" and a third party authority. The demanding party has "no choice" but to ask for verification. "I trust you. But what can I do? The law demands it."

Thomas Schelling offers another example of the same interaction. He recounts how a coercive rule helped the Boston Bruins hockey team overcome the players' reluctance to wear helmets. The players feared ridicule, although all understood the strong need of wearing a protective helmet. The National Hockey League's coercive rule resolved the problem. The players could say: "We had no choice. We were forced to wear this silly thing and look like sissies." [Schelling, 213].

In addition, law can convince people with a weaker moral backbone that honesty "pays."[26] Such people may be convinced not by the right but by the might of the law. They may desire to avoid punishment, to shine in the light of the legal advertisement for honesty, and to gain the approval and trust of others. For whatever reason, they follow the rules.

The Effect of Formal Legal Contracts in Supporting Business Understandings

The law need not spell out in detail how honest people should behave. It helps enforce informal rules when they stand in the shadow of the law. Legal formal rules help support an understanding based on goodwill and honesty. For example, the contracts that people write leave open many conditions. These conditions are left to the parties' unspoken understanding about goodwill and honesty. Do formal rules support or undermine the parties' understanding? As one would expect, the answer is complex and inconclusive. But a recent study suggests that formal contacts complement and support the enforcement of noncontract conditions. Short-term relationships require formal, but simple, contracts.[27] The two interact.

Morality of the Public: Why Do People Obey the Law?

There is a growing literature on why people obey the law voluntarily. I deal with the subject in greater detail in chapter 12. Yet the topic should be noted here as well. How is it that people enforce restrictive laws on themselves? Robert Cooter, Richard McAdams, Eric Posner, Alex Geisinger, Tom Tyler, and Dan Kahan have demonstrated the ways of self-enforcement.[28] Even though punishment may play a role, there is evidence that people follow their internal commands, their peers, their leaders, and the crowd in obeying the law.[29] Thus, people may observe the law voluntarily, depending on how their leaders, their communities, and other people act. The forces of self-limitation are not so much internal, as is discussed in this chapter, as they are societal. Nonetheless, the component of self-limitation and following the law is prevalent in American society. To the extent that self-limitation is a major part of moral behavior, most Americans behave in a moral way.

Morality Helps Enforce the Law

To use an economic measure, morality is the least expensive mechanism for maintaining honesty. It is relatively long term, because moral persons acquire a habit of self-enforced honesty. As to them, the police need not be on constant alert. But morality alone is not enough to prevent fraud when temptation is great, competition is fierce, and pressures to win are very high. Morality must be strengthened, as hard as this is to accomplish. Yet, instead of supporting morality, we have undermined it.

8

The Subtle Changes in Legal Doctrine and Interpretation

The past three decades can be summarized as follows. We reduced the power of morality in the law. We have emasculated the regulation of trusted persons—fiduciaries. We have weakened the laws that govern fiduciaries' honesty, allowed them more freedom, and called the relaxing rules more efficient. But by doing so, we have reduced the efficiency of government enforcement of honesty, increased the risk of abuse, and opened the door to enormous losses to the public and the economic system. We have elevated the role of the markets in preventing abuse of trust. But by doing so, we have shifted the burden of policing fraudulent fiduciaries to the parties who dealt with these fiduciaries, such as the investors in corporate shares, and the patients of physicians. We have changed legal doctrine to reduce the burdens and stigma on embezzling fiduciaries and converted them to salespersons and contracting parties in the markets.

Chapters 8, 9, and 10 show how, in the name of efficiency and freedom from government regulation, we have weakened the controls over the temptations facing fiduciaries, and fiduciary professionals. These chapters show how controls were weakened by recasting the whole world as a market, all fiduciaries as advertisers and sellers of trust services, and their beneficiaries as buyers. These chapters tell the story of how these changes came about and the theories that supported them. "The road to hell is often paved with good intentions." Brilliant ideas and theories carried too far, without caution, and sometimes without judgment, can produce disasters that undermine the good that they brought in the first place.

Changes in the Law

The Movement to "Deregulate" and Hegemony of the Market

The crisis of financial frauds that were discovered in the 1990s did not start in the 1990s. Its seeds were sown in the 1970s. It was then that a slow but basic shift was beginning to take place. The purpose of the shift was to restrict the law's intrusion on market activities and to "deregulate." These were good, creative, and courageous moves. For example, Congress abolished the fixed-commission rates on the New York Stock Exchange.[1] Regulators allowed traders to standardize stock options and develop a market in them.[2] Investment advisors to mutual funds were permitted to develop new structures, such as money market funds.[3] And at the beginning of the 1980s, when mutual funds were hurting and shrinking, advisors were allowed to use the shareholders' assets to finance the sale and distribution of fund shares.[4] As Jim Saxon notes, this innovation, together with the passage of the Employee Retirement Income Security Act of 1974, which favored the professional management of pension plans by registered advisors, contributed to the enormous growth of mutual funds.[5] On the judicial side, the ability of private parties to bring actions for violation of the securities acts was restricted, and, with few exceptions, courts deferred to corporate directors' judgment.[6] All these steps reduced the intervention of the courts of law and left the actors greater freedom from legal restrictions.

Deregulation was accompanied by strong legal support of the "markets" and their judgment. Laws strengthened true disclosure, in the belief that it is crucial to the existence of effective markets. Armed with this information, investors were expected to evaluate the offered securities and products, and pay the "right price" for them. The system emphasized "verify" by available information about the securities and products, and deemphasized "trust" in those who offer the securities and products. And that was fine in market relationships.

Further Deregulation

It made much sense to "deregulate" and shift control of economic activities to the markets. Up to a certain point. But then the envelope was pushed further, undermining the legal requirements for true information about securities. First, there surfaced the efficient market hypothesis. The theory, which was greatly influential,

> says that investors quickly make effective use of available information in buying and selling stocks. What they are willing to pay for a stock depends on how much they expect this stock to return (in dividends and capital gains) in the future. . . . So long as there are rational well-informed investors, who react quickly to changing events and information, stock prices should reflect their future prospects.

Thus, under the theory, the market already has "all the relevant information"; therefore, there is no need for regulation to ensure that such information is indeed available in the market. The price reflects all that investors need to know. But when insider trading showed that market prices do not include all available information and that some information is not available to public investors but only to insiders, the hypothesis was limited to include only "publicly available information" and exclude insider information. While this theory was well accepted in the 1970s, recently the observed facts of the market raised significant questions as to its validity [Mansfield, 153]. The theory reached a full circle. Alon Brav and J. B. Heaton noted that full information no longer represented the right price. *It is the price that represented true and relevant information.* Why should this be? It is unclear why the buyers' information and pricing of securities is more accurate than the information known to the issuers of securities. After all, consumers and investors do not have sufficient and accurate information to calculate the "correct" prices objectively.[7]

Why reduce disclosure requirements? Early on, in the 1970s, scholars like Homer Kripke argued against the legal requirements of publishing to the market information about the issuers. These scholars noted that investors did not read the information that the issuers were required by law to send the investors.[8] Besides, the required data is already available, regardless of legal rules and enforcement. And even if data is unavailable, or not available in full, the intended readers do not care. The price tells them the truth. In addition, sending the information is costly. The regulation of truthful information is wasteful. So why should it be necessary to impose information requirements and their costs on the sellers of securities?

The cost of disclosure became an important factor in limiting the legal requirements for information. But the legal requirements were not eliminated.[9] Because investors do not read the hefty prospectuses written in "legalese," the SEC launched a movement to induce investors to read by providing information in "plain English."[10] Yet this movement created problems as well. The problems stem from the fact that the information to investors serves multiple, and not necessarily compatible, purposes. It can serve as advertising the virtue of the offered securities. It can also serve as protection against investors' claims of misrepresentation. And it can serve as a tool for educating the investors. Plain English may help investors educate themselves and understand what they are buying but might weaken the legal protections of issuers against claims of misstatements and reduce the value of the information as advertising. In addition, the plain English puts the government in the business of writing or rewriting the sales literature of the issuers and the drafting of their lawyers.

An important reason for requiring the publication of true information about the issuers was lost in the heat of these arguments. The requirement for publication is based not only on educating investors and ensuring that they receive true information or allowing the issuers to advertise their securities but also on inducing corporate management to tell the truth under the penalty of law. The need to publicize could prevent management from doing what they would not wish to publicize. Publicity not only informs the public but also cleanses the informants. Behavior changes when one lives in a glass bowl. Yet pressures to deregulate and emphasis on the cost of disclosure created resistance to legal requirements for public full and true information.

The Challenge of Economics to Fiduciary Law

Over the past 30 years, a strong movement of lawyers, scholars and some judges advocated changing the law that regulated trusted persons—fiduciaries. The movement pressed hard for fashioning the law of fiduciaries to mimic the law regulating contract parties. Scholars, such as Daniel Fischel, and judges, such as Frank Easterbrook and Richard Posner, viewed the world of fiduciaries and beneficiaries as the market world, and the relationship of fiduciaries and the people who trust them as contract relationships, buying and selling goods and services.[11] As I shall show, the change reduces the fiduciaries' duty to repay the profits they made off other people's money. Even more important, the change removes the stigma attached to abuse of trust. A breach of contract does not have the strong odor of dishonesty.

The Test of Fiduciary Law's Efficiency: Inefficient Rules *Can Be* Efficient Enforcers *of Honesty*

The regulation of fiduciaries can be viewed as inefficient. It prevents trusted persons from doing what is legal for others. For example, fiduciaries may not transact any business between their beneficiaries and themselves. The principle in fiduciary law is that a person should not serve two masters. He cannot be loyal to both, especially if he is one of the masters. Therefore, a corporate manager may not buy corporate assets, even at market price, and even if the deal benefits the corporation (it may save on commissions). The manager must get approval for such a sale from parties who are "objective" and not interested. These parties can represent the shareholders and decide whether the shareholders would benefit from the deal and whether the terms of the deal are fair. But if such deals are prohibited, then from the point of view of the managers, and sometimes even from the point of view of the corporation, the prohibition is inefficient. It prevents innocent parties from making profitable transactions, and creating value.

The other side of this coin was ignored. These inefficient rules, limiting the freedom of trusted persons to gain, are efficient in limiting the freedom of trusted persons to gain by abusing their trust. To evaluate the efficiency of these restrictive rules, one must consider the cost to the government and to all trusting people of enforcing the fiduciaries' honesty. If weak enforcement results in the harm that we are discovering since the opening of the twenty-first century, then the restrictions on the fiduciaries and their losses of profits pale in comparison. Inefficient rules may be highly efficient after all.

Besides, fiduciaries who are subject to restrictive rules do not lose all. The restrictions bestow on fiduciaries such as corporate directors and officers a reputation for honesty and help them gain the investors' trust. Even if the value of investors' trust is discounted in the belief that investors care more for profits, it may still be worth something. Over the long term, being trustworthy turns out to be good business, and rules that prevent abuse of trust can turn out to be profitable after all.

THE NATURE OF FIDUCIARY LAW: A SHORT REVIEW OF DOCTRINE

Who Is Interested in "Technical Legal Doctrine"?

Why should nonlawyers be interested in legal doctrine, and especially in a long discussion of the topic? One answer is that the changing legal doctrine reflects the evolution of American culture and draws on the developments that have been percolating in America for some time. The more important answer is that this legal doctrine is not in the public domain today but is reserved to the profession. It is time for the public to discover what the latest generation of jurists is thinking. The public ought to understand how these jurists, who affect the law or even make the law, view trusted powerful people on whom the public depends. The public not only ought to know but is entitled to know.

A detailed discussion of contract and fiduciary law is outside the scope of this book.[12] It is unnecessary. My purpose here is to show the direction of the law in regulating fiduciaries. One important example of this direction in the past 25 years is the attempts to subsume the law of fiduciaries into the law of contract. Sometimes a transition of the rules is not very clear. For example, transactions may remain within their historical categories, but the rules within the traditional categories can change, by absorbing borrowed rules and principles from other categories [Corbin, 1:111]. In the case of fiduciaries who hold other people's money, however, there was and continues to be a strong movement, bold and open, to change categories—from fiduciary law category to contract law category.

A battle of categories is no idle pastime. Classification determines substance and image. It makes a great difference whether people who hold other people's money are accused of embezzlement or of failing to keep their word. After all, embezzlement can be subsumed in contract. It can be viewed as breaking a promise not to take other people's money and not to use it as your own. But the difference is significant. Embezzlement carries with it a moral stigma. Breaking a promise is far less pernicious. Even stealing is less abhorrent than embezzlement, because embezzlement is easy stealing. And it is stealing what is voluntarily *given in trust.* When the category of contract absorbs fiduciary relationships, the category colors fiduciary relationships with the moral standards and the rules of a contract exchange, converting the fiduciary into a seller of service, and his embezzlement into a breach of promise.

"Trust" and "Verify" in Contract Relationships

Trust or verification or both are often necessary between buyers and sellers, especially if the parties do not have equal information. But a trusted party to an exchange is not a "trustee" of the money he receives in an exchange. A trusted party in an exchange is not a "fiduciary," who is expected to act for the benefit of the other party. This kind of trusted party has a right to the money he receives and can use the money for his own benefit. After all, that is the deal.

When a trustee receives money in trust, the parties do not intend the money to belong to the trustee. That is not the purpose of the transfer. The purpose of the transfer is to allow the trustee to manage the money for the other party's benefit. The money continues to belong to the person who entrusted the money—the "entrustor." There are gray areas in which the status of the money can be debated. There are gray areas in which the status of controlling other people's money can be debated. But by and large, the models of a contract party and a fiduciary can be clearly distinguished. Money given in a contract exchange belongs to the receiver. Money given in trust continues to belong to the giver.

Many, if not all, the rules that surround the area of contract and fiduciary can be explained in light of this distinction. Shifting a trustee into the category of a buyer or seller confuses the status of property that a trustee receives. It can mislead some trustees into believing that the entrusted property belongs to them when it does not.

TYPES OF FIDUCIARY AND CONTRACT RELATIONSHIPS

The Money Manager and His Client

What are the differences between contract and fiduciary law? Here is an example. When a person hires an advisor to manage his savings, the parties create two types of relationships. One relationship is a contract for hire: an exchange. The advisor offers his services in exchange for fees. The advisor can do with his fees whatever he likes. The fees belong to him.

The second relationship in this transaction is fiduciary.[13] The client hands his savings to the advisor so that the advisor will manage the client's money more efficiently. If the client controlled his money, the advisor would have to involve the client in every transaction, and that is costly and inefficient. Therefore, the only purpose for handing the client's money to the advisor is to facilitate the advisory service. The client can then tend to his business and rely on the advisor to invest the money prudently and honestly for the client's benefit. This money that the client hands over to the advisor continues to belong to the client. The advisor must manage the money and use it for the sole benefit of the client, and according to the client's directives.

The Physician and His Patient

A similar and even more powerful example of a fiduciary is the physician. A physician who performs surgery on a patient gains full control over the patient's body and sometimes over the patient's life. Yet the patient's body continues to belong to the patient. For example, in one case, a physician used a patient's unique cells to develop a new medicine. The physician asked the patient to make occasional visits for tests but did not tell him about the research. When the physician patented the medicine, the patient sued for ownership of the patent. The court held that the physician misappropriated the property of the patient in his body. Even though the patient was not harmed, and the physician patented his own innovation, the physician had to share the financial fruits of his research with the patient.[14] That is because the physician was a fiduciary, and got control over the patient's body as a fiduciary.

The Teacher and His Students

A teacher is also a fiduciary with respect to some of his powers. I sometimes propose to my students a scheme. I want to auction off the grades at the end of the semester. I will give the highest grades to the highest bidder, and the students can even create a market in the grades. Would not that be attractive? It is attractive to me. After reflection, students note that the grades are designed to show how proficient they are, and not how wealthy they are. Therefore, the idea is not very good. But the main point usually eludes them. It is that my power to award grades is not mine to sell. I hold the power in trust for the university. The university gave me the power for a specific purpose, and for no other. That is the main difference. There was no exchange. I received the power as a fiduciary.

SUBSUMING FIDUCIARY DUTIES INTO CONTRACT

The recent revelations regarding corporate top management, mutual fund advisors, and securities analysts show the effects of converting fiduciary relationships into contracts.

Prohibitions on Conflicts of Interest Transactions

If fiduciaries—trusted persons—benefit from deals with other people's money, the fiduciaries are likely to be convinced that the deals are fair. It makes no difference that the market price is a benchmark for self-dealing of this sort. The vision of a fixed, certain "market price" is misleading. There are market *prices*, not one price, for most securities, commodities, and services. There are choices that remain within the trusted persons' power; there is much room for biases. Dealing for themselves and for others, they are likely to lean toward benefiting themselves, even unaware of the tendency. If a fiduciary needs a personal loan and obtains favorable terms from a particular bank that seeks the fiduciary's clients' business, the fiduciary may decide that the bank is also the best bank for his clients. An initial deal that could be fair to the clients may be slowly tilted with time against the clients. A little more to the bank would not hurt the clients; and a little more, and a little more. After all, these are just pennies per share but millions for the bank and the trusted person.

In fiduciary law, with few explicit exceptions, all such benefits are prohibited, that is, unless the client agrees to the arrangements after receiving full information. The client may do with his money as he wishes. If he wishes to give the fiduciary a gift, or if he trusts the fiduciary entirely, that is fine. The principle is, therefore, that for the client's consent to be binding, the client must be fully informed and independent of the fiduciary. The fiduciary may not benefit in any shape or form from the money that the client entrusted to the fiduciary for management or from any power that is vested in him.

This, however, is not the end of the story. How can the client ensure that the fiduciary does not use the money or the vested power for other than the purpose for which it is intended? The cost of supervising the fiduciary and making sure that he does not benefit from the entrusted money is very high. The cost of making sure that the fiduciary manages the money well is also very high. If the client watches over the manager closely, this strict supervision undermines the very purpose of the arrangement. The client would lose the time necessary to tend to his own affairs. Besides, the client may not know how to invest in the securities market, and will be unable to judge whether the manager is doing the right thing. After all, that is why he hired the fiduciary in the first place. Supervision without expertise is useless.

The Operating Surgeon Who Left for the Bank

An example of a conflict of interest is the story of the surgeon published in the *Boston Globe* on August 8, 2002. While he was performing an operation, the surgeon received a cell phone call from his broker. It was a margin call. The price of his shares was falling. Since he used the shares as collateral for a loan, if the price of the shares fell, he had to cover the shortfall by adding money or collateral. If he did not, the shares would be sold (at a loss). The physician left the operating table and rushed to the bank, to deposit more money in his broker's account and prevent the sale.[15]

Luckily for him, the patient survived. Yet this physician lost his license to practice medicine. Why should he, if no harm was done? The answer is that he was a fiduciary. He had full power over the patient's life. He endangered the patient's life, regardless of the probabilities. He succumbed to a conflict of interest (his financial loss versus the loss of the patient's health or life). He abused the patient's trust (that he will perform the operation and that he will operate to the best of his abilities). The patient could not possibly have consented to this behavior in advance of or during the operation. These factors appear in most cases of abused fiduciary relationships.

Disney's Chairman and CEO and His Friend

A thought-provoking story is that of the short-lived tenure of the president of the Walt Disney Corporation. Disney's controlling chairman, Michael Eisner, decided to hire a longtime friend as Disney's president, although the friend had little experience in this position. It soon became clear that the friend and the job were unsuitable for each other. So the friend began to look for other opportunities, and less than a year after he started work he was ready to resign and leave.

The legal arrangement between the new president and the corporation was unusual. No contract was signed when the friend started work. Negotiations on his contract with the corporation continued for some time. And while Eisner caused the corporation to sign and obligate itself to grant stock options to his friend, the friend did not accept the options until later. These options granted the friend the right to receive Disney's stock and pay for the stock at the market price at the time when the options were given. When the corporation signed the options, the price at which the friend could buy the shares froze. But the friend did not sign the agreement then. When he signed, the market price of Disney's stock was higher than the price of the stock that the friend could buy by exercising the options. Therefore, he could accept the options, buy the stock at the exercise price, and then sell the stock and pocket the difference. The difference amounted to a significant amount of money. Moreover, the contract was termed so that it offered the president's friend more money for leaving the job than for staying on the job. He parted with $140 million.[16] The shareholders' challenge in Delaware Court was pending as of March 9, 2004.[17]

The interesting part of the story is how the two friends dealt with each other, the corporation, and the board of directors. Board members, all honorable and experienced businesspersons, were aware of the choice of the friend as president and the contract negotiations. Yet the board hardly interfered, even though under the articles of associations of Disney, the board had the exclusive power to choose and determine the contract terms of Disney's president. The board simply acquiesced. The two friends dealt with each other as if the matter was a private hiring and an amicable termination of the position. The matter was, however, an agreement about other people's money. But neither the chairman nor his friend seemed to notice. There were signs that some board members were uneasy with the choice of the president. But they did nothing formal about it. The case shows how people in power can become less sensitive to the fact that their power does not belong to them.

The Directors Who Have Consulting Contracts with the Corporation

Directors are compensated for serving on corporate boards. The service can be time-consuming and involve legal liabilities. As their duties and responsibilities have increased in recent years, so have their compensations. That is only fair. But what about directors who earn many dollars under consulting contracts with the corporation? What about other benefits that the new directors would receive, such as significant contributions to universities in which the new directors have an interest? The *Washington Post* reported that Enron Corporation donated money to George Mason University, where Wendy Gramm, director of Enron, headed a program on regulatory studies.[18] And a story in the *USA Today* noted that Senator George Mitchell has a consulting contract with a number of corporations on whose boards he serves as a director.[19] These contracts and benefits are granted by the corporation's top management. Yet part of the board's mandate is to supervise and monitor the management's performance. The contracts and donations involving significant amounts may present a conflict of interest.

Even assuming that the independent spirit of the directors-consultants is very strong, as in the case of Senator Mitchell, there is a serious question whether directors should accept such contracts in this day and age. These contracts could *seem* to influence the directors' judgment, even if they don't. If shareholders rely on directors to represent the shareholders in supervising the management, then directors must not only be independent of management but also seem to be independent of management. These contracts give the contrary impression. Under the Investment Company Act of 1940, for example, directors might not qualify as disinterested directors if they receive contracts of this sort from the advisor who manages their funds.[20] But in the case of other corporations, there is no legal prohibition on such contracts, if the disinterested directors approve the contracts. The question here involves judgment and the posture of leadership.

The Shift from Fiduciary to Contract: Does It Make Any Difference?

What difference does it make if fiduciary relationships are subject to contract law instead of fiduciary law? Both contract and fiduciary relationships are voluntary, between consenting parties. But that is where the similarity begins to fade. In a contract of exchange, even as the parties agree to a transaction, they know and recognize that their interests are conflicting. The buyer wants to pay less; the seller wants to charge more. The buyer wants more guarantees of quality; the seller wants to minimize them. Each party wishes to maximize its advantages, and the other party knows it. The law recognizes the parties' own awareness of the conflict and expects each party to protect his interests from the other. To be sure, the law prohibits fraud, and requires the parties to tell each other the truth (when asked). The law requires them to abide by their promises, with a few exceptions, such as events beyond the parties' control. Nonetheless, the basic principle is that once a party receives true information, he is expected to make his own decision in his own interest. Rarely do contract parties promise each other to take care of each other's interests. And if they do, the court may recast these promises as fiduciary obligations.

Years ago, I was asked to render an opinion about a contract that was clearly a sale, except that in a certain situation, one party was entitled to set up a fair price for the other party. In the arbitration among the parties, the defendants' lawyers were surprised as the words "fiduciary duty" arose. When they consulted me, I told them that as to the price, a fiduciary duty did indeed arise (within limits). The defendants had bargained for the power to decide a fundamental condition of the contract that would bind the other party. They could no longer ignore the interests of the other party. They were bound to be fair.

Why does the law impose stricter duties on fiduciaries? What business is it of the lawmakers to interfere in deals among independent parties? Let each party take care of himself. And if the weaker parties are hurt, they will learn the lesson and protect themselves better in the future. They can pay less for the product to compensate for their risks. They could organize and combine to become a more powerful counterparty.

They will be more careful to research and interact only with those who are proven to be trustworthy. Let them find their own shields. This is the contract model.

There are a number of answers to these arguments. First, public policy encourages people to resort to services in medicine, law, banking, and investment management, to name a few. Yet, for the financial system to flourish, investors must be players in the markets. Government regulation of fiduciaries signals the importance that the government assigns to these services. Second, if the risk of fiduciaries' dishonesty is high, people will not trust fiduciaries and will either refrain from using their services or will demand guarantees, or pay less for the services. Law reduces these risks, and the possible reaction of the trusting people. Third, the inequality among the parties in fiduciary relationships can relate to specialization, not necessarily to bargaining power alone. A person may be wealthy and powerful but lack the time to check out his manager, or lack the expertise to supervise and ensure the ability and honesty of his physician. Fourth, regulators can check the fiduciaries better than small investors, or single patients, can. The costs of legal enforcement are distributed over the taxpaying population, or among the members of the professions. By reducing the peoples' risks, the costs to the fiduciaries in establishing their trustworthiness are reduced as well.

Different Remedies

The remedies for breach of contract are different from the remedies for violating fiduciary duties. Usually, a party that breaches its contract must pay the other party the damages caused by the breach, including, sometimes, anticipated profits. If a party to a contract suffered no damage from the breach of the other, the breaching party is likely to pay nothing and keep its profits from the breach. For example, suppose Jones sold Able 100 shares of "Bargain Corporation" for $100. Before delivering the shares, Jones finds a buyer willing to pay $110 for these shares. Jones sells his shares for the higher price. Able then buys the same shares on the market for $100. Jones breached his contract. But Able cannot prove damages (except, perhaps the added transaction costs, if he had any). Jones will keep his profit, even though it arose from a breach of contract.

Abuse of trust is treated differently. For example, the fiduciary buys 100 shares of Bargain Corporation from the estate that he manages as trustee. He pays $100 to the estate—the market price. He then sells the shares to another person for $110. The trustee need not pay the estate any damages, because the estate did not suffer any loss: It received the market price for the shares. But regardless of whether the estate suffered damages, the trustee will have to account to the estate for his profits of $10. He must pay the profits even though the estate was not harmed at all. That is because the trustee benefited from his power over the property that belonged to the estate. The law will view him as the estate's agent. He misappropriated the power over the estate's assets and must pay the estate every penny he earned as a result of this misappropriation.

In the case of *Securities and Exchange Commission v. Warde,* a fiduciary profited by violating its duties.[21] But in the same transactions, the fiduciary's profits were unrelated to the violations. The court held that the fiduciary was not entitled to any of the profits, including those that were gained without relation to the abuse of trust. This court squeezed all profits that the fiduciary gained in connection with the wrongful acts and required these profits to be paid to the beneficiary.

The story of Frank W. Snepp offers an extreme example of this principle. Snepp was a CIA agent. His contract with the government prohibited him from publishing information about the agency without government permission. After he left the CIA, Snepp published a book about the agency without permission, and was sued for breaking his contract. The material he used was public information, and the government failed to show damages. However, the court held that the *information* Snepp received during his employment was the property of the government, and, that Snepp misappropriated the information for his own use and benefit. Having reclassified the relationship as fiduciary *with respect to the information,* the court required Snepp to account for his profits from the publication of the book, and pay the profits to the government. This remedy made it unlikely that he or any other agent would write such a book for profit without the government's approval.[22]

The Role of the Courts

Another difference between a breach of contract and abuse of trust in fiduciary relationships is the role of the courts and legislatures. These lawmakers determine many fiduciary duties, and impose strict rules of behavior designed to reduce temptations. In contract law, the parties determine most of the terms. "Hard bargains," as unfair as they might be, are likely to survive attack in the courts [Restatement (Second) of Contracts, § 208; Uniform Commercial Code § 2–302 cmt. 1; Williston, 3:383–386]. The attitude is a "too bad" attitude, a "you should have been more careful" attitude. Under the fiduciary regime, the beneficiaries, such as the investors or the patients, are more protected from unfair treatment. By definition, the dependent party to a fiduciary relationship is less able to protect itself. Therefore, the courts assume that the dependent trusting party would not have agreed to an unfair behavior of the fiduciary, and attribute these results to the relationship with the fiduciary [Restatement (Third) of Trusts, § 2 cmt. b; Scott & Fratcher, 1:43].

The Very Different Stigma

A different stigma attaches to those who breach their contract from those who breach their fiduciary duties. A breach of contract is a breach of a promise. Some breaches of fiduciary duties constitute misappropriation of property vested in trust. If the breach reaches the level of embezzlement, it becomes more than a stigma. It becomes a crime! In 1949, Edwin H. Sutherland noted that the claims against corporations were rarely criminal, even though the violations are crimes. White-collar criminals that manage corporations were shielded. Even if they were found *liable,* they were not found *guilty*. The stigma attached to the wrongs was different. One of the reasons for the different treatment, he asserted, was the status of a corporate manager as a businessman [Sutherland, 56]. The move from fiduciary law to contract law represents a further downward step, with similar results. Perhaps, in part, the move is driven by the same motive, to protect the good name of corporate management. Yet it allows the wrongdoers to be covered by the good name of those who did no wrong.

How Does the Shift from Fiduciary Law to Contract Law Occur?

A shift from one legal category to another need not be made in one drastic step. One does not wake up one morning to find that one's relationship has changed from a fiduciary partner to a contract partner. The change can be creeping up in different ways and directions. Names may change even if the contents remain the same. Or the names may remain the same, but the meanings and content change, and the names are added to changes that were already made.

The Shift in Academia

In 1993, a renowned academic, Daniel Fischel, and an academic turned judge, Frank Easterbrook, wrote an article in which they argued for viewing fiduciary law as contract law.[23] They started with the fact that the relationships are voluntary, based on an agreement between the parties. And no one could dispute this. Then they distinguished between relationships by the unequal information among the parties. Like the buyer of a used car and the holder of 401(k) savings in mutual funds, a trusting person knows little about the car or the service he is about to buy. No one could dispute this conclusion either.

Then Easterbrook and Fischel suggested that the fiduciary law rules are the rules that the parties would have themselves negotiated had they known what to negotiate. Fiduciary rules are contract terms that have been incorporated into law instead of repeating them time and again. The rules requiring the fiduciaries to be honest and fair to their beneficiaries are the rules on which the parties would have agreed had they been asked. But if the parties wish to write the implicit rules into their contracts, or change them explicitly, they can do so, with the stroke of their pen.

Under these very rational arguments, a number of fundamental protections are swept out of the window. Whether fiduciary rules were drawn from an imagined agreement among the parties cannot be proven. Whether this is the approach that the courts ought to take is an open question. I have shown that regardless of origin, honesty has become a rule of law, and not a contract term. The parties may explicitly agree to eliminate some of the protections against fiduciaries' abuse of trust, but not all. If all, or even many, protections are waived, most courts are not likely to enforce the waivers. It would take far more unreasonable terms in a contract for the courts to deny enforcement of honesty by trusted persons.[24] More important, the rights against fiduciaries stem from the fact that they hold other people's money, not merely from promising honesty in an exchange. All the rest of the differences stem from this very fundamental fact.

The Shift in the Corporate Law

In the area of corporate law, a similar shift from emphasis on fiduciary duties to emphasis on contract has occurred. In the 1980s–1990s, scholars on corporation law began to speak of the corporations as a "nexus of contracts." They borrowed this term and the concept it represents from economic and business literature.[25] Because economic literature did not consider the legal differences of contracts and fiduciaries, and because the substance of the discussions was not the doctrine of the law, the use of the word "contract" to describe the constitutional documents of a corporation was inappropriate. But as they were "law and economics" scholars and were paying less attention to the words, sliding from fiduciary to contract was not as noticeable. This shift, however, changed the image of the relationships, and with it, the view of corporate management's duties.

The Delaware General Corporation Law, under which about half of the large corporations in the United States are registered, was amended to allow the basic documents of the corporation, that is, the corporate "constitutions," to contain waivers of management's legal fiduciary duties of care.[26] These are the duties of management to be alert and use its abilities in the service of the corporation. Not surprisingly, shareholders voted for the amendments. No shareholders will launch a costly proxy fight against such a change. Thus, under the new provisions, management that partly sleeps at the helm would not be liable, or would be far less liable, for the damage its negligence has caused.

The Delaware General Corporation Law distinguishes the duty of alertness and "care" from the duty to serve the corporation without conflicting interests, and to use the power and control of management for the benefit of the corporation. This is a duty of "loyalty." The Delaware General Corporation Law does not allow the management or the shareholders to waive such a duty of loyalty. But the pressure in the 1990s continued. In 1996, for example, Richard Epstein, a renowned legal scholar and teacher, called for allowing limited waivers of the duty of loyalty, although he emphasized exceptions. He would not have allowed corporate directors to take for themselves business opportunities that came to the corporation, and that they discovered as board members.[27] It is not certain whether the suggestion to relax other aspects of the prohibition would be considered after the recent scandals.

The Shift in Partnership Law

During the 1990s, the Uniform Partnership Act has taken a similar approach in melding contract into fiduciary law. In the past, partners had a fiduciary duty toward each other, unless they explicitly waived the duties, after they received full information. The duties of a partner as a fiduciary were described in the *old* section 21 as follows.

> (1) Every partner must account to the partnership for any benefit, and hold as trustee for it any profits derived by him without the consent of the other partners from any transaction connected with the formation, conduct, or liquidation of the partnership or from any use by him of its property.
> (2) This section applies also to the representatives of a deceased partner engaged in the liquidation of the affairs of the partnership as the personal representatives of the last surviving partner.[28]

This is a general provision of fiduciary law, without many details, and sufficiently vague to catch in the net disloyal activities and hidden conflicts of interest. Unless the partners agree to specific, disclosed conflicts, the conflicts are prohibited.

The new approach is declared in the Revised Partnership Act of 1997. The Act is more specific and detailed. It "includes a more extensive treatment of the fiduciary duties of partners." The new version "continues the traditional rule that a partner is a fiduciary" but "also makes clear that a partner is not required to be a disinterested trustee. Provision is made for the legitimate pursuit of self-interest, with a counterbalancing irreducible core of fiduciary duties."[29]

Contract prevails, with exceptions. Section 103 of the Revised Partnership Act of 1997 provides that the partnership relationship is governed by the contract, except for listed provisions that cannot be waived.[30] As the first comment to the section says clearly: "The general rule under Section 103(a) is that relations among the partners and between the partners and the partnership are governed by the partnership agreement."[31] The balance between the contract provision and the court's ability to impose duties drawn from a more general source has shifted. The relationship has changed. Trust less. Verify more.

The Shift in the Courts

The movement from fiduciary to contract has touched some of the courts. The Court of Appeals of the Seventh Circuit has shown its aversion to fiduciary law by adopting an interesting approach. In *Wsol v. Fiduciary Management Associates*,[32] the court retained the traditional definition of a fiduciary duty and the remedies that are available on breach of these duties. Then the court eliminated any remedies in the situation at hand by resorting to contract remedy principles. The result was a possible *breach of fiduciary duty but no judicial remedies*. How could the court reach such an amazing result? The story is a bit long but is worth telling. This is the story of Fiduciary Management Company (Fiduciary) and the Teamsters Union Pension Fund (Teamsters). Fiduciary hired Blizzard to solicit new business, and Blizzard made a deal with a broker. The broker would introduce Blizzard to the Teamsters. In exchange, the broker would receive some brokerage business of Fiduciary's clients. In fact, the introducing broker did not execute these brokerage transactions. He "farmed them out" to reputable brokerage firms. But these firms did not receive the full commission for executing the transactions. Part of the commissions remained with the broker.

What did each party gain from this exchange? Fiduciary gained from the introduction to Teamsters $260 million in new money under management. In a competitive environment, that contract of management was quite valuable. Not so, said the court. Fiduciary received *nothing*. The introduction was worth *nothing*. What did the broker receive for this worthless introduction? It turns out that Fiduciary's clients were charged 6 cents per share, while the executing brokers only charged 2 or 3 cents per share. Therefore, the introducing broker got about two-thirds of the brokerage commissions or more. According to the court, he received these fairly large amounts for nothing. But the court held that this was fine. A client cannot complain if he is charged the "market price," that is, 6 cents per share, even if the service was in fact offered for 2 cents a share and the rest was pocketed by an intermediary.

It does not matter that there are reputable brokers who are willing to give a discount of 3 or 4 cents a share to get the business. The introducing broker "guaranteed" the excellent execution of the transaction—that is, even if he was a "shady" character, as the court describes him, because he *bribed* two Teamsters trustees into giving Fiduciary the management of $260 million.

In fact, Fiduciary receives the benefit of $260 million dollars under management. That, in and by itself, is valuable. For that introduction, Fiduciary had to pay the introducing broker. Had it paid with its own money, that would have been fine. But Fiduciary did not pay its with its own money. It paid the introducing broker with clients' money. The clients were charged more than what the actual executing brokers were paid. The clients did not benefit from the "guarantee" of a crook. Besides, the clients paid Fiduciary to ensure satisfactory execution.

The most important part of the story is in the conclusion of the court that the *clients should be happy with payment of the "market price" of 6 cents a share.* The discount of 4 cents a share is not their business. That is a contract view of the relationship. The clients bought services and can expect to be charged the market price. That is the implied condition in the contract. But fiduciary law views the arrangement differently. In the fiduciary model, the court would have made the reverse decision. The brokerage business is the client's business. The discounts are the clients' assets. Using the discount is a misappropriation of the clients' assets. Fiduciary was not entitled to benefit from that discount in any form, including the form of new business.

The Shift in the Legal Power of Politicians

Political language and image have been touched by the contract model as well. The difference between an elected official as a fiduciary and an official as a contract party was also marked in the political area. The Republican Party published the "Contract with America." President Clinton solemnly entered into a "covenant" with America. They misspoke. Neither the Republican Party nor President Clinton had anything to give in an exchange with the American people. Both the party's and the president's power belong and continue to belong to the people, and both held this power in trust for the people. Neither the party nor the president was a contract party. Both were fiduciaries.

The view of elections as an exchange of political power between the voters and the elected officials has consequences far beyond language. In corporate law, once the directors are elected, they owe a duty not to only the shareholders who elected them but to all shareholders—to the corporation. The majority of the shareholders may not dictate to the directors how they should act. Similarly, if the power of elected officials is vested in trust, these officials may not use the power to strengthen their position after the expiration of their term, or to prefer those who elected them to those who voted against them. The officials must use their power for the benefit of the country as a whole, for the benefit of the population at large. The power is not theirs to use and was not given to them in an exchange.

Not all academics, courts, and laws have made the shift from fiduciary to contract and from trust-based political power to contract-based political power. But a sufficient number of important actors have led this shift, and it became a movement with marked results.

9

The Shift from Professions to Businesses

D<small>URING THE PAST 25 YEARS</small>, the professions, such as physicians and the lawyers, have undergone a shift. They have become less professional and more like businesses. The impact of this change has been felt in the 1990s.

PROFESSIONALS, BUSINESSPERSONS, AND FIDUCIARIES

Who are professionals? Historically, are professionals different from businesspersons? How does the distinction relate to trust? Are all professionals viewed as fiduciaries? What are the consequences of the shift of professions to businesses? I deal with each of these questions in the order they are presented.

How do professionals differ from businesspersons? The ideal model of a professional is a person who is public service–oriented. He seeks money secondarily, for he needs to make a living. In contrast, the model of a businessperson is that of a profit-oriented person who is exchanging service or goods for the money.

In his article "The Professions in the Society Today," Roscoe Pound, the late dean of Harvard Law School, told the story of an old man who was prosecuted for practicing medicine without a license. The judge called him an amateur. "At this the old man broke-in protesting. He said: 'Your Honor is calling me an amateur? Why, I have made more money in my business each of the last five years than all of any three licensed doctors in the country put together.'"[1] Dean Pound added:

> I have not found it easy to impart the conception of a group of men pursuing a common calling as a learned art and as a public service—nonetheless a public service because it may incidentally be a means of livelihood. From the Middle Ages, the formative era of our social institutions, we had received this idea of a profession, and medicine, the law, the ministry and teaching had grown up in its pattern.[2]

Pound lists three important ideas that relate to professions: "organization, learning and a spirit of public service. The gaining of a livelihood is not a professional consideration. Indeed, the professional spirit, the spirit of public service, constantly curbs the urge of that instinct. It is no disparagement of honorable trades and callings." Dean Pound notes that while an engineer may claim a patent for innovative ideas, the lawyer may only claim a copyright for his words. The ideas of the lawyer belong to the public and cannot be patented.[3]

In his book *The Lawyer from Antiquity to Modern Times,* which followed the article, Dean Pound reiterated the same ideas. The money that a professional earns is but "an incidental purpose, pursuit of which is held down by traditions of a chief purpose," that is, public service. The term *profession* "refers to a group of men pursuing a learned art as a common calling in the spirit of public service—no less a public service because it may incidentally be a means of livelihood" [Pound, 4–5]. He adds: "It is of the essence of a profession that it is practiced in a spirit of public service. 'A trade . . . aims primarily at personal gain; a profession at the exercise of powers beneficial to mankind'" [Pound, 9]. One of the distinctions between professions and trades writes Pound is that "the member of a profession does not regard himself as in competition with his professional brethren. He is not bartering his services as is the artisan nor exchanging the products of his skill and learning as the farmer sells wheat or corn." He does not strike for better wages. "This spirit of public service in which the profession of law is and ought to be exercised is a prerequisite of sound administration of justice according to law" [Pound, 10].

At commencement, Dean Paul M. Siskind of Boston University Law School used to explain the origins of the hood that academics wear with their gowns. The hood has a baggy part on the back of the wearer. It looks like the bag in which infants are carried. Dean Siskind noted that the academics of the past, the monks, taught or gave religious services but did not ask for compensation in exchange. The monks did not hold out their hands to the givers or even face the givers. Payment was not charity. The monks performed services and had to subsist. This was a "nonexchange" giving, preserving the professional image of the monk. Respectfully, people paid by putting food or money or valuables into the back pocket of the hood.[4] Reality was probably more pragmatic. The hoods kept the monks warm. Cynthia W. Rossano wrote: "In some areas during the Middle Ages the hood was an alms bag slung around the necks of begging friars; in others, the medieval cowl was worn simply for warmth drawn tightly around the face by the liripipe."[5] The practical and symbolic use of the hood can be applied to the professions. Money is important but comes second to public service.[6]

Both businessperson and professional can be productive, innovative, and brilliant. Their motivations, however, are different, and their emphasis on the monetary rewards is different. The differences are not mutually exclusive. Some businesses, such as the original Ben and Jerry's ice cream enterprise, are oriented toward public interests. Some professions are closer to making money, such as financial managers. When expertise involves making money for others, it is only natural that the experts would use their talents and knowledge to make money for themselves as well. Nonetheless, the origins, basis, and distinction of a profession are its objective of public service.

Even if there are differences between professions and businesses, do these differences concern trust? After all, there are businesspersons who are moral and professionals who are not. However, a professional evokes more trust than the businessperson. If service comes first, the interests of the patient, the client, and the dependent customer come first. The model did not always fit the reality but was the aspiration to which the professions were upheld, sometimes through the media. In the 1938 movie *The Citadel,* Robert Donat plays the physician caught in a very lucrative service to neurotic upper crust ladies. He finally leaves for a very low-paying service in a mining town where his services are truly needed. The dilemma is old. In the film, the solution highlights the profession's ideal of public service. This aspiration commands trust in those who must rely on professionals and cannot verify their expertise or judge their advice. In contrast, the focus on the payment for the services puts the actor's interests first. His question is: "What and how much is there for me?" The trust of the patient, client, and dependent customer is lower. Doubts about the trusted service are higher.

The image of professions as public service counts. As part of the culture, it builds expectations by those who deal with professionals, and requires professions to honor these expectations. It condemns those who do not comply. The reverse can happen as well. At some point, the image can change, and people reclassify professions as businesses, with different and lower expectations of commitment to service and accompanying reactions.

The models of a professional and a businessperson just described are ideal models. In fact, they are not so separated. There always were fiduciaries who behaved like businesspersons and businesspersons who were trusted and behaved like fiduciaries. A businessman tells me with nostalgia about the times when a deal was closed with a handshake. A manufacturer tells me with the same feeling about the relationships with employees. While his father did not hesitate to help his employees, his son hesitates to give advice, lest he be sued for bad advice. But as models, the morality of professionals was traditionally expected to be higher than that of businesspersons.

Historically, professionals' duties of self-limitation and moral behavior were heavier, in part because of their great expertise. Those who became more expert organized their group to signal their superior knowledge and sometimes asked for a legal distinction, by requiring examinations and registration. The evolution of the nursing profession is one example. Expert practical nurses sought legal licensing to control the membership and to ensure the higher standard.[7] In addition, the law provides expert professionals with business. Public corporations must employ certified public accountants to certify their financial statements. Lawyers have the exclusive right to represent others in court. Rating by rating agencies is necessary to gain certain exemptions from the Investment Company Act[8] and other securities acts. These privileges come with duties. The experts and their certifications should be trustworthy more than the sellers of services and commodities in the marketplace.

The price for the experts' monopolies and privileges is the public service aspect of their activities. For example, the lawyers must participate in the enforcement of the laws that granted them their special status. That is the deal.

Why aren't bankers and insurance providers professionals? They fit the definition of professionals in that they offer a public service and it is hard to monitor, understand, and supervise their activities. One difference between bankers and insurance providers and professionals is historical. Professionals included physicians, lawyers, and teachers. In the Middle Ages, people who dealt with money, especially moneylenders, were not included. Perhaps they could not be deemed professionals because they dealt with money.

Another difference between professionals on the one hand and banks and insurance on the other relates to regulation. Today banks and insurance companies are microregulated by the government, while physicians and lawyers are not. That may be the reason why financial advisers, who are not as micromanaged, are considered professional trusted advisors. And yet, these distinctions are not precise. In sum, professionals include a broad category of trusted people, whose activities are difficult to monitor and judge. They are trusted people who are not subject to close government micromanagement. Therefore, if people are to ask them for help, and if they must be trusted, these professionals are expected to feel constrained to give service, and to control their temptations, even though there are no police around. Sometimes they are expected to give service even if they are not paid in advance or might not be paid at all. A doctor is expected to come forward to the cry: "Is there a doctor here?"

THE RECENT TRANSFORMATION OF THE PROFESSIONS AND ITS CONSEQUENCES

In the past three decades, the professions have lost their special status and have been recast as businesses. Professionals have become the producers and sellers of commodities in the markets. Richard Posner compares the legal profession to the seventeenth-century merchant guilds [Posner, 33–70]. The guilds were groups of merchants who organized fairs and maintained the reputation of their members for honesty. Posner predicts: "Something like the evolution of the textile industry from guild production to mass production, and the concomitant decline of artisanality, is occurring today in the market for legal services" [Posner, 47]. It should be noted that the judge compares professional services to the production of textiles. He predicts that lawyers and physicians will render mass-produced services, rather than personal services, like the recent producers as compared to the weavers of the preindustrial era. Perhaps the professionals' advice would be based on an efficient use of statistical data. This economic theory for the industrial age may be unsuitable for today's information age. But then, the professions are not sufficiently efficient. Therefore, it may be that the wealthy will benefit from personal services, while the less wealthy will be put into the mass-production of a standardized service machine. In that case, the controls may have to shift to those who design and operate the machine. Their professional status can be hidden under the facade of businesses that sell their machines.

The Effects of Competition among Professionals

Historically, professionals, such as lawyers and teachers, belonged to fraternities. They did not compete. Their institutions created roles that made them more interdependent. These institutions resulted in greater reciprocity and fairness and more trust among their members [Misztal, 226]. This form of institution makes sense when all members of the fraternities aim at public service. Competition is the antithesis of such fraternities. Competition makes sense when each member serves his own interests and is therefore in conflict with the aims of all other members of the group.

Advertising accompanies competition. Until 1977, lawyers were barred from advertising, and the states approved the prohibition. In *Bates v. State Bar of Arizona*,[9] the Supreme Court ruled that the ban was unconstitutional and permitted lawyers to advertise. First Amendment rights served as the basis for the decisions to allow advertising.[10] Advertising and competition could bring benefits. Advertising could offer more information to clients. Competition would reduce the professionals' fees. Market forces could discipline the lawyers' and doctors' transgressions, and empower clients and patients. These expectations did not materialize; the fruits of these changes were not so sweet. In the words of Justice O'Connor: "In one way or another, time will uncover the folly of the approach [of allowing lawyers' direct and targeted solicitation]."[11]

The expected competition among the professionals did arrive, perhaps with unexpected fierceness, and seemed to bring the morals of the profession down to the level of the marketplace. The prophetic concerns of Dean Pound about the competition among the professions have materialized. Among the four related dangers to the ideal of the professions, Dean Pound noted the "magnified economic exigencies of the individual." Prophetically, he noted the developments of the large law firms: "the creation of partnerships and the reduction of individual responsibility of the lawyers, which make it difficult to resist business methods, which can easily become the methods of competitive acquisitive activity."[12]

Indeed, as Gregg Bloche noted in discussing trust in the medical field, the contract and market image have changed the medical profession.[13] With these changes have come decreased patients' trust and lower respect for the doctors.[14] Among the gruesome stories is an example of a doctor who attempted to hurry up the death of his dying mother in order to save blood-clotting cells.[15] In the late 1980s, medical professionals were also investigated for a typical marketplace crime: price fixing.[16]

As lawyers moved to offering revenue-producing advice, lawyers were drawn to search in the gray areas of law and accounting. Discovering or creating loopholes through which clients could crawl would reduce the clients' costs and gain for the clients a competitive advantage, at least until the competitors discovered the same loopholes and used them too.

David Wessel wrote:

> The decay of professionalism—and codes of ethics that distinguished a profession from a job—intensified in the 1990s, but it didn't begin then. Reflecting on his 23 years in corporate management [treasury secretary Paul O'Neill] recalls a parade of Wall Street professionals who came to his office with plans for "new and exotic" financial maneuvers to reduce his company's tax bill or report debt levels in ways "not clearly prohibited by the tax code or law."

He continues, citing Professor John Coffee: "This disturbing pattern is the biggest reason why the abuses of the 1990s can't easily be dismissed as the fault of a few immoral human beings. 'The professional gatekeepers were greatly compromised by finding they could make tremendous profits by deferring to management.'" [17]

Sometimes they did more. Law is not a precise science. Attorneys could justify saying no to almost every new design of a business that had not been tested in court. In the 1980s, they developed a more flexible attitude. A lawyer might decline to approve a prohibited transaction but might help the client design an alternative. The alternative might be less profitable, but still profitable, with the minimal risk of illegality that a new design presents. This trend, which started in the 1960s, reached much wider dimensions in the 1990s.

The search for "creative" transactions, financial assets, and accounting became the order of the day. For example, the large accounting firms KPMG and Ernst & Young have put their energies into marketing "leveraged" tax law and tax shelters. [18] The legal effect of these innovative arrangements was not ascertained. In KPMG, money was the main driver. The firm did not comply with the rule that required it to register as the creators of tax shelters. As a partner in the firm wrote in his memorandum: "Penalties [for failure to register] would be no greater than $14,000 per $100,000 in [the firm's fees]"; and: "as the size of the deal increases, our exposure to the penalties decreases as a percentage of [the] fees." [19] Breaking the law was factored into the cost of doing business and was indistinguishable from the cost of rent and office supplies. The tax shelters involved paper (sham) transactions, designed to show losses and cover the capital gains of the clients, and were later disallowed by the IRS. The clients, who had paid handsomely for these "shelters," were left with tax bills containing not only the taxes but also interest on the taxes due. [20]

With the new marketplace environment in the legal profession, clients began to shop around, but not necessarily for lower fees. Sometimes they shopped for better revenue-producing legal opinions and transaction structures. Sometimes they shopped for skewed legal opinions that other lawyers refused to give. It is unclear whether the cost of legal services went down. There are lawyers who demanded part of the clients' revenues from creative advice, and the revenues of large law firms rose dramatically. As already noted, between 1987 and 2003, "revenues at the top 100 firms quintupled to $38 billion, while profits quadrupled to $13.5 billion."[21]

Money became an objective of professional teaching. The American Bar Association's Section on Law Practice Management offered a training seminar, advertised in a fax entitled: "Beyond the Billable Hour." It described ways to make money in law practice, including publishing and selling books on the Web, developing a referral network, partnering with web sites as a content provider, providing adjunct services to clients, and creating and selling "legal commodities."[22] Everything in this advertising was focused on developing the law service as a business and viewing legal advice as a commodity for sale.

Recently, lawyers have been turning on each other, attacking the fees other lawyers were to collect in class action settlements. Litigating lawyers who bring class actions receive significant fees when the actions are settled. There is a recent surge of litigation lawyers called "objectors," who object to the settlements for various reasons, including the lawyers' fees. For example, Lloyd Constantine, who settled a class action suit against Visa USA for $3 billion, requested about $600 million in fees and expenses. The objecting lawyers represented claimants who questioned the terms of the settlement, including the attorney's fees. Judge John Gleeson reduced Mr. Constantine's fees to approximately $200 million, to be paid after the claimants were paid. The judge granted the objecting lawyers $12,316, instead of the requested $398,000. The beneficiary of this conflict is the defendant. While objecting lawyers view themselves as the protectors of the claimants, the initial litigating lawyers view them as "parasites" who bring frivolous actions. Some suits objecting to settlements may be frivolous, but, as one objector noted: "Any system has abuses."[23] As with other expressions of acceptance noted throughout this book, he did not condemn the abuse, nor did he promise to try and limit it. His statement reflected an acceptance of the system.

Competition did not seem to bring quality services either. As sales became the main value for some firms, marketing diverted the focus from quality performance. While "rainmakers" were traditionally rewarded more than those who "only" did the work, rainmakers were also performers, and usually had enormous experience and reputation.

In contrast, specialized salespersons need different skills. They focus on presentation, influence, and relationships. Once a sale is made, they have less interest in performance. Their reputation is more sales based than performance based. Marketing by the less-experienced but gifted salespersons brings embellishment, and could result in the clients' skepticism. Marketing comes to be highly rewarded; performance is downgraded. In fact, the legal profession followed the market trend in emphasizing the sale at the expense of the product or service. Eliot Spitzer expressed the same view: "The customer ceases to become important once you've signed him up—it's capturing the next one that's important. . . . Too much emphasis on that bottom line means you don't often think of the other person, whether it's the shareholder or someone else for whom you're a fiduciary."[24]

The Effect of Advertising

If advertising was intended to offer clients better information, it does not seem to have achieved the purpose. One study found that the average client rarely shops for legal services.[25] Advertising is hardly informative. For example, the advertisement for "Shuman & Ross, P.C., A Civil Litigation Law Firm," lists some of the firm's jury verdicts, 29 settlements, four successful trials, and five instances of recovery, ranging from $360,000 to $3.813 million.[26] There is no mention of the total number of cases or the results in the others, the period in which these verdicts were obtained, the amounts of the claims, the net amounts that the plaintiffs received, or the fees that the litigation firm received.

It may be that information about professional services of this sort does not lend itself to precision. Perhaps it does not lend itself to this advertising style. Perhaps no advertising offers information with precision. On the scale of "trust" as against "verify," people look to verifying the information in advertisements. On this scale, people expect from professionals more accurate and reliable information. But if professionals provide business advertising, the readers shift the balance. They now trust professionals less and expect to verify their statements and promises more. This shift presents a problem. It presents a problem for a patient, who is not an expert and for whom verification is very difficult. It presents a problem for the physician, because he needs to provide the patient with greater proof of trustworthiness.

Don't Trust Me—Verify!

Generally, professional experts must be trusted more than verified. The experts have superior knowledge and information to that of those who seek their help and advice. Only experts and people who are close to professionals can supervise and judge the performance of other experts. Product prices usually signal quality and reliability. But that is less true of professional services. The results of the services do not necessarily signify quality, either. These services cannot be guaranteed by a promise of "your money back." A physician may be superb, but his patient might die. A lawyer may be outstanding, but the client may be found guilty.

Most important, if clients and patients should verify the quality of the professional services, professional advice will be less useful, both to those who seek their help and to society that benefits from specialization. And if everyone had to protect himself by verifying what the professionals do and how they do it, the professions would be of little use. It is in the interest of society that sick people will seek doctors, trust them, and rely on them. Therefore, in general, professionals must be trusted more than market-dealers.

In the past decade, physicians and hospitals have required patients to sign consents to various treatments. In relationships that require a high level of trust, as do relationships with professionals, the trusting person should have a legal right to rely on the trusted persons, without checking on them. True, many patients may appreciate information about their state of health. They do not necessarily wish to have a paternalistic relationship with their doctors. But that is not the issue. The issue is not disclosure. The issue is the patients' *consent to the treatment.* Getting the patients' consent to a treatment after disclosure is acceptable when the patients can make a judgment. But shifting the burden of their *professional decision* to the patients dilutes the value of the professionals' own advice and expertise.

When I had my eyes examined, the doctor proposed to inject a dye mixture into my bloodstream. I was told that the injection poses a very small risk of an allergic reaction. The risk was quantified at less than 1 in 125,000. "What is the risk?" I asked the doctor. "You will die," answered the doctor. How could I possibly evaluate this piece of information? I had to have the eyes examined. I signed the consent. This highly qualified doctor felt constrained to make me sign—I was a potential plaintiff. I trusted the doctor, even though I signed, but felt the perversion of reciprocal mistrust.

In addition, as physicians became the owners of pharmacies, laboratories, and the like, they welcomed payment from pharmaceutical companies and agreed to market their products. They prescribed drugs for their patients from their pharmacies, favored these pharmaceutical companies, and ordered tests in their laboratories. In short, physicians moved to conduct their services as businesses. And these activities created conflicts of interest. The activities required the good doctors to decide what is good for their patients as well as for their own pockets. A number of articles in the October 2004 issue of the *New England Journal of Medicine* highlight the emerging concerns and reaction to the self-regulation, as well as looming government regulation. One article puts it quite clearly: "Apprehension over conflicts of interest in medicine is rooted in a concern that professional judgments about the welfare of patients may be inappropriately influenced by a secondary interest—in this case, the personal gain derived from relationships with pharmaceutical companies."[27] In the same issue, another article, by Dr. David Blumenthal, said:

> When a great profession and the forces of capitalism interact, drama is likely to result. . . . On display in the relationship between doctors and drug companies are the grandeur and weakness of the medical profession—its noble aspirations and its continuing inability to fulfill them.[28]

The pressures are not insignificant. After all, the physicians prescribe the use of the drugs. The marketing costs of the drug industry were estimated at $12 to $15 billion, and its sales force in the United States numbers approximately 90,000 persons, that is, one salesperson for every 4.7 office-based physicians during 2003. The effect on the patients is not clearly marked. But the effect on the profession's credibility is noted.[29]

The story of the employee-scientists in the National Institutes of Health (NIH), a government agency, is instructive. During the 1990s, renowned scientists demanded high salaries, which the government could not pay. In order to attract these scientists, the agency significantly relaxed in 1995 the restrictions on its scientists to collaborate with private-sector companies. They were allowed to consult with private-sector companies, own stock in these companies, and sit on the companies' boards, so long as the scientists did not deal with the companies in their capacity as government employees. In 2003, eight years after the rules were relaxed, congressional investigation uncovered serious abuses. For example, "a clinical trial of a company's drug was apparently derailed shortly after the researcher in charge of the trial received consulting fees from a competing firm."[30] Upon these discoveries, the NIH severely limited the permissible contacts of its scientists with the companies whose drugs these scientists were charged to test. The article in *Scientific American* that told the story ended on an insightful note:

> Ultimately these issues will have to be decided by the scientists themselves. Government posts will never pay as well as drug company jobs. The most the NIH can do is to set clear standards and to enforce them—and hope its employees continue to choose public service over private gain.[31]

The scientists were professionals in the service of the public, and they became businesspersons. They had to revert to their vocation or leave.

When fiduciaries face conflicts of interest, they may take steps to turn their fiduciary relationships with the clients into contract relationships. They can disclose to the clients the conflicts, give the clients full information, and enable the clients to decide whether to engage in the conflict-of-interest transactions with their trusted persons. But consent for an operation or for choosing a medicine or for using the laboratory in which the testing will take place is more problematic. Theoretically, a patient may refuse to buy his medicines from the physician's pharmacy. But that is not the issue. The question is whether the patient needs the medicine in the first place. And that the patient cannot decide. So long as the physician is in charge of the patient's health, the patient is in no position to question the physician's decision or to bargain.

The patients' consent did not help physicians much. The physicians' protection from court cases has remained limited, as is shown by rising litigation and insurance costs, and by their pleas to put a ceiling on the amounts of judgments against them.[32] The patients' consent did not help much. Disclosure is binding only if the consenting party understands what it is consenting to, and can evaluate the information. The doctors' search for protection might backfire and create a vicious circle, if the courts begin to apply consumer protection laws to physicians. Historically, members of the professions were exempt from consumer protection laws. The exemption was based on the higher standard of behavior that professionals followed. It is not surprising that courts are beginning to consider clients and patients as consumers, and ponder whether consumer antifraud laws should apply to lawyers and doctors.[33] In the case of *Macedo v. Dello Russo*, the court wrote: "When professionals engage in common commercial activity designed to attract the patronage of the public, they should be held to the same standards of truth and completeness that govern the sales activities of all other persons or entities."[34] The vicious circle continues and may be closing in.

Whether the court claims or the malpractice came first is hard, if not impossible, to tell. It is easier to determine that the physicians' image as trusted persons is tarnished. Most important, I maintain that the tarnished image has come in part with the impression—right or wrong—that the professionals' goal has changed from public service to business: from "caring first for patient; money comes second" to "money comes first; caring for the patient second."

Weaker Fiduciary Law by Interpretation

The movement from fiduciaries to contract parties, from professions to businesses, was accompanied by changes in the way the law is interpreted. The rules concerning the distribution and sale of securities offer an example. To raise money from public investors ("public offering"), a corporation must file a statement (registration statement) with the SEC. The statement contains information about the corporation and the securities (stock, bonds) that it offers.[35] The government officials then review the materials and may require additional information. When they are satisfied, they will declare the registration "effective," and the securities may then be offered and sold to the public. Part of this registration statement becomes the "prospectus," which must be offered to public investors with the stock. But if the investors are sophisticated, the corporation can offer them its securities in a nonpublic distribution, or "private placement." The corporation must then offer these investors adequate information but bypass the registration with the government. Instead, it just sends the government a notice and a copy of the documents that it offers to the investors. How does one decide when a distribution is a "public offering" and when the distribution is a "private placement"?

In a 1953 case of *SEC v. Ralston Purina Company*, the Supreme Court offered guidelines and a list of factors to define "private placement."[36] It emphasized that those who are offered securities in a private placement must be sophisticated and have access to information that would have been included in the registration statement. A later 1977 case, *Doran v. Petroleum Management Corporation*, provided a more detailed list, including the number of the persons who were offered the stock, their financial situations, their knowledge of the corporation's business, and access to information about the corporation.[37]

The pressures arose to turn the lists of factors into detailed rules. The SEC published regulation D, which detailed with specificity who are sophisticated investors, and how a private placement is to be made.[38] Specific rules seem more efficient, because they are presumably clearer. But experience has shown that specific rules are not necessarily clearer. The more specific they are, the more questions of interpretations they can raise [Cass, 106]. There are now volumes written about regulation D on private placement. Specific rules are assumed to be fairer. After all, people ought to know what is permitted and what is not. The government should tell people *precisely* what to do and *precisely* what not to do. Otherwise, people ought to be free to act or not to act as they please.

This approach may be reasonable for tax and criminal laws. In fiduciary law, this approach raises serious problems, precisely because of the precision that it advocates. No rule can list all that is prohibited to fiduciaries, even if the rule filled the Library of Congress. When fiduciaries have broad discretion, such as managing large corporations, and billions of dollars in financial assets, there are always ambiguous and new situations, which abusers of trust can interpret their way. They can construe the law narrowly: What the rules do not specifically say, the rules do not cover. This is a hostile view of the law as an intruder on the trusted persons' freedom to exercise their powers. Another interpretation would inquire into the purpose of the rule, ask how reasonable people would explain it, and impose a broader or narrower interpretation accordingly, depending on the danger of abuse. This is a view of the law as a protector of trust and the public good.

It may be argued that specific rules limit discretion and standards broaden discretion. That may be inaccurate in many areas. As Frederick Schauer points out, specific rules are not as specific as they seem, and standards are not as broad as they seem.[39] But for fiduciaries, specific rules can be used to broaden discretion, not narrow it. And standards can be used to limit their discretion.

A strictly literal interpretation of a rule can drain it of its spirit and subvert its goal. The proponents of precise rules strive to free trusted persons from legal constraints as much as possible. Under the banner of the rule of law, they wave the flag of market freedom. This approach allows for easy manipulation. If a law prohibits corporate officers from buying corporate real estate but does not mention leases, then the officers may acquire leases—that is, even though the purpose of the law was to prohibit corporate officers from sitting on both sides of any bargain, as representatives of the corporation and as representatives of their own interests. Or if the prohibition mentions leases but does not mention loans, then corporate officers may borrow from the corporation. If borrowing is prohibited, but no mention is made of using corporate power to obtain business opportunities that should belong to the corporation, then such use would be permitted. And if the rule does not describe with precision and prohibit the manner in which officers of Enron managed seemingly independent entities that in fact held Enron's assets, the actions would be permitted. And if the rule does not prohibit Enron's officers to deal with these seemingly independent entities on behalf of Enron, and draw compensation in the millions from both Enron and the entities, these actions would be permitted.

An example of a literal reading is instructive. The SEC reached a settlement that disqualified a corporate officer from sitting on a board of directors of a "corporation" for five years. Literally, the settlement did not disqualify this person from serving as director on the board of a not-for-profit corporation, or perhaps as trustee on the board of a large trust. It may well be that the settlement was truly limited to corporations, and that the officer was not disqualified from sitting on the boards of other types of entities. But suppose the spirit of the settlement meant full disqualification. In such a case, the interpreters would include in the term "corporation" similar large organizations. After all, the message of this disqualification was that this officer, who was in charge of a large corporation in which accounting frauds had occurred, should not be allowed to manage similarly large organizations. A literal interpretation of the settlement emptied it of its substance. In fact, it could make a mockery of the settlement, as this officer could head a large not-for-profit corporation during the disqualification period.[40]

A literal, precise interpretation of a rule invites trusted persons and their lawyers to search for ways to "con the law," that is, escape a rule without openly breaking it. An interpretation of the spirit of the rule invites trusted people and their lawyers to search the gray area around the rule in order to avoid entering the gray area and breaking the rule. One approach leads the lawyers to look for an escape route from the law; the other posits them as the law's gatekeepers, inducing their clients to halt at the gate. Following the literal meaning of a rule can eliminate and subvert its spirit and meaning. Using gimmicks based on literal meaning can protect or even promote fraud.

The experience in the accounting area is similar. Accounting rules are highly detailed, replete with bright lines, checklists, and percentages. These details were interpreted and followed blindly. The staff of the SEC reached the conclusion that a literal interpretation of detailed rules is inadequate. It recommended that these accounting rules be interpreted in light of the principles on which the rules are based, and the purposes for which the rules were enacted. A staff report concluded that interpretations based on *rules only* or *principles only* do not provide optimal results. It recommended that "those involved in the standard-setting process more consistently develop standards on a *principles-based* or objectives-oriented basis." The staff's study noted that it considered the principles-based regime adopted by the European Commission in its International Financial Reporting Standards (IFRSs), and recommended a middle road: specific interpretation in part and interpretation on principles in part.[41]

This may be the better way. The meaning of the words in a rule must be decided not by their dictionary meaning but by the purposes that the rules address, and the problems that the rules are designed to resolve. Looking to the objective of the rules is similar to paying attention to the tone in which the same words are uttered. The tone determines whether the words "You rascal!" are said in anger or in jest, and whether the words are designed to hurt or to show tender affection. Similarly, the objectives, rather than the dictionary, help determine the meaning of the rules.

Legal imprecision sends a message to trusted persons: "When in doubt, don't do it!" Rules that increase the legal risks (uncertainty) for trusted people produce a self-enforcing mechanism that keeps trusted people from coming too close to the forbidden boundary. A wrongful act can be deterred when surrounded by other possible but uncertain violations.[42] For example, if the government prohibits healthcare service givers from offering physicians cash and other benefits, one can interpret the rule to mean that paying physicians for work done (research) is permitted—that is, because paying cash or other benefits is limited to situations in which the physician does not provide anything in exchange. Or one can examine the purpose of the rule and conclude that it is designed to prevent conflicts of interest, in which physicians will order drugs unnecessarily. In that case, every financial arrangement between the drug company and the physicians is prohibited. A lucrative research contract presents conflicts of interest just as cash does. Both should be avoided.

But would this idea not backfire? After all, imprecise rules may give the fiduciaries more room for maneuvering and for justifying undesirable activities. The answer depends on how the law is interpreted. If the purpose of the rules is examined instead of their literal meaning, then the situations that violate the purpose of the rules will be prohibited even if the situations are not specified.

There is also a psychological reason for creating a region of uncertainty for people who hold fiduciary power. Rules and procedures that increase uncertainty "can make people imagine themselves in another's place" and induce them to consider others who may be affected by their actions. Such rules and procedures could increase interdependence and reciprocity among people [Misztal, 226].

Weakening the Law in the Name of Efficiency

From the point of view of efficiency, fiduciary rules are inefficient because they severely limit the fiduciaries' freedoms to engage in tempting (*but not fraudulent*) transactions. The rules rob fiduciaries of opportunities to profit. Why should law prohibit corporate officers from buying corporate assets for themselves or their family and friends, if the price is right, for example, the market price? If the corporation needs the assets, wouldn't both parties save the cost of brokers' commissions? The corporation is not hurt, and the fiduciaries benefit. Similarly, the rules to keep entrusted money separate and require them to earmark trust property [Scott & Fratcher, 2A:497–506, 506–511] are expensive to the fiduciaries. As a result, fiduciaries try to pass the costs to the customers and charge customers higher fees. It is irrational, critics say, to impose these costs just by reason of the probability, especially a low probability, that the fiduciaries will misappropriate the entrusted assets. Leave enforcement of honesty to the markets. And if you need to regulate, regulate just the truth of the fiduciaries' statements. Investors will take care of themselves at lower cost.

During the past 30 years, the efficiency argument has won many battles and gained a large following. The investigations of Enron Corporation showed how the rules were "softened." Prohibited transactions were permitted if independent third parties (e.g., the board of directors) gave their blessings to conflict-of-interest transactions, and if the shareholders were notified of the transactions and either consented to them or did not object.[43]

Policy-makers worried less about a little embezzlement and more about rewarding trusted persons and supporting businesses. They worried that talented persons would move elsewhere—where more money is to be had and more freedom is available to gain more money. When the focus shifted to cost reduction for the fiduciaries, both the regulators and the fiduciaries began to make a cost-benefit analysis. They started with the idea that the laws are too paternalistic. Investors should be encouraged to educate themselves and protect themselves from fraud. As Victor Brudney wrote, the question became whether the laws imposed excessive costs of providing and verifying true information and guaranteeing promises, that is, whether the costs of selling and advertising securities could be reduced. And they were reduced.[44]

Public policies underlying the regulation of the securities markets were also relaxed. The clear congressional mandate of protecting investors was watered down to include the cost of "capital formation." This is an economic term. It obscures the nature of the transaction that the law regulates, that is, a transaction in which investors part with their money and hand it over to others. "Capital formation" highlights the good part for the corporation and its managers, that is, the infusion of money into corporate coffers. But under the newer guidelines of Congress in 1996, investors' protection should be balanced against the cost of regulation to the sellers of the securities, that is, the cost of "capital formation."[45]

We Ended Up with Less Law and More Opportunity for Fraud

During the 1990s, as pressures and opportunities to defraud rose, the legal constraints on fiduciary behavior were sometimes lifted. For example, in March 13, 1997, Enron received an exemption from the Investment Company Act of 1940 and the Commodity Exchange Act of 1936.[46] In the year 2000, Congress exempted energy and minerals commodities from the jurisdiction of the Commodity Futures Trading Commission.[47] As the *Wall Street Journal* reported, Enron lobbied successfully for this legislation.[48] The relief from the restrictions may have been driven by the interest in deregulating the supply of energy and creating a free market in energy. After all, this company was boldly breaking new ground in an exciting new experiment. Relief from restrictions could have been driven in part by ideology and true hostility to the law. In any event, the relief from restrictions was not accompanied by alternative controls. Senator Fred Thompson during the investigation of the Enron said: "The real scandal here may not be what's illegal, but what's permissible."[49]

We encouraged innovations and "privatizing" but imposed no protective barriers. Entrepreneurs and their innovations should not be constrained in a straitjacket of rules that did not anticipate the new environment. Innovations may fail, but if they are not tried, we will never know whether they would. "A large part of Enron's failure can be traced not to any misdeeds, but simply to the failure of its business plan," as Douglas Baird suggested.[50] And yet, although regulation had to be changed to allow Enron to pursue the plan, no barriers were imposed to ensure that the corporation would not engage in manipulating the market, and in other well-known activities that undermine efficient markets. After all, the policies may have changed, but not human nature. And America has experienced market failures of this sort before. The balance between the opportunities for illegal gains rose, and barriers to these gains were removed.

10

In Markets We Trust

THE WORLD IS A MARKET. The vision of the world as a market and the vision of relationships as exchanges are useful views for many situations. But in the past few decades, the market and exchange images have overshadowed and subsumed all other views of the world and all other kinds of relationships. The Supreme Court has spoken of the market for ideas;[1] Roberta Romano wrote about the market for corporate laws.[2] Daniel A. Farber and Phillip P. Frickey discussed the market among legislators.[3] I wrote about a market for power.[4] Robert C. Elickson examined the market for social norms;[5] and Richard A. Posner analyzed the market for babies.[6] The word "product" includes trust services and is used to emphasize what is sold rather than what and how it is produced. Thus, consumers are offered financial products, trust products, and legal products—or "legal commodities," as one of the courses for practicing lawyers on how to make money described what lawyers do.[7]

All relationships are an exchange. No more giving without receiving in return. The transformation of the world to a market had an effect of transforming relationships into exchanges, and affecting other types of relationships. When blood donors, who used to donate their blood free, started to be paid, they refused to donate blood when the payments stopped. Their habits and views had changed. Converting a gift into a commodity and an exchange may have had a permanent effect on gift giving [Radin, 95–101].

Another example of the shift from donations to self-interested exchange is the evolution of the forms of donation. In the past two decades, a type of donation has developed that allows the donor to have his cake and eat some of it. The donor gets the income from his donations during his lifetime.[8] The laws were amended to recognize these donations as tax-deductible today, presumably because many donations would not be given otherwise. The Philanthropy Protection Act of 1995 amended the definition of charitable institutions that were excluded from the regulation of investment companies. Under the amendment, charitable institutions include charities that accept tax-exempt donations, even if the donors receive lifetime benefits.[9] These arrangements move closer to an exchange and further away from full giving.

They redefine charity. Now charity includes giving to others but retaining a healthy portion of the gift to the giver.

Reciprocity, which is a kind of an exchange, is also evident in other forms of charitable giving. Armin Falk reports on the effect of a gift by a charity to the solicited donors. It turns out that donation increased by 17 percent if a small gift was included, and by 75 percent if a large gift was included. The report concludes that "gift-exchange" is important for charitable giving, in addition to the "warm glow" of emotional satisfaction.[10] However, when requests are accompanied by a gift, the pressure comes not from the donors bargaining to retain part of their donations but from the solicitors of the donations. The gift pressures the donors to reciprocate. Yet the need to offer a gift signals the added pressures that must be exerted to gain a donation.

Believers in the markets have negated the need for immediate legal response to fraud. Why not wait for the market to react to minor embezzlements? In the long run, the market will punish wayward corporate management that went too far, and purge itself of the few "bad apples" that have grown in its midst. Yet a "little embezzlement," especially if it appears in the higher ranks of private or public government, created the problem. As the story of the low-echelon accountant at WorldCom demonstrates, a little embezzlement rarely stops with the first move. Habits can slide down a slippery slope, starting small and fleeting and growing large and entrenched, for good and evil.

Law did not prevent the fraud of Enron, and government enforcers rose to action only after the corporation went bankrupt. Why pay the legal "tolls" and not let the markets take care of such situations? When I mentioned my proposal to auction the class grades to the highest bidder, my law and economics colleagues had a similar reaction. They argued that there was nothing wrong with my auction. In time, the value of the grades will deteriorate. Employers will not consider them a reliable evaluation of the students' abilities, the price of grades will fall, and the market for my grades will disappear. Then, other teachers will move in and offer grades without pay. The chastity of the grades will be advertised, and their value will rise, perhaps until another teacher has the brilliant idea of auctioning the grades off.

Yet this solution is not desirable. Leaving the grades to be determined by the market introduces instability in the students' evaluation and the employers' reliance. Employers will demand additional customized proof of the students' evaluation, which is costly to the teachers, and is harder for the employers to compare. The students will learn less and seek to earn more to pay for the grade. Every part of the educational system will suffer, except me, the teacher. I will collect payments from the power to grade—a power to which I am not entitled in the first place. This is precisely a situation in which law is more effective and more desirable than the markets.

Like highways, markets create spontaneous rules. Like highways, they require rules. Highway traffic can move by spontaneous rules that are not imposed by any authority. These are rules that emerge from the behavior of many people, as if by common design. The movement of the drivers cannot be planned or dictated. It can change, depending on mood, distraction, and weather. Spontaneous rules help regulate the traffic. But if accidents are to be reduced, spontaneous rules must be supported by central rules. These rules dictate, for example, whether people should drive on the right or left side of the road, and require drivers to obey the traffic lights. As some drivers veer to a free space, and some stay in their lane, both lanes are less congested. And yet driving in Italy, Argentina, Sudan, and India, for example, becomes truly dangerous because drivers attempt to fill any open space. There is a balance between spontaneous rules and regulation imposed by authority. Both are necessary to reduce accidents.

Spontaneous rules can grow into customs and become part of the culture. Courtesy or lack of courtesy plays a crucial role in maintaining safety. In some countries, trying to get into a lane aggressively is necessary, because no one is likely to stop and let you into the lane. Accidents occur. In other countries, drivers allow each other to get into the lane, and the drivers who wish to get in wait more patiently for the opportunity. Accidents occur less frequently. Law supports this custom by a sign that reads: Yield!

Markets are more complex than highways, but many market rules emerge essentially the same way. Frederick A. Hayek argued that the markets could solve all problems spontaneously [Hayek, 1:39–43, 2:115–120]. But Thomas Schelling analyzed a case of two roads leading to two similar grazing fields. He attempted to find a formula for a spontaneous way to avoid congestion in one road at the expense of the other and failed to reach a decisive result. Spontaneous highway rules cannot fully regulate the highway traffic [Schelling, 223–243]. They alone cannot fully regulate the markets. To be effective, the invisible hand of the market needs the supporting visible hand of the culture of self-limitation and the government.

Therefore, as I have written elsewhere, paradoxically, "free" markets are free in part because they are regulated.[11] Law fills the gaps that are left open in spontaneous rules; spontaneous rules fill the gaps that exist in law. As Professor George Dent wrote:

> The order of law alone . . . is not enough in itself to sustain a market economy: a capitalistic system also requires what might be called an order of custom—a cultural infrastructure of norms, learned dispositions to respect property and keep promises and pay taxes and refrain from private violence to settle disputes and of a certain degree of mutual trust—confidence that others will, within limits, for the most part, also respect the norms. . . . Yet custom also needs the support of law.[12]

Frederick A. Hayek's extreme views have followers today. To name a few, Warren Grimes would rely on the markets to solve antitrust issues. Regulation is not necessary.[13] Mathew M. Sanderson would rely on the hypothesis of the efficient capital markets to solve securities frauds. If everyone accepted the hypothesis, there would be no need to regulate the securities markets. The hypothesis would become the market reality. [14] William J. Brodsky voiced a typical complaint about the unnecessary burdens of securities regulation. [15]

BALANCING MARKETS AND THE LAW

The difficult question is not whether markets need the law's support. They do. The more difficult issue is the right balance between law and market regulation. To what extent should legal regulation intrude on market practices and rules? To what extent should legal rules adopt and enforce market rules? And to what extent should market sanctions suffice and no legal rules need apply? On these issues, the last three decades have seen a shift. The balance between law and markets has been changing. The legal standards and enforcement have given way to market standards and private-sector enforcement.

The private-sector markets have produced many different private enforcers. One kind of enforcer of truth and reliability is the other party to the transactions. Both buyer and seller are interested in protecting themselves from each other's dishonesty. Each party will therefore try to ensure that the other party tells the truth and keeps his promises. They will create a protective process. One example is the usual way in which people design the sale of a house.

When the parties agree on the sale of a house, the buyer pays the seller a few thousand dollars and receives in exchange an informal receipt. When the parties sign a formal contract, the buyer deposits a far greater amount of the value of the house (e.g., 10 percent) in exchange. The buyer is not ready to pay this sum directly to the seller. The seller demands a stronger commitment from the buyer before he takes the house off the market. Therefore, usually, the amount is deposited with the broker as an escrow agent. After the buyer checks the house and seeks financing, and if all goes well, the final exchange is made at closing in the lawyer's office. One can view each stage as an exchange of a similar value: the informal receipt for a few thousand dollars; a signed contract for an escrow of 10 percent; and the full payment for the house in exchange for registration and the full possession. But this market arrangement is supported by many laws. For example, in Massachusetts, the law regulates the formal contract, the house inspections, the registration to pass ownership to the buyer, the brokers' licensing, and the escrow arrangement. [16]

Parties to continuous transactions can organize in a group for each party's protection. An interesting example is the diamond exchange, which regulates the relationships among its members. When a jeweler's business depends on the membership in the group, the sanction for breaking a rule can be expulsion, which means terminating the member's ability to engage in the business. Therefore, as Lisa Bernstein explains, in this group, handshake agreements are usual, and the sanctions for breach can be brutal. [17]

Trusted parties who are interested in attracting customers organize groups to protect their members' interests. Among the main interests of these groups is the protection of their members' reputation for honesty. They impose rules of behavior and sanction members who misbehave. For example, the National Association of Securities Dealers has developed a large book of rules and a separate enforcement arm. Members who are found guilty of violations may lose their license to practice their trade, subject to a final decision on appeal to the SEC.[18]

The markets are populated with private enforcers and "truth guarantors." They verify particular facts or a general trustworthiness of a business or an individual. Some of these guarantors are regulated. For example, the SEC regulates the stock exchanges and the National Association of Securities Dealers. The SEC approves the rules of the exchanges and the broker dealers in dealing with stock transactions, and hears appeals from brokers who have been sanctioned by their organization.[19] There are credit agencies, such as Moody's and Standard & Poor's, that rate the risk and creditworthiness of corporate bonds. Moody's offers "trust packages" for customers who plan to do business with foreign entities. Customers who do not know the foreign businesses ask the agencies to investigate and report. Who are their true owners? What is their personal and financial history? What is the history of the entity, its financial position, its bank arrangements, its reputation, and so on?

The Internet has become a fertile ground for trust verifiers, such as Verisign, which ensures the identity and signatures of people and institutions. There is even an enterprise that guarantees the color of materials displayed on the Internet. It assures buyers that the materials ordered will be of the same color as the materials displayed on the Internet.[20] SquareTrade offers online programs that verify, authenticate, and assure merchants' reliability. It also offers an online mechanism to resolve dispute.[21] Barry Minkow, a self-proclaimed reformed con artist, is a trust creator; he established the Fraud Discovery Institute, which helps investors, corporate management, and law enforcement agencies uncover frauds.

Two other kinds of system provide a high level of assurance for the honesty of individuals. They verify the trustworthiness of persons. Both are built on reputation. One type of program is operated by eBay. It can build (and destroy) an individual's reputation for honesty. The reputation is based on the aggregate evaluation of those who traded with the particular individuals. It is not foolproof. One can establish a reputation by dealing honestly in small amounts and then deal with many people on a much larger amount and disappear with the money. But by and large, the system works.

The other type of program for verifying the trustworthiness of individuals is LinkedIn. In this system, users offer information about themselves, and invite others to network. As the *Washington Post* describes it:

> Not every user is visible—only those who are four or fewer "degrees" (or people) connected to any given users, and those who agree to let anyone contact them. The names and profiles are visible, but a user can't get contact information unless the target agrees to an introduction. To contact any user, you first must seek an introduction from someone else in that person's network.[22]

The requests can travel from one person to another, and as they do, each person takes responsibility for the final meeting online. By having a direct contact to 89 persons, one acquires a potential contact to 48,700 people.

This technology substitutes for, or adds to, efficient trust in organizations. A person who knows two people can vouch for one to the other, increase the network of trusted people, and enable people to deal with strangers. This could be done only with the aid of technology. All these mechanisms have a price, but to judge by the demand for them, it seems that their costs do not exceed the benefits of more robust trust. Nonetheless, like the government regulators, these hordes of private verifiers were not effective in uncovering recent frauds. The guarantors themselves were not immune to collaboration with the institutions they were expected to monitor.[23]

Law helps close the information gap between the parties. Buyers and sellers who do not have the same information, talent, and qualifications to determine the right prices are expected to take care of their deficiencies. In an analysis of antitrust law, Kevin Mitchell has shown that consumers' knowledge has an effect of enforcing market discipline.[24] As George A. Akerlof explained, when the information gap between the parties is great, buyers discount the seller's price. Or the parties fail to reach an agreement.[25] The informed party's advantages can end up in its loss, and even undermine the market. The law can reduce the risk to the buyers, and induce them to offer the sellers a higher or "correct" price. Law can require sellers to offer buyers true information on penalty of civil and even criminal prosecution. Under these conditions, the buyers are more likely to believe the seller's information and agree to pay more. This is one way the buyers or the markets can exert their discipline more accurately. They don't pay too little. But they also don't pay too much.

When both the law and the verifiers fail to convince the buyers, the market-for-lemons phenomenon appears. Investors' uncertainty brings down the price of all shares. This may be one reason why the market crash of 2000 may have brought the stock prices lower than they should have been. The depressed prices could reflect investors' uncertainty about the truth in all corporate financial statements. As more corporations restated their financial information, investors' perceived risks rose.[26] They discounted the prices, like the buyers of used cars.

The markets reacted. Issuers have attempted to regain their lost trustworthiness. The *New York Times* reported that companies like Spain's Telefonica took steps to show their reliability by voluntarily binding themselves to obligations. Companies began to pay dividends, for the first time since 1998.[27] *Business Week* noted that "the average dividend-paying company has upped its payout by 18 percent this year. But a high dividend alone won't hack it—a company needs to be growing its earnings and have healthy free cash flow, too."[28] Dividend payments signify that companies have sufficient funds to pay, and their continued timely payments remind the shareholders that the companies are reliable; they keep their promises. As Yuval Rosenberg noted in *Fortune*, "There's nothing like money in the bank. That's why many savvy investors look to lock in a certain amount of yield when they're designing a portfolio, no matter the market cycle."[29]

Legal changes have supported these market attempts to reestablish trustworthiness. Congress passed the Sarbanes-Oxley Act. The New York state attorney general, Eliot Spitzer, and the federal SEC initated prosecutions. In the past five recent cases, the Delaware Court has begun to show far less deference to corporate management.[30] There is no proof that the steps taken by the particular corporations were effective in maintaining their stock prices, or that the rising legal enforcement has contributed to the maintenance of the current stock market prices.

ECONOMICS CAPTURING THE LAW

One change that has taken place in the past 30 years is the rising impact on the law of a branch of economics, named "imperial economics" by George J. Stigler, in his article "Economics: The Imperial Science?"[31] This type of economics has affected the approaches of lawyers, teachers, and judges. It has changed the attitudes to trust relationships and the legal protection from abuse of trust and deception. It has weakened self-limitation by trusted persons and legal limitations by the government. It has raised the self-protection that each party is expected to exercise against the other. It has also raised the importance of the sanctions of the markets—the aggregate of the parties in the markets. In sum, it has diluted the value of "trust" and increased the value of "verify."

When law is captured by economics, or by any other discipline, the law loses its autonomy, its language, its soul, and its role in society. Captured law and the search for an "efficient law" in the economic sense can significantly reduce the legal duties imposed on trusted persons and the limits on deception and abuse of trust.

The language of economics and the language of law reflect their different focuses, values, and objectives. When economics subsumes the law, the law reflects these different focuses, values, and objectives. When economics subsumes the law, it also makes changes in the law's culture by changing the underlying assumptions about how people view society and their relationships with each other, as well as how they view the law. We can study group culture on

> three levels: its artifacts, the level of its values, and the level of its basic assumption. . . . If one does not decipher the pattern of basic assumptions that may be operating, one will not know how to interpret the artifacts correctly or how much credence to give to the articulated values. [Schein, 26]

The difference between the basic assumptions and the values of the law and economics appears in the language of the two disciplines.

"Capital formation" is the language of economics. "Duties, liabilities, and rights of investors and issuing corporations" is the language of law. When economists say "capital formation," they mean corporate raising of capital in the markets. Law has no such expression. It speaks of "issuers"—companies such as Google that issue and sell their securities to investors in the securities markets through broker dealers such as Merrill Lynch. The two descriptions are interrelated, but their objectives and emphasis are different. The economists focus on the *money that corporations get*; law focuses on *who pays to whom, for what, and under what conditions,* and uses words like *duties, liabilities,* and *rights.* Economists are less concerned with these issues, unless they involve costs.

Law aims at creating a fair balance between trusting investors and trusted corporate management to support their raising of capital. Businesspersons see duties, liabilities, and other people's rights as constraints on "capital formation," at least short term. Law helps corporations achieve the goal of "capital formation," which economists and businesspersons applaud, but also limits the freedom to raise capital and imposes costs on capital formation, which some economists and businesspersons criticize.

"Agency costs" is the language of economics. "Breach of fiduciary duties and conflicts of interest" is the language of law. Economics focuses on the cost of abuse of trust and deception. Law focuses on preventing and punishing abuse of trust and deception. The two are interrelated; but their objectives and emphasis are different.

"Moral hazard" is the language of economics. "Abuse of trust and embezzlement" is the language of law. Economics looks to the risk from fraud. Law judges fraud as a wrong and considers its punishment. They are interrelated; but their focus and emphasis and objectives are different.

Economics reaches the end of its inquiry at the stage of capital formation, agency costs, and moral hazard. Its objective is to create wealth. Law reaches the end of the inquiry at the stage of declaring wrongs and their punishment. Its objective is to prevent antisocial activities, even if they create wealth. The two are interrelated but do not coincide, and may even clash.

When law becomes a branch of economics, rather than an autonomous discipline, it will adopt the traditional economics approach. That is the danger of the theory. Law will then consider wealth and cost as the main guides to justice and fairness, to greed and lack of empathy, and to the balance of self-interests with commitment to the community. The objectives of the law will change. No longer will the law have as its *primary and unconditional objective* the prevention and strict punishment of deception and abuse of trust. No longer will its emphasis be on wrongful or unfair behavior. Even though economics sees harm in deception and abuse of trust, their prevention is not its main objective, and costs are its main guidance. When the goals of the law become the goals of economics, law loses its independent goals. Preventing fraud becomes subsidiary to creating wealth.

The dangers of a theory are not in the opinions of its creators; not even in the misleading impressions that it produces. Opinions, impressions, and ideas enrich us, whether we agree with them or not. A theory becomes dangerous when it is implemented and is used to support antisocial behavior, abuse of trust, and deception.

Legal principles should consider cost. In fact, this book considers costs and benefits in many of its discussions. But legal principles should not be locked into the straitjacket of cost. Not everything can be measured in terms of dollars and cents. The world is far richer and more complex. For example, medical care involves very difficult considerations, other than money, such as priorities among young and old, wise and foolish, individuals and communities. Therefore, law parts ways with economics at the very foundation on which the discussion is based. We should reject a law that is exclusively founded in economics over everything, views the whole world as a market, quantifies everything, and models people as "rational" according to these measures.

There is a hostility of the legal economists to government intervention in economic activities. Milton Friedman opened his 1962 book *Capitalism and Freedom* with an attack on President Kennedy's statement: "Ask not what your country can do for you—ask what you can do for your country" [Friedman, 1]. For Friedman, these words implied dependence of those who ask the country to do something for them and subjugation of Americans by having to do something for their country. For others, John Kennedy's statement could mean that people should not seek to exploit the commons—the country—but to replenish the commons; that people should not try to selfishly take from their fellow citizens but unselfishly give to them. Where Friedman heard a ruler's command, one could hear a chosen leader's call for voluntary patriotism. Those who cheered John Kennedy were not slaves but lovers of their country. With him they berated those who aimed to selfishly take advantage of their country. Freedom, for Friedman, was freedom from government and from arbitrary actions on the one hand and empowering individuals on the other. But his freedom may include freedom to take other people's property, unless prevented by the owners, or freedom from government protection of weak owners.

Most dangerous is the erosion of public trust in institutions. One example is the attitude of people in eastern European countries after they established their independence from the Soviet Union. Not surprisingly, people in these countries mistrusted institutions, including the police and the parliament. "The past forty years of undemocratic rule devalued the importance of law, destroyed in people's minds any connection between law and the behavior of authorities and eroded the image of law as the protector of individual rights" [Misztal, 230]. In those countries, people became risk averse, distrustful, intolerant, and lacking in self-confidence. The question is whether the loss of respect for the law could lead to similar results in the United States.

Morality and law have declined in the past three decades, and the belief in the markets as regulators has risen. Notwithstanding these changes, there are many laws on the books under which it is possible to prosecute fraud and abuse of trust. Yet, enforcement of these laws has remained very weak. The next chapter inquires into this puzzle, suggesting criteria and possible ways to strengthen some of these weaknesses.

11

Why Did Legal Enforcement Fail to Stem the Avalanche of Fraud?

THERE IS ENOUGH LAW on the books. Why did legal enforcement fail to stem the avalanche of dishoneshty during the late 1980s and throughout the 1990s? To be sure, as the materials in chapters 7–10 have shown, the rules that imposed barriers to temptations were relaxed in the past three decades. But there are sufficient prohibitions on abuse of trust, and even more recent tougher federal punishment guidelines to stem the tide. Criminal and civil sanctions are attached to the regulation of the stock market and distribution of securities.[1] In addition, some elements of fraudulent activities, standing alone, were made crimes long ago. For example, sending false advertising; money laundering;[2] posting fraudulent materials through the mails;[3] and obtaining money under false pretenses are all crimes.[4] There are still many institutions and individuals to enforce the laws. So why did the legal enforcement fail?

WEAK DETERRENCE

Deterrence of abuse of trust and deception has been weak. Early discoveries can prevent many such abuses from ever occurring in the first place. It takes time and effort for white-collar criminals to gain millions by abusing other people's trust. Even if the money is entrusted to fiduciaries voluntarily, abuses start in small doses. They increase over time if they remain undetected. In large corporations, most of the frauds do not occur once. They are long-term progressing patterns of behavior. Only then can the schemes bring significant gains for the abusers and losses for their victims. If the abusers know that they will be discovered very soon, they are less likely to try. For example, at WorldCom, salespersons reported the same sale more than once. That showed higher profits and allowed the salespersons to collect double or more commissions for the same sale.[5] But this system could not bring much unless it was repeated over a long term. If the fraud could be discovered quickly, the salespersons and their approving-managers would have been less likely to try this technique in the first place.

Professor Gordon Tullock has suggested that increasing the chance of being caught is more effective to prevent crime than increasing the severity of the punishment.[6] In the white-collar crime area, an early discovery has an even greater preventive effect. But early discovery of white-collar crime is very difficult. Bill McDonald, chief of enforcement for the California State Department of Corporations, was quoted as saying that it is virtually impossible to track illegally operating investment advisors unless somebody complains.[7] The problem, according to experts on white-collar crime, is that such crimes are too easy to hide.[8] As compared to violent crimes, for example, financial frauds by trusted persons can be well hidden. Corporate diversified business, complex structures, far-flung enterprises, and innovative accounting can shelter deception. Fraud can be buried in the massive documentation of these enormous organizations, even when employees know or suspect it. To be sure, there are new technologies that help discover and publicize the dangers of financial crimes. But technology is evenhanded. It helps white-collar criminals hide their identities, their actions, and their assets. Therefore, it is unclear whether new technology tilts the scales toward stronger enforcement.

Who are the people and institutions who can detect white-collar criminal abuses early? *Those who have both access to the information about fraud and the incentive to report it.* The markets, and especially the markets for information, may fall into this category. Others include employees and newspaper reporters, the securities traders who sell securities short (short sellers), and analysts and rating agencies, whose business is to follow the performance and fortunes of the corporations. They could detect fraud. Large investors and recipients of corporate donations might receive sufficient signals of fraud.

The Markets as Discoverers and Reporters of Fraud

Markets can discover deception in some cases, for example, in the sale of products that can be tested. Buyers of low-quality goods that are advertised as high-quality goods quickly discover the difference. The defrauded consumers spread the word around, and reduce the sales. But in practice, market discipline may be too weak to prevent financial abuse, as Timothy D. Lane claimed in a publication of the International Monetary Fund.[9] Years can pass before stock prices based on deceptive accounting signal the fraud. Professor Frank Partnoy testified before a Senate committee, in the Enron hearings, that most investors cannot distinguish abusers from trustworthy persons or quality securities from worthless securities.[10] In addition, David A. Hirshleifer showed, in his book *Investors Psychology and Asset Pricing*, that even if investors receive true information, they do not necessarily make rational investment decisions.[11] In the words of Don Langevoort, investors can be swayed by brokers who sell their clients "hope and risk."[12]

Honest firms find it difficult to distinguish themselves from fraudulent ones, especially if the honest firms cannot compete with fraudulent firms on showing high revenues or sales. The more difficult and costly it is to distinguish between honest and dishonest actors and their actions, the weaker market discipline becomes. Therefore, information about deception and abuse of trust comes to the authorities far too late. The key to limiting deception and abuse of trust is early detection, and today the key is missing.

These conclusions are passionately rejected by some law and economics scholars. Stephen Choi, in an article entitled "Regulating Investors, Not Issuers: A Market-Based Proposal," argues that investors in the market can distinguish between true and false information, because a sufficient number of expert investors can learn the truth and can lead the rest.[13] In accordance with the efficient markets hypothesis, investors just follow the price, and thus distinguish between the fraudulent and the true. Therefore, the market prices of particular securities tell the story. Robert Prentice, in *Whither Securities Regulation? Some Behavioral Observations Regarding Proposals for Its Future*, vehemently rejects these proposals.[14] These arguments are based on the role and credibility of market prices and on what they truly represent.

Part of the debate centers on how investors and regulators make their decisions. For many years, economics, and the lawyers who follow it, worked on the model of "rational investors" making rational investment decisions, according to some rational criteria. But as more evidence piled up that investors are not rational by economic rationality standards, the arguments came to focus on the virtues of market regulation versus regulation by the SEC, or, more broadly, versus government regulation. If investors have biases, the arguments ran, so do government regulators. If investors are influenced (by advisors, brokers, and the like), so are government officials.[15] For these and many other reasons, markets that are free of regulation are deemed better.

The recent history of abuse and deception does not support the claim that the markets or the government are effective discoverers and reporters of fraud. The frauds were hidden from the public and from the government until it was too late. John A. Weinberg noted that the number of corporations that have had to restate their accounts has risen in recent years, "significantly above the dozen or so per year that was common in the 1980s."[16] As described in chapter 1, Huron Consulting Group's *Annual Review of Financial Reporting Matters* reported that in 2002, 330 companies restated their earnings recently; 270 restated their earnings in 2001, and 233 in 2000. In addition, 414 companies restated their financial statements in 2004, an increase of 28 percent from the 323 reported in 2003. The report noted "a rising trend in the number of periods contained in each restatement."[17] One earlier example is Goodyear, which restated its earnings three times in a six-month period.[18] As compared to the 1990s, the number of companies that have conceded to having misinformed the public has tripled. But this number, although much higher than in the past, represents only 1 percent of all publicly traded companies,[19] or 4 percent in 2004. At most, the number can show a trend toward fraud, but it teaches us little about markets and market prices as discoverer of abuse of trust.

Drawing generalizations from chaotic systems, such as the markets, can lead to many conflicting conclusions. So much affects so much else, and is affected by so much else. In the context of this discussion, it is enough to conclude that there is no convincing evidence that the markets could and did discover fraud. The results of all the debates and information on whether markets can best discover and regulate honesty or whether government regulation is necessary are inconclusive. Perhaps the markets can help discover some frauds and the law and regulators can help discover others, and the astute investors can discover yet others. The strong ideological arguments seem to suggest that neither mechanism alone is the best, and that the recent avalanche of discoveries may be due to the changes in the balance between the rule of law, the rule of the markets, and the diligence of the "rational investors." It may also suggest that we have gone too far in relying on the markets as discoverers and reporters of fraud. Perhaps a mix of the regulators' bias and the biases of the participants in the markets would yield better results.

Employees and the "Snitching" Syndrome

Many frauds in large enterprises are inside jobs that only insiders could detect. Few outsiders can find the necessary information. In cases of abuse of trust, those who could discover the frauds and put an end to them early on are not talking. Generally, these are the employees, and they remain silent. The abusers know and anticipate this reaction as well. Employees of fraudulent corporations face conflicting choices. They should be loyal to their employers, but they should not help perpetrate frauds, actively or passively.

The employees' loyalty to the employers conflicts with the employees' civil duty to honesty. The employees' commitment to the employers may be linked to self-interest. They can be offered a raise to help in the fraud, or paid to say nothing about it. They may fear losing their jobs unless they help in the fraud or say nothing about it. Personal relationships may make the choice even more difficult.

In the case of Equity Funding, the company established a special group to forge death certificates. Sixty-four thousand such certificates were forged, with a face value of over $2 billion [Dirks & Gross, 3]. Twenty-two persons, including officers and directors, were found guilty of the fraud.[20] A witness "reported that he had attended a dinner in New York with several other Equity Funding officers, and that some of them had joked openly at the table about 'the Y business' . . . the euphemism by which the insurance fabrication program was known within the company."[21] The fraud was reported by a former employee, an insider, who had left the company.[22]

In contrast to the reporters of violent crimes, those who reported suspicious activities to outside authorities or to higher authorities within the organization were usually viewed as "snitchers."[23] This attitude may be changing. A sign of this change is the treatment of Sherron Watkins. After she testified that she admonished Enron's CEO about a number of the fraudulent transactions, she went on to write a book about Enron [Swartz & Watkins]. Positive stories about her appeared in *Newsweek* and the *Wall Street Journal.*[24] And in December 2003, the *Wall Street Journal* devoted a front-page column to the persons who discovered and acted in connection with corporate fraud, such as Noreen Harrington, who disclosed Edward J. Stern's Canary Capital deals in mutual funds.[25] The publication bestowed legitimacy on these persons and their actions. They were not "snitches" but concerned citizens and committed employees. Changing the view of reporting employees is tremendously important as a model for other employees and for management: "Fraud will be discovered and publicized sooner than you think." Whether this is a signal of a future trend remains to be seen.

Employees' reporting is problematic. Corporations cannot survive without the employees' loyalty to the organization and to management. Corporate productivity will diminish if collegiality among its employees gives way to snooping around to uncover wrongdoing. But management can convince the employees that protecting the enterprise from fraud maintains their job security and will be recognized. In such a case, the employees' loyalty and sense of doing the right thing can converge with their self-interest and self-protection. This balance, however, is hard to achieve.

Former employees are also a source of information about fraud. In the case of *American International Assurance Company v. Bartmann,* two employees who resigned from a company alerted a prestigious law firm and a very large bank to signs of a possible fraudulent scheme. When management denied the allegations, the stories of the former employees were ignored. Later, it turned out that their information was true. The company was engaged in a Ponzi scheme that cost investors many millions of dollars.[26] In the case of Equity Funding, an analyst, Raymond L. Dirks, heard a story of a massive fraud from Ron Secrist, a former employee of Equity Funding [Dirks & Gross, 3]. Dirks alerted the *Wall Street Journal* and the SEC. He did not succeed in convincing the paper to publish the story, nor did he move the SEC to investigate the allegations.[27] Former employees are a direct source of information, but they are not always a reliable source. Their information may be colored by negative feelings toward their former employer. In sum, both employees and former employees can help uncover internal corporate frauds. But employees do not offer such information readily. Former employees might not be objective, and their information may not be easily verified.

Newspaper Reporters

Newspaper reporters can be effective fraud detectives. They can dig out information and ask questions more freely than the police. Because reporters do not have the coercive power of the law, the rules that limit police interrogation do not apply to them. Rather than threaten, reporters can offer publicity to those who are interested, and send the messages of those who wish to remain anonymous. Reporters have the privilege of keeping their information sources confidential. And even though the press has greater immunity from liability for defamation, reputable newspapers take great pains to check the truth of the information they publish.

Newspapers follow and publish the details of frauds once they are discovered. The *Sacramento Bee* publishes a standing column about scams.[28] The *Wall Street Journal,* the *New York Times,* the *Washington Post,* and the *San Francisco Chronicle,* among many others, reported daily on frauds that have been unfolding in the corporate and mutual funds areas. Newspapers can alert the public. Their circulation is wide, and their warnings are in the form of readable stories and explanations. Equally important, newspapers have incentives to disclose rather than to hide this kind of information. News about frauds, especially scandalous frauds, makes for interesting reading material, for which newspapers are rewarded. Exposing deception and abuse of trust is also virtuous, serving the public interest. Newspapers can arouse public opinion. They can also affect the readers' view of the discoverers of fraud. Newspapers therefore help uncover fraud some of the time, and educate the public about fraud. It was a reporter who discovered the prison history of Charles Ponzi and triggered Ponzi's demise. It was the *Phoenix New Times* that published a series of investigations into financial frauds replete with researched facts.[29] It was the *Washington Post* that disclosed the Watergate scandal.[30]

Reporters, however, did not discover the recent scandalous frauds. Enron's scam was self-proclaimed, by a straightforward bankruptcy. And in the case of Equity Funding, the *Wall Street Journal* hesitated to publish the information brought to it by Dirks. The story was too preposterous. It required full verification.[31] In that case, even the SEC refused to follow Dirks's lead until later. In sum, newspapers can help discover fraud some of the time.

Short Sellers

A group of expert traders, called short sellers, indirectly serves to police publicly traded companies and may signal deceptive practices in such companies. Short sellers investigate companies to discover overpriced stock. When they find such a stock, they sell the stock at the (inflated) market price even if they do not own it, and promise to deliver the stock within a certain period. During that period, they hope, the true value of the stock will be discovered, and its price will fall. Short sellers will then buy the stock at the lower price, deliver the stock, and pocket the difference between the price at which they bought the stock and the price at which they sold it.

The value of short sellers as sleuths is significant, except that they do not inform the public or the authorities of their specific findings directly. They trade on the basis of the information that they have gathered. Through their trading, market prices may change, and these prices provide vague signals to those who watch. If a company is supposed to be very successful and its financial statements were "too good to be true," the drop in its stock price suggests that "the financial statements are not good, and might not be true."

The short sellers' signals not only are ambiguous but also might not be always reliable. There are no cases on point, but there are many speculations. Short sellers might be tempted to manipulate the market by rumors that would send stock prices down, and would do that after they sold the stock but before they bought it to deliver to the buyers. The very actions of short sellers may signal to other investors that it is time to sell. If the investors are convinced, they will sell, and the price of the stock will drop. If the short sellers were mistaken, the drop will be short-lived, but some investors will be misled. Academic research offers support for both sides of this debate.

Robert L. D. Colby and Michael J. Simon argue that short sellers can create the appearance of a declining market to increase their own profits, and thereby cause the market to decline in reality. The writers note that short sellers can demoralize a market by knocking out buying interest through short sales.[32] Corporations use defensive measures to stop short sellers from making "bear" raids on their companies' stocks. Thus, short sellers are active in evaluating stock prices for their own benefit, and their activities *could* provide an early signal of fraudulent corporate schemes. And yet short sellers do not prevent corporate fraud, and it is unclear whether they discover it. Besides, stock price fluctuations do not single out fraud. They can be based on many other flaws in corporate performance and other events in the environment.

Analysts and Rating Agencies

Analysts and rating agencies are in the business of monitoring issuers whom they evaluate and rate. And yet neither the analysts nor the rating agencies seem to have discovered the recent frauds in advance of public disclosure. In fact, rating agencies do not have the history of such discoveries. Analysts may disclose the reasons for their recommendations, but not necessarily. The analyst Raymond L. Dirks advised his clients to sell the stock of Equity Funding after the SEC refused to investigate fraud allegations against the company. His clients were more trusting of his advice. They sold, and their sales began to bring the market price down. It was only then that the SEC started investigation, which led to the full discovery of the fraud [Dirks & Gross, 152–182]. It is difficult to know what analysts discovered and what is publicly disclosed.

Recipients of Donations

Large charitable, educational, and political institutions often know personally the management members of large donors and contributors. Presidents of universities and colleges grace the boards of large corporations, and corporate presidents are active fundraisers for charitable and political organizations. Contributions and donations are not entirely one-sided, however. When reputable charitable institutions and the powerful political figures accept the criminals' donations, and when they recognize the donations publicly, by naming buildings after them and bestowing honorary degrees, they cover the donors in a mantle of respectability. This does not mean that the recipients of the corporations' largess knew of the frauds within the corporations. But they did receive tainted money, all the same. They might have recognized the donors' problems before the public became aware of these problems. At that point, they may wish to disassociate themselves from the criminals. But they are unlikely to go to the police. They would be loath to admit to association with a fraudulent management, knowingly or unknowingly. Instead, they may slowly distance themselves and say little or nothing.

Helpers in Planning Fraud

The recent discoveries of abuse show that fraudulent managers had professional helpers, including outside firms of lawyers, investment bankers, accountants, and consultants. These helpers could have known or suspected that part or all the schemes were fraudulent. For example, an investment banker could arrange with a corporation a disguised loan in the form of two transactions: a sale of a note by the corporation to the banker and a subsequent purchase of the note by the corporation from the banker at the same price plus 7 percent. Put together, the two transactions constitute a loan. Separately, they look like two legitimate transactions of sale and purchase. Whoever created the idea, and perhaps whoever prepared the documents, if they were prepared at the same time, must have known of the deception. Since the banker took part in the transaction, someone in the organization may have had at least a suspicion that the sale and purchase were in fact a loan. Yet these knowledgeable persons had no incentive to notify the police, even after they realized that the transactions were fraudulent. The discovery and their close involvement would induce them to forget they ever participated in the deal.

The accountants in Arthur Andersen, who considered Enron to be their client, chose to shred documents rather than to present them to the SEC, as it demanded. This example demonstrates how unlikely these knowledgeable and informed parties are to bring their information to the police.

FAILURE OF DETECTION BY THE SOPHISTICATED INVESTOR

Those Who Suspect Fraud Do Not Report; They "Cash Out and Run"

Sophisticated investors may have negotiated directly with the issuers, or have personal contact with the management and the leaders of the fraudulent organizations. These investors might recognize "red flags" and discover or suspect the frauds before the events become public. But even as they suspect, these investors will not necessarily call the police. Instead, they may cash out and run. These investors may send signals to the markets, especially if they are insiders. Insiders may have to report their trading.[33] But the sales are ambiguous signals. They need not reflect suspicions of fraud. They can reflect other reasons for selling. Investors who cash out and run may help shorten the life cycle of fraudulent schemes. Frequent cash-outs can signal that something is wrong, even without spelling out the details. This is the way a run on a bank or a particular stock develops. Roy A. Schotland showed that reports of problems cause bank depositors to lose confidence in the bank, and then to withdraw their money from the bank en masse.[34] If people sense that something is wrong, they often do not ask for details but want to get their money back as fast as possible. While banks can often seek the help of the government, the credit of corporations is more limited, and the credit of individual white-collar criminals may be even lower.

A "run" does not necessarily prevent fraud, and may not be the best way to shorten it. A run may press the corporate or individual deceivers to recruit new unaware investors, whose money will be quickly lost in paying creditors, shoring up the stock prices, or paying former investors. And yet a run has advantages. It is self-enforcing. It is a market mechanism that costs the government close to nothing. In addition, although a run can intensify the efforts of the criminals in the short term, it is likely to shorten the fraudulent scheme in the long term. Those who cash out and run send negative signals to the market and help terminate the fraud earlier. Losses, however, can be devastating. For example, when a market run began on Enron's stock, it took about two months to drive the share prices from over $75 to 28 cents a share, ending at 14 cents a share.[35]

Suspicious investors who cash out would prefer to keep quiet. One reason for their secrecy could be to avoid a "run" by the other investors. If all investors cash out, no investor is likely to be paid in full. If investors have the right to demand their money from the issuer of the securities, they are unlikely to be paid in full either. Much of the money may have been spent and lost.

There are other reasons for investors' silence. The U.S. Department of Justice suggests that the victims may be reluctant to "get involved" if they have insufficient information on the precise details of the scheme. They may not have a direct proof that the scheme is fraudulent. After all, risky but legitimate businesses can deteriorate. Voicing suspicion can become an embarrassment.[36] Besides, testifying and being cross-examined in court does not promise much pleasure. Sophisticated and wealthy investors who invested after direct contact with white-collar criminals may prefer to lose money rather than lose face, respect, or the trust of their clients. If the investors are fiduciaries, such as investment managers, they have little incentive to report the frauds. Why advertise their inept handling of the money entrusted to them by others? Institutional investors who received special treatment or participated in the fraudulent scheme have hoped to gain. They will not report if the scheme failed. When such investors suspect fraud, the last thing they want is to publicize the fact. Even after they cash in on their investment, these investors may wish to keep quiet in order to shield themselves from the wrath of the losing investors once the scheme is discovered. That is especially so if they had recommended this investment to others but did not recommend that they cash out quickly as well. And if the white-collar criminals or their corporation declared bankruptcy, these investors who cashed out may have to account for their gains. Better to keep quiet.

Careless Investors Who Do Not Heed the Red Flags

Too few investors who are the targets of fraud recognize or heed the red flags of fraud that are waving at them. There are warnings in books, articles, newspapers, government publications, and on the Internet, advising investors to verify offers that are "too good to be true," to check with government agencies and their web sites, and to obtain information about the promoters who promise enormous short-term gains. After disastrous losses and painful experiences, the Department of Justice's Office for Victims of Crime offers support to victims.[37] In spite of these admonitions to the victims, most investors do not report financial fraud.

I noted earlier that investors were blamed for "greed" and lack of prudence. One way to avoid large disastrous frauds is to teach investors "prudence." If investments are too good to be true, they are not true. There is much truth and wisdom in these cautions. But they were not heeded. Fraudulent schemes send red-flag signals to those that can see and care to see. Perhaps one item does not raise a sufficient warning. But two or more of the following signals should.

- Promises of very high returns at low risk are unlikely to be true. Either the returns are lower, or the risk is higher.
- The promised returns are from a business that the investors do not understand and cannot easily verify. If the explanations of the business are too complex, the red flag must be raised.
- There is minimal government supervision. The offerings are of securities or advisory services about securities that are not registered. The offerors are not registered broker dealers or advisors. Such a registration is no assurance that the transaction is free of deception. But no registration shows that a certain protective mechanism does not exist in the particular case. That should raise a red flag and require investors to take greater care.
- The issuers of the securities continue to issue securities even though they are not financial institutions. This continuous offering can signal a Ponzi scheme by which the money of the later investors is being paid to the old investors.
- Lavish large donations and huge entertainment budgets on behalf of the issuing corporation or the advisory business rather than personal donations may raise a red flag. Grand generosity at the expense of others is suspect. In one case, the *Indianapolis Business Journal* reported that an investment advisory firm sponsored investor trips to exotic places at great expense. That should have been especially worrisome, because competing investment professionals did not offer investors such perks.[38] Donating one's own money is a sign of sincerity. Donations of other people's money can signal abuse of investors' trust.

Many of these red flags fit Enron. Its stock prices were very high and continuously on the rise. Its financial statements and business strategy were complicated and very hard to understand. The company enjoyed exemptions from three crucial federal statutes, and was therefore subject to minimal government supervision. The company issued securities continuously, even though it was not supposed to function as a financial institution. Enron had made large generous donations to educational institutions and political parties. Yet, as Jonathan Macey noted in his article on Enron, large and small investors bought the stock, and Wall Street analysts hailed it as an excellent investment.[39] The warnings to investors were not effective.

Relying on small public investors to protect themselves from fraud did not work in the past, and may be a double-edged sword. If investors become truly cautious and questioning, the incidence of fraud may fall. But suspicious investors, who refuse to take the risk of uncertainty, impose high costs on the issuance of securities. Investors would demand more evidence of truth and guarantees of reliability. Or, following the theory of the market for lemons, they will offer lower prices for securities that are not accompanied by such evidence and guarantees. Or, as in the 1930s, they may refuse to buy equity securities altogether, and acquire only bonds, or put their money in the bank. All these reactions could raise the cost of capital and reduce the liquidity of the markets. Therefore, shifting the burden of verifying and caution to investors is not the optimal way to reduce fraud.

The Board of Directors

How many boards of directors have discovered frauds within their organization? It is doubtful whether anyone knows. Yet it was not the investors or the market but the board of Nortel Networks Corporation who found "accounting tricks" as the source of its profits in the year 2003.[40] The company's executives told its board to expect losses of $112 million in the first quarter. But then, in February, the losses shrank to $32 million, and a week later fell to $20 million. March 30 ended in a profit of $40 million. Bonuses began to flow to employees, and millions—to executives. It turned out that the profits were attributed to unacceptable accounting "gimmicks." The rise of profits from the ashes of the losses should be a red flag, as it seems to have been with the company's board. It should be clear that boards do not have detailed information about the operations of their companies. They cannot micromanage the operations. It is not their function either. But sensitive boards can detect suspicious changes; the kind of red flags that would lead them to demand more information and explanations. The boards also have ultimate clout. As a last resort, they can fire management.

INEFFECTIVE PUNISHMENTS

Historically, punishments of white-collar criminals were not heavy. These criminals can "feel" less threatening than thieves and robbers, even when they cause well-publicized disastrous losses to many investors and to the financial system. The *San Francisco Chronicle* noted that white-collar violators are often connected to "influential circles, sometimes hobnobbing with politicians, law enforcement officials and business leaders. It is all the more difficult to make charges stick when the judge is the [alleged criminal's] golfing buddy."[41] Therefore, as Clinton Leaf complained in

Fortune, until recently at least, the chances of going to prison, even for committing very large-scale frauds, were quite low. The white-collar criminals "got away with it."[42]

In addition, in the United States, there is less condemnation of "victimless crimes" such as drug use, gambling, or drinking, where no specific individual is a "victim." It is assumed that individuals who smoke or take drugs can change their habits, if they only wanted to do so hard enough. Therefore, the question becomes a matter of a cost-benefit analysis to society: Is the gain to society from preventing the undesirable conduct worth the cost to society of preventing it? This question arises even when these activities are enormously harmful to society as a whole. "When all of the parties involved in the activities are consenting adults, the harm to society does not approach the level of crimes with true personal victims" [Loewy, 303–304]. Alderman Rodney Barker is quoted as saying: "What I'd like to see police do is deal with important issues and not these sorts of victimless crimes when society is riddled with problems."[43] This attitude directs the blame to the investors who sustained great losses. The attitude may stem from the greater weight that the American culture puts on individual freedom to decide as compared to society's right to interfere in the individual's decision.

In the period 1992–2001, the SEC referred 609 cases to the Justice Department for criminal prosecution. Of these cases, 525 were disposed: 187 defendants were prosecuted, 142 were found guilty; and 87 went to jail.[44] Research statistics cited by *Fortune* noted that "the starched-collar S & L [savings-and-loan association] crooks got an average of 36.4 months in the slammer. Those who committed burglary—generally swiping $300 (U.S.) or less—got 55.6 months; car thieves, 38 months; and first-time drug offenders, 64.9 months." The lowest estimate of the costs of the 1989 savings-and-loan associations fraud scandals was $1.4 trillion.[45] The highest estimate, by the General Accounting Office, was $285 billion, over the next three decades.[46] Some of the white-collar criminals that have corrupted and endangered the stock market in the 1980s have not only endured less than three years in prison but also were not necessarily left destitute. For example, one such prisoner, Michael Milken, was worth $800 million in 2002, while two others, Ivan Boesky and Charles Keating, managed to hold on to millions, a far cry from the amounts left for the investors.[47] To be sure, it is possible that they have earned all or part of these amounts after they left prison.

As reported in the *San Francisco Chronicle*, Bill McDonald and Robert Crowe suggested that the penalties "aren't stiff enough to deter the criminally minded."[48] It is unclear whether prison sentences deter repeat violations or rehabilitate white-collar criminals. Anecdotal evidence suggests that the punishments are not necessarily strong deterrents. One reporter who paid a visit to the con artist in jail while the con awaited sentencing told the following story. He was going soon to "camp," said the con artist.

"When I walk out of here I'll probably be seen as the biggest son of a bitch," he said. In the [prison] he was a hero, the hundred-million-dollar man. He said two things about his long-term future. ["First,] I'm going to start all over again. . . . I've got all the energy in the world. . . . [Second,] I'm going to play golf four months out of every 12."[49]

Even when they finally land in prison, white-collar criminals are likely to be treated gently, and for good reasons. They are usually model prisoners. They are intelligent, pleasant, and obedient. Therefore, they end up managing the library, working in an office, and providing services to prison officials. Services that make life more tolerable for imprisoned white-collar criminals make sense from a cost analysis perspective of the prison administration. Prisons are not overly populated with obedient, eager-to-please, and qualified prisoners. Such services reduce the prison costs. White-collar prisoners are generally the least expensive to the government.

Top management withstands prison sentences surprisingly well. It was assumed that for members of the corporate management group, being branded as a notorious criminal and losing prestige was what they feared far more than fines. Yet a study conducted by Michael L. Benson in 1988 contradicts some of these assumptions.[50] The study suggests that these offenders have "greater emotional resources than ordinary offenders" and that they are "more adept at coping with psychological stress of prison life." They feel superior to the other prisoners and do not interact with them. This attitude also helps these white-collar criminals to maintain their dignity and cope with prison life.[51] In addition, they have the support of their peers outside prison. When the membership of the support group includes political and business leaders, the prisoners withstand their sentences quite well.

What Is Better Punishment for White-Collar Crime?

Would harsher punishment be more effective? In a 1974 article entitled "Does Punishment Deter Crime?" the economist Gordon Tullock examined the issue of punishment and deterrence from economic and sociological viewpoints.[52] His approach as an economist which was an innovative approach at the time, was to examine the demand-and-supply curve of crime. "If you increase the cost of something," he wrote, "less will be consumed."[53] Therefore, if you increase the cost to the criminal, you have a good chance of reducing the incidence of crime. He believed that tougher punishments would help empty the prisons. Tullock suggested that deterrence should involve unpleasant experiences. If prisons are more like educational facilities and do not inflict pain, they may not be effective deterrents. He maintained that severe punishments deter, while rehabilitation practiced with tenderness "never has worked."[54] As Eliot Spitzer suggested, the signals of potential prison sentences and possible stigma, the added burdens of disclosure regulation, may be an effective deterrent to potential wrongdoers.[55] There are conflicting opinions on this point. Suffice it to say that it also has followers.

What are the economic standards for an efficient enforcement system? We assume that illegal deception, fraud, and abuse of trust cause harm to individuals, society, and the economy, even as they benefit some people (at the expense of others). Here I focus on the possible avenues for preventing this illegal behavior, drawing on economics and behavioral science.

In economic analysis, the most efficient legal system would be the one that provides the greatest reduction of abuse of trust and deception at the lowest cost. Following this approach, one should evaluate the harm from deception and abuse of trust to investors, the society, and the economic and financial systems on the one hand and the costs of discovering the violations and punishing the offenders on the other. Losses to the economy and financial system are hard to measure, but they are real and should be given approximate weight.

One can estimate punishment cost as a stand-alone item. Some punishments, such as fines, cost the government less than other punishments, such as imprisonment. But the costs of enforcing the law and the harm to society have a symbiotic relationship. Spending more on enforcing the law may be worthwhile if the social harm is reduced by even more. If, for example, an additional dollar spent on a more expensive punishment saves two dollars of social harm, the choice of the less expensive punishment is inefficient. Therefore, a habitual white-collar criminal who is likely to continue defrauding unsuspecting investors should be imprisoned. That is, even if prison is more expensive to the government than imposing a fine.

The punishments of white-collar criminals should be evaluated also by their deterrent effects. Richard Posner suggested that white-collar criminals "should be punished only by fine and other money penalties, because for the white-collar criminal a fine or imprisonment makes no difference 'in principle.'"[56] Yet determining whether imprisonment makes a difference to white-collar criminals should not be based on reasoning but on empirical research. Does social harm from the white-collar crimes fall by more than the cost of stricter, though costlier, punishment? Testing punishments by cost alone should be limited to those cases in which different punishments have the same deterrent effect on offenders.

Professor Robert Cooter offered a cost-benefit analysis to evaluate the level of punishment's pain and the probability of being caught as against the immediate gratification and the level of the satisfaction from breaking the law. People make different probability calculations and valuations of these factors, and some may break the law, while others will abstain. Older people may be deterred by relatively severe punishments with low probability of being caught and punished, while younger people may be deterred by relatively severe punishments only if the probability of being caught is much higher.[57]

Perhaps in the case of white-collar criminals, one size does not fit all. Not everyone feels the same anguish when "hit in the pocket." Not everyone feels the same shame and stigma of a prison history. Corporations can be repeat offenders as well, because corporations do not operate by themselves. People operate them. And people can be repeat offenders [Clinard & Yeager, 116–122]. When they escape punishment, one can expect the corporations to continue to behave in a fraudulent manner until their leaders and managers, and their culture, change to prevent these activities. Therefore, in addition to, or instead of, criminal punishments, other measures of deterrence should be considered.

Preventive Punishment: Licensing and Revocation

For repeat offenders, fines can be higher, and prison sentences can be longer. Yet another punishment can protect society from repeat offenses by preventing the wrongdoers from legally engaging in, or occupying positions of, trust. This punishment applies to occupations that require licensing. Most physicians, nurses and pharmacists, lawyers, securities broker dealers and accountants, investment managers, and investment advisors must obtain licenses to practice.

To be sure, qualified practitioners invest much to acquire their licenses. But there is a balance. Qualified practitioners receive rewards in the form of a partial monopoly that increases their gains and prestige throughout their careers. Nonlicensed persons may not practice and compete with licensed persons, and are punished if they do. The government regulates licensed persons' professional activities but bestows on them the mantle of trustworthiness and protects their reputation as reliable actors. The public can easily find out whether people are licensed. For example, the law requires doctors to clearly display their licenses. Anyone who wishes to know whether a securities broker is licensed can easily find out by looking at the website of the SEC. The absence of the name warns the investor to beware.

For the government, licensing, supervising, and disqualifying licensed practitioners as a punishment have a number of advantages. Licensing enables an authority (whether the government or a private sector governing body) to sift through the applicants and prevent unqualified persons from practicing. Thus, licensing can have a preventive effect of weeding out unqualified persons in advance, even before they start practicing. In addition, licensing enables the government to impose restrictions on licensed persons and to withhold benefits from them. Licensing allows the government to disqualify licensed persons, who were found to lack expertise and to have violated the law. Disqualification is relatively inexpensive to government and expensive to the licensees. Licenses make it easier to prosecute repeat disqualified offenders, since practicing without a license becomes an independent offense that is easier to prove than fraud. Further, part of the government's costs of licensing are covered by fees, and the practitioners of some of these occupations, such as lawyers and physicians, provide self-regulation as first-tier protection to clients and patients. A number of regulators control the honesty of these occupations: the markets and the public consumers, other practitioners in self-regulatory organizations, and the government.

License revocation bars the holders from reaping the benefits that they expected from their initial investment of getting the license, which can be very significant. But license revocation does not prevent them from earning a livelihood any other way. When a licensee poses a danger to clients, the protection of the public trumps the rights and protection of the licensee to practice in the area of his choice. Besides, revocation of a license need not be for life; it can be for a limited period. Such a revocation imposes the equivalent of a fine, coupled with a warning about future illegal activities. For repeat offenders, the sanctions of the SEC, such as denial of registration, may not be an effective cure, as is shown by the continued securities violations of brokers who have faced charges.[58] The fact that their registration was revoked may not alert all their potential victims either. The SEC publishes the names of registered brokers, but victims continue to deal with people who are not on the list.

Licensing can be criticized as a constraint on entrepreneurs. Customers are far better judges of qualifications. Customers could try the licensed persons and find out whether they are reliable and qualified. And that is true. Yet some services are too dangerous to try, if the experience requires a high level of trust. One does not try a lawyer in an important case to determine whether he is qualified, or a pharmacist to find out whether he prepares the right medicine. If we want people to seek healthcare from physicians they do not personally know, patients must be assured of their physicians' qualifications.

Physicians can regulate themselves better that the government can regulate them. But because their desire to do good for others is mixed with desire to do good for themselves, and because they may be biased on certain issues and toward their own prestige and pockets or those of their friends, government regulation is superimposed on self-regulation. These are the reasons for involving the patients' self-protection, the physicians' self-regulation, the government's regulation, and for balancing the three for optimal protection and freedom to practice.

Licensing, like government regulation generally, can present problems. Regulators might identify with the regulated persons too closely, and "be captured" by the regulated industry and profession. The judgment of government officials is not necessarily beneficial to society. Their views may be myopic. They may lack knowledge or understanding. They may be locked into a mistaken ideology and beset by biases. Nonetheless, in a service that has significant effect on society, like brokerage, for example, licensing may benefit more than it can harm.

Eliminating the Power to Abuse: Disqualification of Corporate Management

Relatively few white-collar criminals must be licensed. The elite group of white-collar criminals does not sell securities nor give advisory services. This group manages those who sell securities and give advisory services. The elite occupies positions of power as officers and directors of corporations or as top executives of broker dealers and investment bankers. They may have had licenses in the early stage of their careers, and have outgrown them.

A proposal to "professionalize" corporate management did not go very far.[59] After all, directors are the elected and chosen representatives of the shareholders; that is their qualification. Directors are expected to heed and represent the interests of their shareholders. In closed corporations, directors' power is limited. The shareholders, and especially the shareholders who hold a large number of shares, may be in partial or full control. In public U.S. corporations, with thousands of shareholders, who do not own even a small fraction of controlling shares, the management, rather than the small shareholders, chooses the directors. The key power to choose is to pick and nominate the proposed candidates for directorship. Even large institutional shareholders, such as pension funds, do not have this power. Small shareholders seem to have as much power to remove the directors as voters have to remove the president of the United States. The shareholders' clout is to "exit" by selling their shares. But that exit may involve costs for them, and the effect of their sales on the managers is unclear. After all, lower share prices can provide managers with an opportunity to buy the shares and gain tighter control over the corporation—the managers' main source of livelihood.

Under the existing law, the courts and the SEC have the authority to disqualify directors and officers of public corporations. Disqualification precludes such managers from serving in this capacity if they are found guilty of deceptive practices in connection with securities trading.[60] However, like many laws on the books, until 2002, the disqualification punishment has remained close to a dead-letter law. The courts did not use it or impose it, perhaps because no clear guidelines have been developed on imposing this penalty. Besides, removing elected directors, as opposed to hired managers, may present a fundamental issue of the shareholders' rights.[61] Private litigants did not press for removal, perhaps because removal does not bring the hoped-for dollars to the litigants and their lawyers. The SEC has used disqualification to a greater extent than the courts. In settlements of claims on securities violations, the SEC bargained for disqualification of top management. But until recently the SEC has not done so aggressively.

In 2002, Congress extended the power of the SEC to impose disqualification.[62] As I show later, the number of disqualification orders has gone up dramatically. From 1972 until June 2003, the SEC requested a total of 291 officer and director bars in 192 separate complaints.

In 97.92 percent of the 192 cases, the SEC alleged a violation of insider trading rule 10b-5 under the Securities Exchange Act of 1934. Of the 192 cases, 48 percent were settled, 34 percent are pending, 11.4 percent were court cases, including judgments by default, and 2 percent were SEC orders (4 percent of the complaints included both settled and pending cases); 86 percent involved at least one request for a permanent bar, and 81 percent involved public companies, counting only those cases where I was able to determine whether or not the company was public or private. Of the 192 cases, 50 percent involved financial fraud, such as illegal loans, inflated earnings, and other accounting fraud. Only four of the companies were ranked on the current *Fortune* 1000 listing. Another three cases involved companies that have been recently dropped from the list: Tyco, Enron, and WorldCom.[63]

Disqualification can be effective only if the elite group of corporate management adopts a self-policing approach. Without positions of power, the bonds of disqualified directors and officers with other group members may slowly weaken. They might meet, work together, and reciprocate less often. The criminals among the group members may become "marginalized," and their influence may be reduced. This waning of influence is especially important if the disqualified officers were the CEOs and leaders of a large corporation.

For directors and officers who enjoy the position of power, disqualification can be a very strong deterrence. But the deterrent effect depends mainly on the attitude of their peers. Disqualification will be very effective if competitors who use aggressive accounting methods and seek unlimited compensation, no matter what it takes, are shunned rather than emulated. Disqualification will be powerful if abusing people's trust by deception is viewed with contempt rather than admiration.

Removal from one board but not from another emasculates the deterrent effect of disqualification. Corporate managers recommend and nominate each other to high-level positions. One might assume that they are unlikely to nominate or appoint disqualified members in violation of a legal order. A recent case, however, suggests that this assumption may not be quite accurate. If the case is symptomatic of other corporate boards, disqualification may be ineffective. On June 5, 2003, the CEO of Xerox settled with the SEC a claim against him. He agreed to pay a fine of $1 million, and account to the corporation for $7 million that he gained from alleged illegal activities. He was disqualified from serving on the board of a corporation for five years.[64] But on July 8, 2003, the *New York Times* reported that this man, who also served as chairman of the Ford Foundation, was reappointed to that position "despite accusations by federal regulators that he participated in accounting fraud when he was chairman and chief executive of the Xerox Corporation."[65] It seems that after perusal of the order, it was discovered that the disqualification applied to serving on the board of a "corporation" but did not apply to serving on a board of a "not-for-profit corporation." It also seems that the members of the Ford Foundation board did not consider this man to be sufficiently tainted to preclude him from serving as their leader and the symbol of their institution.

Two important lessons emerge from this story. First, the settlement order of the SEC was interpreted literally, and the word "corporation" was therefore not "expanded" to include a similar position in the Ford Foundation. Perhaps this reflected the deal with the government. But if it did not, then the interpretation is the result of the demand for specificity in the area of regulating fiduciaries. The dangers of this form of interpretation surface here. Even if the SEC's staff members were farsighted enough to include the words "and not-for-profit corporations," this itemization would not have included credit unions, some of which are quite large and pay quite well. And there are other forms of associations, such as pension funds, in which this man would be permitted to serve as a leader. Besides, the word "board" may not include a "commission" and a "committee," and the word "director" may not include a "trustee of a business trust," a form in which many huge mutual funds are organized.

Unless the order was intended to limit disqualification to corporations, the interpretation of the settlement with specificity constitutes a subversion of the order. To be sure, there is an argument for interpreting the settlement in this way. The violation of the settlement agreement is punishable by law, and such provisions are usually interpreted strictly. Yet this is not a case of depriving someone of a livelihood. It does not prevent the person from working in any other capacity. It prevents the person from holding a powerful office. Was the intent of the settlement so narrow? Was it designed to allow this man to sit on other types of boards and continue to exercise much power over enormous amounts of money?

The second lesson of this story concerns the decision of the Ford Foundation's board. The reinstatement of this man constitutes an affirmation that the settlement did not affect the board members' affection for the chairman or their respect for his integrity. The reinstatement is a declaration that his continued tenure will not hurt the Foundation's finances or reputation. The chairman remains in the position of prestige and power—revered as ever. The board is making its position defiantly public. This man remains a leader.

Even if there is no doubt that the chairman is an able and experienced person, he has also shown experience in heading a corporation that practiced deception and abused public trust on a massive scale. Perhaps there is no danger that the Ford Foundation would be found to have "cooked its books." But he did head an organization that did just that, and presumably the disqualification was aimed in part as a punishment and in part as a public statement for others to take notice. And yet the criminal activities of Xerox did not seem to taint him. As one board member of the Ford Foundation said: "We are committed to doing what we considered and consider the right thing, and that is what is best for the foundation, which is to stay with a man who has been an exemplary leader."

In fact, the decision of the board of Ford Foundation demonstrates not only a statement of support for the chairman but also a statement of criticism of the SEC. The SEC and its staff are viewed as the zealots who are after blood for their own aggrandizement. Attributing bad motives to the opponent is a well-known defensive practice against the accusation of criminal behavior. Gary Johns noted that to justify their own behavior dishonest people will attribute dishonesty to their victims: the people whom they will deceive.[66] This approach is apparently being used in this case.

If the disqualification was designed as a punishment, it failed to achieve its purpose. If it was designed as a preventive measure, to prevent this person from leading a large organization for at least five years, it failed to achieve its purpose. If the disqualification was designed to reduce this man's power and his role as a leadership model, it failed to achieve its purpose. And if the disqualification was designed to deter others, if must have failed to achieve its purpose. Had he been fully disqualified, his effect as a leader would have diminished. He would have been left at the edge of the power network. He could not have recommended others to positions of power or be recommended by others. But with the help of the Ford Foundation and other such organizations, the chairman will retain his power with little, if any, change in the next five years.

Not all boards reacted this way, however. Here is an example of a board that did not wait for the SEC to disqualify its top management. The *Wall Street Journal* reported that on June 23, 2003, the board of directors of the Federal Home Loan Mortgage Corporation ("Freddie Mac"), a government-sponsored corporation, revolted against top management. The board removed top management after discovering that its employees had "sought to 'smooth out' the company's earnings through its hedging and accounting practices" and that the corporation could be required to restate its financial statements by more than $3 billion. The board took the further precaution of examining whether the newly installed CEO was involved in the accounting irregularities. The company's historical culture is a familiar story. It stretched the envelope, looking to "dampen [the] volatility" of its earnings, while attempting to do that within the government's rules. The directors fired the executive after they discovered that he had failed to provide them with full documentation.[67] All in all, three top executive officers, including the chief operating officer, were removed from office.

Repay the Money

Embezzlers, who directly put their "hands in the till," are required to return the money they stole. But *embezzlement* cannot be the word applicable to compensation of top management. This compensation was approved, and supported by legal documents. But some managers presided over deceptive accounting. The accounting was aimed at driving up the stock prices. That allowed management to exercise stock options. These options were exercised with money borrowed from the corporation. The stock was sold at enormous profits. The compensation some managers received during the 1990s is now examined and investigated, but the question of how such management would be required to repay to the shareholders its enormous compensation is not as easy to answer. What portion of this compensation was acquired by fraud? Should the compensation of these managers be linked to the price of the shares after the fraud is discovered? Would that approach at least equalize management's financial position with that of some of the losing shareholders? One justification for the link would be the invalidity of all the validating legal instruments. After all, these validations were based on incorrect and fraudulently presented data. The other basis for repayment would be simply the damage to the corporation and its shareholders. And yet another could be accounting for profits that fiduciaries who used their beneficiaries' assets should repay to the beneficiaries. Otherwise, even after years in prison, the managers of such corporations can come back to a life that was denied to many of their employees and shareholders who invested in the shares of these corporations. As of November 2004, this issue is unresolved.

Prompt Prosecution

As of 2004, relatively few of the top managers who headed fraudulent corporations for years have been tried and sentenced. In June 2003, the former CEO of ImClone Systems became the first CEO to be sentenced following the scandals.[68] No former Enron executive was sentenced until September 2003.[69] In October 2003, a former chief executive of two divisions of Enron pleaded guilty and faced a possible prison sentence.[70] As of November 2003, neither the former chairman nor the former president of Enron had been charged, although other former Enron executives had been.[71] By and large, very few of the top executives involved in the large-scale corporate frauds of the 1990s have been sentenced. Prosecutions take a very long time. Months pass without indictments.[72] On May 14, 2003, Lou Dobbs reported on the CNN television program *Moneyline*: "Well, it has now been 527 days since Enron filed for bankruptcy, 65 executives charged, 15 of them from Enron. No one's gone to jail."[73] As of July 3, 2003, not one Enron executive had been sentenced.[74]

The pace has picked up in 2004. But it is still slow. As of July 22, 2004, according to *Wall Street Journal Online*, of a group of 27 officers of firms involved in eight noted corporate scandals (including a broker and brokerage assistant for two officers) who have faced criminal charges, seven have been sentenced. Nine others have been found guilty or pleaded guilty, and 11 others have been indicted (including three who pleaded not guilty); two of those indicted were acquitted, and mistrials were declared in the case of three others.[75] In August 2004, another officer of Enron Corporation pleaded guilty to fraud.[76] And court cases proceed slowly.

Financing prosecution. One reason for the weak and slow enforcement against deception and abuse of trust is cost. Without sufficient financing, the SEC cannot enforce the law as it should. A comparison between the amounts spent to ensure the safety and honesty of our banking system and the amounts spent to ensure the integrity of the securities markets and the mutual funds shows a staggering difference. The 2003 budget for the SEC was $712 million, while the 2003 budget for the FDIC—only one of five federal bodies that regulate the banks—was $1.113 billion.[77] It is true that banks require more control. Even so, the enforcement personnel of the SEC increased to only around 400 people in the year 2003.[78] The Federal Reserve Board earns and keeps the money it collects to manage their operations. The SEC earns by fines and fees, but delivers the money to the Treasury and receives a far smaller budget from Congress.[79]

Enforcement against corporate white-collar criminals, and especially against institutional defendants, is very costly and time-consuming. As the *Economist* noted, the truth is buried in large amounts of information. And managers of large corporations "fight back," continuing expensive court processes and depleting the resources of the government prosecution.[80] Large law firms are at the defendants' disposal. They resist long before they agree to settle. In some cases, both or one of the parties refuses to settle, as in the case of Frank Quattrone.[81] The high costs influence the government to settle rather than to conduct full-fledged trials. Another reason for the government's settlements is to gain the defendants' collaboration in uncovering other serious and widespread frauds. As Eliot Spitzer, who was criticized for agreeing to such settlements, explained in an interview published in the *Harvard Business Review*, the government often gains by the collaboration of the wrongdoers. The collaboration saves government resources.[82] Yet, as the *Atlanta Journal and Constitution* commented, the government settlements have not served the prosecutions' purpose. After all, there is a need for strong examples that would deter future fraud.[83] Thus, financing may restrict government investigations and trials. In principle, the purse strings are a desirable and effective tool of controlling prosecutors' excessive zeal. But when an avalanche of fraud is discovered and the purse strings are not sufficiently loosened, law enforcement weakens.

THE WINDS OF CHANGE

The Changing of the Guard

There are signs of the changing of the guard. During the past four years and especially during 2004, a number of corporate leaders have left their posts, for many reasons. Some were removed. Motorola suffered poor performance and termination of thousands of employees. The CEO had to leave.[84] American Airline's president left when he did not disclose the benefits for top management while he was negotiating with union members for a 15 percent cut in salary.[85] Freddie Mac's CEO and chief operating officer resigned "following the company's recent accounting problems."[86] The CEO of the New York Stock Exchange resigned after outrage over his compensation package and dissatisfaction with the trading system.[87] In August 3, 2004, the chairman and CEO of Callaway Golf resigned.[88] And Citigroup substituted its CEO status for that of a chairman.[89] In the six months ending on May 5, 2004, 46 management officials of large corporations have resigned or have been removed and replaced by the boards of directors.[90]

These are signals of change. However, one item does not seem to have changed. Corporate management compensation has not been reduced. In fact, as Matthew Boyle notes in *Fortune*, instead of stock options, which are worth far less in this stock market, executives receive stock, which is worth something even if the price of the stock falls.[91] It is cash. It is unclear whether and how corporate culture is changing.

Reform by Wall Street Leaders

There are structural reforms on Wall Street. Not all reforms are voluntary. Settlements with government prosecutors require 10 of the largest Wall Street firms that offer research to clients to attach to their research the materials of independent analysts.[92] This procedure sends signals of doubt as well as assurance. It is similar to the requirement of verification by certified public accountants. And if the in-house and outside analysts differ, investors may have to decide whom to believe or on whom to rely. The firms themselves took voluntary steps to reinstate their reputation. For example, the *Wall Street Journal* noted that the firms changed the way analysts were paid. The firms prohibited their research analysts "from being paid based on the amount of investment-banking business they bring in and limiting the communications between [the analysts and the brokers]."[93]

On June 15, 2004, Paul Schott Stevens, the president of the Investment Company Institute, spoke at the National Press Club in Washington, D.C.[94] The Institute is the trade organization of all or almost all management companies of mutual funds. Stevens had assumed this office only two weeks earlier, but he was a familiar figure to the firms, because he had served about 10 years ago as the general counsel of the Institute. In his speech, Stevens blamed no one in particular. He made no excuses for the scandalous behavior of many fund advisors. The speech was a clear statement of the duties of mutual fund managers. They are fiduciaries who hold other people's money, Stevens said. Whether the industry will follow remains to be seen. But the statement emphasized the culture of "old-fashioned" trust.

The question is whether American leadership will adopt, in actions, words, and signals, a more balanced model of behavior and the use of the power entrusted to the leadership. "Nearly every man can stand adversity," Abraham Lincoln said, "but if you want to test a man's character, give him power." American leadership's character is now being tested.

More Government Oversight

The light is beginning to shine on competition for government contracts. Large government contractors have gained contracts by what seem to have involved undue influence on the government decision-makers. Presumably, this was "the way things were done." Aggressive corporations provided government officials with fine positions in exchange for information about competitors' bids on contracts. Other corporations fought back with the same tools. The cycle may be coming to an end; the competitors may have had enough. As *Defense Week* noted, there are attempts to stop these practices.[95] More important, the news sends an important message that such behavior is no longer acceptable. The *New York Times* on January 21, 2001, noted that Wendy Gramm received a consulting contract and a directorship at Enron Corporation after she left the chair of the Commodity Futures Trading Commission. The Commodity Futures Trading Commission granted exemptions from constraints of the law and these exemptions affected Enron's business.[96] The question is: when may high-ranking government officials accept such contracts in similar circumstances?

Less Protection of Corporate Boards and Increased Duties for Lawyers

There are some departures from the historical strong protection of corporate boards. For example, in the past two decades, the Delaware courts, where about half of these large corporations are registered, were reluctant to make corporate directors liable for the wrongs committed by their corporations. The courts respected the directors' business judgment and, with a few notable exceptions, shielded the directors from the claims of shareholders. The burdens on shareholders who sued the corporate directors were very heavy.

In the past few years, the Delaware courts have shown that they can change their attitude in response to abuses. Of the five large shareholders' suits brought since 2002, all five were allowed to proceed.[97] The tone of the courts has changed. In the case involving the compensation to a departing president of Disney Corporation, the court said:

> It is of course true that after-the-fact litigation is a most imperfect device to evaluate corporate business decisions, as the limits of human competence necessarily impede judicial review. But our corporation law's theoretical justification for disregarding honest errors simply does not apply to intentional misconduct or to egregious process failures that implicate the foundational directoral obligation to act honestly and in good faith to advance corporate interests. Because the facts alleged here, if true, portray directors consciously indifferent to a material issue facing the corporation, the law must be strong enough to intervene against abuse of trust. Accordingly, all three of plaintiffs' claims for relief concerning fiduciary duty breaches and waste survive defendants' motions to dismiss.
>
> The practical effect of this ruling is that defendants must answer the new complaint and plaintiffs may proceed to take appropriate discovery on the merits of their claims. To that end, a case scheduling order has been entered that will promptly bring this matter before the Court on a fully developed factual record. [98]

The court opened the door to the litigation.

Under Sarbanes-Oxley, lawyers must report violations they discover within the organizations to the upper echelon, and—if the violations remain uncorrected—to the board of directors, and if the board does not act, the lawyers may have to resign "noisily," giving signals that something is wrong.[99] These duties and actions raise the lawyers' awareness.

More Punishment and Enforcement

The punishments for abuse and fraud have increased. Prison terms have become longer. The prison sentences of white-collar criminals used to be relatively short, although prison sentences for securities frauds were the longest among fraud violations. Russ Mitchell noted in the *New York Times* that in the past, an imprisonment term for white-collar criminals could turn out to be much shorter by parole.[100] However, in 1984, Congress abolished parole for federal crimes.[101] The only basis for reducing a prison sentence is for satisfactory behavior.[102] Yet this basis is flexible, and white-collar prisoners are likely to be well behaved. The Sabanes-Oxley Act of 2002 increased the maximum prison sentences for some crimes, such as "attempt or conspiracy." This crime, which was deemed separate from the underlying crimes, now carries the same maximum punishment as the crime attempted or conspired.[103] The punishment for mail and wire fraud was increased from 5 to 20 years imprisonment.[104]

In addition, the Sarbanes-Oxley Act directed the United States Sentencing Commission to promulgate stricter sentencing guidelines for certain white-collar crimes.[105] In January 2003, the Commission passed new rules for offenses that affected large numbers of victims, such as 100 or 250 persons. These offenses relate to conduct that seriously endangers the solvency or financial security of certain organizations, such as banks. In addition, the new rules cover criminal actions by officers and directors of publicly traded companies. The rules provide a range of permissible sentences for different offenses. The changes in the rules have increased the level of these ranges. They allow the courts and juries to impose longer sentences for these offenses. In May 2003, the Commission further increased the sentences for economic crimes that carried with them a maximum sentence of at least 20 years.[106] Even assuming that the courts and the juries will impose such heavier sentences, it is an open question whether this possibility will deter white-collar crimes.

A few enforcement results have also emerged in 2004. Large brokerage houses that paid analysts to recommend stock without much analysis have settled with the SEC. By July 14, 2004, the fines paid up were: Salomon Smith Barney—$400 million; CSFB—$200 million; Merrill Lynch—$200 million; Morgan Stanley—$125 million; Goldman Sachs—$110 million; Bear Stearns—$80 million; J. P. Morgan—$80 million; Lehman Brothers—$80 million; UBS—$80 million; Piper Jaffray—$32.5 million. Thomas Weisel Partners is in negotiation for paying $12.5 million. [107]

In the year 2004, a number of prosecutions started coming to closure. On May 3, 2004, Frank Quattrone, "the most prominent Wall Street figure to face a criminal trial in years," was found guilty on three charges of interference with a federal investigation in December 2000.

Management's nervousness concerning claims of improper accounting practices is demonstrated by the settlement of Bristol-Myers of a private litigation brought against it. Bristol-Myers *won* the suit. Nonetheless, the *Wall Street Journal* reported that the company agreed to pay the plaintiffs $300 million to settle the case. The judgment was subject to appeal, and the company had yet to settle a criminal investigation concerning its financial statements.[108] The payment of $300 million signals concern about the corporation's financial statements. It shows management's awareness of the corporation's disclosure situation.

A Little More Uncertainty about Drug-Taking Athletes

Nike, sneaker manufacturer, has been using Marion Jones in its advertising. Jones is the winner of five medals at the 2000 Olympics. The *Wall Street Journal* reported that she is being investigated for drug use. Although she has denied the allegations, and has not been charged, Nike hesitated to engage her in its advertising. Finally, Nike decided to engage her but not her partner.[109] Nike has a high stake in its reputation. Its hesitation demonstrates the shadow of drug allegations in the year 2004.

Questions remain. How long will the memory of the wrongdoings and the pain of their settlements last? How deeply will the new internal structures remain, and how effectively will they prevent further abuses? Would the barriers to deception hold out when temptation knocks at the door again? Would a better balance between law and the markets and a stronger concern for morality take hold to become the American Way? Will all these changes turn American culture around toward a honest society?

PART III

Conclusion

12

Toward an Honest Society

The Essential Role of Culture

If America is to retreat from the precipice of abuse of trust and deception, how can it move toward more pervasive honesty? The answer: It must redirect its culture. The mechanisms that obstruct abuse of trust and deception are rooted in the culture of a society, and in the shared assumptions that do not require proof and do not lend themselves to debate [Schein, 12]. It is culture that sets the broad definition of trust and honesty, as well as the acceptable limitations on abuse of trust and of deception.

The interpretation of rules differs depending on the culture in which they apply. In an orthodox Jewish community, "meat" does not include pork. No one needs to specify this interpretation. Working with Chinese officials, I soon discovered a different meaning of "contract." For me, "contract" meant closure and finality. For them, "contract" meant a basis for renegotiation. Lawyers can be viewed as the expert finders of legal loopholes for sale, or mainly as "gatekeepers" of law, giving advice as a public service. Shared assumptions could view all of us as self-interested, bent on maximizing our wealth and success. Shared assumptions could expect each of us to protect himself from others. If these shared assumptions are that this state of affairs is not only natural (which is doubtful) but also good (which is even more doubtful), then people will behave accordingly. They will tend to their interests, ignore the interests of others and of society, and protect themselves against other people. The reverse will be the exception.

According to Harold Garfinkel, culture, like habits, "feels" predictable. Therefore, people attempt to "normalize" unexpected changes, to return to stability and to the comfort of the familiar and known. Yet, even though culture is stable, it is not frozen. "Normality," he wrote, includes a number of features: how typical the events are; how likely they are to occur again; and "how comparable they are with past or future events, and among other factors also their necessity according to a natural or moral order."[1] As Matt Ridley has reported, research suggests that individual genes have a "culture" of their own. They do not freeze the individual's character, but establish tendencies. These tendencies change in response to the environment.[2] Culture, like people, has tendencies, but can change.

How Does the Direction of a Culture Change?

Like changing a habit, changing a culture starts with awareness, shaking off the "automatic behavior," and reexamining what one is doing and where one's behavior is leading. That is where choice enters the scene. Only then can people decide on the kind of society in which they want to live. And if they find that they are going toward harmful and destructive habits, they can then determine whether they are ready to make the efforts necessary to redirect their habits. Sir Winston Churchill is quoted as saying: "A nation that forgets its past is doomed to repeat it."[3] One must remember the past in order to learn from it and be free of it.

Thus, after awareness, the next step in changing the culture is an analysis to understand the behavior, to recognize its dangers, and to realize the benefits of change. The third step is action. Without action, change remains in the land of good intentions. People who have quit smoking may recognize the process and the difficulty of breaking a habit. Society is no different.

Yet these are generalities. How actually can we change the direction of a culture? One source of information is the literature on why people obey the law. After all, the culture that threatens American society is the culture of dishonesty that is prohibited by law.

Obedience to the law must be essentially voluntary. That depends on social habit. Charles Camic describes Max Weber's views: "At the base of modern political-legal orders . . . 'the broad mass of the participants act in a way corresponding to legal norms, not out of obedience regarded as a legal obligation but [in a great many cases] merely as a result of unreflective habit.'"[4] If this cultural habit did not exist, and if a significant number of people did not obey the law, law enforcement in a democratic society would be impossible. The history of Prohibition in the 1930s teaches us this lesson.

Law is built on broad voluntary compliance. No matter how many laws are on the books, no matter how many police are on the beat, if the majority or leadership of the population does not obey the law, law is likely to remain a dead letter. Even in this litigious society, state and federal courts entertained only 15 million criminal cases in 2003.[5] Assuming multiple convictions, that's less than 5 percent of the population involved in criminal litigation in a year.[6] According to the Justice Department, only 2.7 percent of adults in 2001 had ever served time in prison.[7] And these numbers strain the justice system. If the numbers were higher, law enforcement would be practically impossible. So why do most people obey the law, knowing that their chances of being caught and punished are fairly slim? Corporate environment is the same. The rules within large corporations are enforced differently from the rules of law. But these rules, too, must be based on voluntary obedience by most of the employees.

Voluntary obedience to law has a flavor of ethical and moral behavior. "We can't legislate ethics," said Commissioner Cynthia Glassman of the SEC, in an interview with a *Christian Science Monitor* reporter in June 28, 2004. "But we can motivate people to do the right thing." However, she added: If fear of investigation (rather than ethical constraints) motivates the board of directors to enforce the law within their organizations, "that's OK with me."[8] Yet, depending on the culture, fear of this sort may not be enough in the long run. For a culture that values honesty there is little satisfaction in a fear-based behavior. But in a culture that values "getting away with circumventing the law," fear can turn into an excitement that can produce satisfaction. Such a fear may not bring voluntary obedience in the long run. Or fear may drive people "underground." The cost of violations will rise. But so will the cost of discovering the violations.

Edward Johnson, the head of Fidelity, the largest mutual fund complex in the United States, put it unconditionally: Nothing will be effective to enforce the law but the "moral fiber" of the leaders, he was quoted as saying in a *Christian Science Monitor* article. In that article I summarized this book's message: "Unless people are self-limiting, unless there is a culture of honesty, a law change won't work." And Charles Elson, a corporate governance expert at the University of Delaware, noted: "We have to look at our own culture."[9] These statements raise awareness—the first step in a change of culture. But morality alone cannot change culture. It has no coercive power to begin and push toward the change. It can only strongly support it. The law can aim at the same objective as morality, and achieve it by *coercion*. Yet law alone cannot coerce a whole population. Law alone cannot change the habits of a society, and its tolerance for dishonesty. In a conflict between culture on one hand, and law on the other hand, culture is very likely to win.

How can awareness of morality and law affect the activities within large corporations? Millions of Americans work in corporations and large institutions. They are governed by internal corporate rules. These rules are backed by private sector sanctions and rewards, such as demotions and promotions. Law enforcement within organizations depends on their culture. Like culture in society, corporate culture, being the habit of members of the corporate community, evolves through repeated experience. This experience reflects the corporation's history, its population—its old-timers and new recruits. But what most determine corporate culture are the attitude and the signals of top management—sometimes only one or two people at the head of the corporate pyramid. They set the tone and direction of the organization. In corporations, the signals of top management are closely watched and followed. When the chief financial officer throws a lavish party that costs $2 million and charges part of the expense to the corporation, the door opens to employees to help themselves to corporate assets—on a smaller scale, of course. When top management travels frugally and distinguishes between corporate business and private use, the word quickly spreads. Which employee would dare order the corporate jet for private travel? Top management can signal the corporate population to obey the law or to ignore it. "Once you as CEO go over the line, then people think it's okay to go over the line." Lawrence Weinbach was quoted as saying.[10]

Why Do Most People Obey the Law?

Much has been written about the ways in which people can be induced to obey the law voluntarily, that is, to internalize the behavior and self-enforce it.[11] But, as Alex Geisinger shows, there is no agreement on the right approach.[12] One reason for the disagreements could be that people obey the law for many different reasons.

Fear of punishment. Gordon Tullock suggested that early detection and stricter laws and appropriate punishments induce people to obey the law.[13] He believed that people would obey the law for fear of punishment. And if punishment is unlikely, they will not obey. The past history of fraud and abuse may support this view. Fraud was not detected in time, and when it was detected, it was not energetically prosecuted. The violation of the law was sometimes eliminated by redefinition, or was made easier by explicit exemptions.[14] Following Tullock's theories, swift detection, strict laws, and heavy punishments produce a culture of obedience to the law. The flavor of this culture is concern and fear.

Reciprocity by the members of the community. Professor Dan Kahan has a different view about why people obey the law. He suggests that people follow the law to gain favor and avoid disapproval of others. People assume that legal rules represent the views of the majority in the country. In addition, people may feel a need to reciprocate and contribute to the general welfare, if others do the same. For example, if people believe that others pay their taxes, they too will pay their taxes. But if people believe that others do not pay their taxes, they will refrain from paying their taxes as well.[15]

Following other people. An analysis of signaling leads to a similar conclusion. Most people follow the behavior and judgment of others, as well as the expressions and beliefs of others. Most people wish to belong to a group, and are influenced by the activities and attitudes of their peers. They follow their leaders, doing good or evil, exercising mercy or cruelty.

If everyone around obeys the law, a violator will be stigmatized and shunned. But if everyone around violates the law, a violator will not stand out and will not be shunned. His behavior conforms to the general behavior. Similarly, if most people in the community do not have a prison history, then the person who served a prison sentence is likely to be stigmatized. But if many community members spent time in prison, the sharpness of the stigma will be dulled. In that case, the "square" or "preacher" will be stigmatized. In groups of white-collar criminals, the rights and wrongs differ from those of the law, but the same rules of stigmatizing apply. George C. Homans described high-crime areas where the criminals were "far from being neurotic and outcasts. They were healthy, hearty, happy, and much admired. . . . In these areas only a person who was *not* a criminal showed any sign of personality disorder" [Homans, 337].[16]

I am speculating that for a similar reason, there is a difference between a general disapproval of breaking a contract promise and a much greater disapproval of abusing trust. More people engage in contracts than in offering trust service. If people believe that more people are likely to break their contract promises, as compared to abusing the trust that other people vest in them, then the stigma attached to a breach of a contract promise is likely to be lower than the stigma attached to abuse of trust. These distinctions may also relate to contract violations. The stigma attached to the late payment of a small bill is likely to be lower than the stigma attached to a breach of contract that causes enormous damage to the other party.

Following American leadership. America's leaders include government officials, regulators and congressional leaders, the heads of corporations and educational organizations, the leaders of religious and civic groups, and outstanding performers in the arts and sports. They have a great impact on America's culture as they move from one role to another. The late President Ronald Reagan was an actor, a union leader, a governor, and a president. Arnold Schwarzenegger, the current governor of California, was an actor. Presidents Carter and the younger Bush were governors. Presidents Kennedy and Johnson were senators. These leaders' views and guidance are followed and can become embedded in America's culture. If the leadership obeys the law, so will the people; if the leadership disobeys the law, so will many of the people.

Corporate leadership affects not only the culture of the corporations but also the general culture in the United States. On behalf of their corporations, management has contacts with the political leadership and the lawmakers. Through lobbyists, these leaders have access to the other powerful leaders here and abroad. Their attitudes toward the law affect the substance of the law as well as obedience to the law. Needless to say, corporate leaders also affect the marketplace, which can be a barrier to fraud. In many respects, corporate America is not merely the leader but the keeper of American culture.

Members of American leadership have a culture of their own. They interact among themselves. They sit on each other's boards, share information networks, and gather in social affairs. They know each other or about each other personally, because their number is relatively small. Therefore, this group tends to be homogeneous, governed by a dominant culture.

Corporate employees spread their leadership's culture as well. They spend most of their waking hours within an organization, absorb its culture, and take home not only their pay and experience but also their assumptions about how people behave and should behave—that is, the society's culture.

The leadership's attitude toward law is important to the culture of obedience to law. If the authorities, corporate leaders, and lawmakers denigrate the law and preach the market gospel, people will take these signals to heart and resist the law or tend to ignore it and minimize its impact. People need not be told what leadership's attitude is. They may even be told the contrary: to obey the law. But if the words come with conditions and strong criticism of the law, they will get the "correct and true" message, and follow it.

The same can be said of corporate leadership.

> Culture and leadership are two sides of the same coin, in that leaders first create cultures when they create groups and organizations. Once cultures exist, they determine the criteria for leadership and thus determine who will or will not be a leader. But if cultures become dysfunctional, it is the unique function of leadership to perceive the functional and dysfunctional elements of the existing culture and to manage cultural evolution and change in such a way that the group can survive in a changing environment.

And if leaders "do not become conscious of the cultures in which they are embedded, those cultures will manage them. Cultural understanding . . . is essential to leaders if they are to lead" [Schein, 15].

If too many leaders belittle the law and criticize the very institution of the law, others will do the same. By so doing, they will cause enormous harm to the legal system, leading a movement that undermines the respect and obedience to law. Leaders may offer and request changes in the rules, but they should do so with great caution and deference. They can provide justifications for relaxing the rules but take fraud prevention into account. If the influential members among American leaders talk disparagingly about the law and deny the legitimacy of its rules, those who listen to these leaders will follow in words and perhaps in deeds. They may accept the views of their own leaders rather than the views of the law enforcers.

Too many American leaders have preached faith in the market to protect the public against dishonesty. The resistance of the leadership to the law and its constraints on the leaders' power is complemented by the elevation of self-interest and the markets. "If each person took care of himself, and if each person catered to his interests, and protected himself from others, society would be served best," they say. "Trust" has given way to "verify." At most, law should help trusting persons to obtain true information. But let them make their own decisions. And if they have no expertise, they should seek the advice of private-sector experts. Yet law should be least intrusive in regulating the experts. This message empowers the powerful and releases them from the constraints of accountability to the less powerful and less expert.

The puzzle is that most American business leaders are truthful, honest, and law-abiding. They were hurt by the recent scandals because the scandals tainted all of them. And yet, by and large, these business leaders are silent, or speak faintly. Strong denunciation is missing. Could it be that even those law-abiding businesses agree with the resistance to law?

Trust in the law enforcers. One reason people do *not* obey the law, says Professor Tom R. Tyler, is that they suspect the motivations of the authorities. A general perception that the enforcing authorities are the captives of corporate criminals prompts people to ignore and disobey the law.[17] Therefore, the government's attitude toward law affects the culture of obedience to law. People tend to obey the rules if the government makes it clear that no complaint will be left untended, and no discovery of a wrong will be compromised, and that those who disclose fraud will be protected from powerful criminals.

In sum, obedience to law must be largely voluntary. It is built on the perception that everyone else is complying with the law. This perception is affected by the behavior of leadership in the public and private sectors, the attitudes of peer groups, and the approach of the population at large. The pressures to conform to the culture of these groups bring about the voluntary obedience to the law.

It follows that people will disobey the law for the same reasons they obey it. Obedience will erode as more and more people in the society, including leadership and peer groups, denigrate the law and belittle its enforcers. The materials in this book support this conclusion. Deception and abuse of trust have spread throughout the population—that is, even if the number of violators has not risen relative to the numbers in the past. That means that pockets of peer groups from students to athletes and from top management to healthcare providers, from job applicants to employees, draw support for such a behavior. Honesty can be practiced in a competitive business only *if most businesses act the same way.* An honest business must not only ward off temptation but also be fairly sure that its competitors are warding off temptation as well. If circumventing the law is the "way things are" for almost everyone, then it is quite likely that almost everyone will circumvent the law.

One can say: "A society gets the culture it deserves." Americans got the culture they deserve. But perhaps the American people are moving toward a culture that they do not deserve or choose. They simply follow passively. They merely do not get involved.

How Should American Culture Be Redirected?

Awareness

Changing a habit in society should be similar to changing personal habits. The first and usually the most important stage is to raise awareness of what we are doing and what we are taking for granted. In the case of abuse of trust and deception, awareness is not entirely dead in the United States. It has been raised by the reaction to the discovered corporate frauds of the 1990s. Congress and regulators reacted. There are debates and emphasis on moral (ethical) behavior in business.

The law signals to the population that the lawmakers condemn the latest abuses and raise the stakes of violation. Congress has enacted stricter laws, and the SEC has followed with detailed and demanding regulations.[18] As mentioned earlier, about half of the largest corporations in America are registered in Delaware;[19] the courts there have signaled stricter supervision over corporation management by opening its closed doors to more shareholder suits.[20] These developments increase the awareness of top management to the possibility of shareholder suits. They also increase the awareness of their lawyers that their legal opinions, which have sheltered top management, may be subject to closer critical scrutiny by the courts.[21]

Awareness, however, is not enough to change the direction of culture. There is resistance to upsetting the comfort of predictable behavior. Instead of changes that drive corporate and national culture toward honesty, drastic events may increase pressure to continue the old ways—for example, to beat the competitors by stretching the envelope toward forbidden areas. Resistance to change is natural, just as is resistance to breaking a habit. Thus, in October 2003, Henry A. McKinnell, chairman and CEO of Pfizer and chairman of the Business Roundtable, complained that the recent legal requirements divert CEOs from their main task of managing large and profitable enterprises.[22] He was aware of the congressional message but resisted the change. But honesty cannot be separated from everyday activities. It cannot be taught twice yearly in an ethics seminar. A better way is to include law in considering new and innovative activities. A better way is to inculcate the habit of asking whether these proposed activities are legal, or whether there are legal limits on such activities. Included in the awareness is another awareness: that competitors follow the law and engage in the same exercise. The ultimate question is whether the latest pressures to obey the law will continue for a sufficient period to support the transition to law-abiding habits.

American law schools can heighten students' awareness about the honesty of their clients. Traditionally, American law schools have taught students to view court and congressional decisions critically. Yet in the past 25 years, the movement has been toward questioning the very necessity for the law and looking to the market or other alternatives for solutions to problems. American law schools have raised generations of lawyers who have less respect for legal rules and government enforcement than lawyers had in the past. Raised on ideals of economics as law, it is not surprising that the lawyers were enthusiastically engaged in ways to relieve their clients of the constraints of the law—for a hefty compensation. Yet the objectives of law schools are not to turn out experts in undermining the legal system. While economics expands the understanding of the law and the economic system, the values of economics are not the values of the law. And if this point is questioned, students should at least be clearly aware of the two sets of values and debate them.

Examination and Analysis

Once awareness is aroused, we must face the issue of transformation. A change in habit induces uncertainty, produces anxiety, and imposes costs. The process requires uncovering the basic assumptions of individuals and of the corporate management and its employees and dealing with the anxiety that arises when these assumptions are challenged and changed. All this takes time. There are difficulties if the existing underlying assumptions in corporate culture are that no change is required [Schein, 27]. A change of assumption means not only altering "our assumptions" but also substituting what is "right and good," and proved to be successful in the past, for unknown plans and actions that may not be as successful in the future.

We take culture so much for granted, and put so much value on our own assumptions that we find it awkward and inappropriate even to discuss our assumptions or to ask others about their assumptions. . . . If we are forced to discuss them, we tend not to examine them but to defend them because we have emotionally invested in them. [Schein, 12]

Overcoming the habit of padding clients' bills could be as stressful as overcoming the habit of not padding the bills.

Kenneth A. Baumerger suggests that to be effective, the regulation of a corporation must draw on understanding how it functions and on how it "learns" and changes. Like society, a corporation is not one unit but a conglomeration of individuals who act and interact mostly automatically, by practices and habits, some good, some pathological.[23] To control the pathological behavior of a corporation, that part of the behavior must be identified. Then and only then can the corporation learn to change its ways. Law that is not responsive and reactive to corporate culture is unlikely to change the culture or the behavior of the corporate institution.

Action by Corporate Leadership

How should corporate leaders introduce cultural change? Leadership must understand the problem at hand and the role of culture in their organizations. That done, the change becomes easier to implement [Schein, 147–168]. The materials in this book suggest that some corporate leaders, academics, and legislators have not yet reached the bottom of the cultural barrel to clarify for themselves and for their followers the assumptions that must be reversed if the road to a culture of dishonesty is to be bypassed. Boeing's new CEO stressed ethics as well as cost cutting, according to the *Wall Street Journal*, reporting on July 14, 2004. Yet he violated accepted rules of behavior and had to resign.[24]

There are many cultural issues that face corporate management in dealing with the workforce. These include feelings of denial and fear, self-interest, anomie, and the existence of underground subcultures. When the culture is influenced by these forces and is hidden partly in underground subcultures, keeping to principles is difficult, and perhaps hopeless [Deal & Kennedy, 169–187]. Therefore, changing particular rules and actions may not make much difference unless there is an attempt to change the culture.

Before changing the culture of corporations, leadership must change its own culture. Too many well-known corporate leaders have been found to lack integrity. Ultimately, without integrity, they not only lose leadership but also downgrade the value and definition of integrity. The importance of the way leadership is perceived cannot be underrated. "In a 1998 survey conducted by the Society for Human Resource Management ('Importance of Trust,' 1998), a national sample of respondents indicated that the number-one attribute they look for in managers is credibility and trustworthiness. Being trusted shows up continuously as the top attribute associated with exemplary leadership [Avolio, 159].

As one CEO said, his generation lost its idealism. CEOs were diverted from doing their jobs and being committed to their corporations.[25] The change, like a change of habit, must come not only with awareness and understanding the issues but also with actually transforming the practices.

WHO SHOULD LEAD? ACTION BY THE AMERICAN PEOPLE: THE META-NORM

America must move to a better balance among morality, law, and markets, between self-limitation and self-interest, between trust and verify, and between fiduciaries and their beneficiaries. Leadership alone cannot achieve this better balance, however. Leadership is not united on the need for change, the means of change, and the ultimate objectives of change. As noted in this book, some believe that the storm will pass soon and everything will go back to normal. Others are not ready for change. Yet others are ideologically committed to the hegemony of the markets and are hostile to law. Who can redirect America? The answer is: "the majority of Americans and the leadership that will rise from its midst."

The Effect of a Passive Majority on Culture: Americans Should Get Involved

The majority that stands by, does nothing, and fails to contribute to the enforcement of the law allows the minority to create the culture that will rule the majority. In chapter 4 I discussed the experiment of Philip Zimbardo. In that experiment students were divided into "prisoners" and "guards." Two-thirds of the students who participated in the experiment allowed the remaining one-third to inculcate a culture of cruelty in the "prison" that was the scene of the experiment—so much so that the experiment, which was to last for two weeks, was terminated after six days. The majority of the students did not join in the cruel behavior toward the student "prisoners." But the majority did not prevent the cruelty to those "prisoners" either. In this case, the majority did not lead; the sadistic minority was the leader. It introduced a culture of brutality by the default of the majority. The wrongs persisted. They ended up as part of the (temporary) culture. Therefore, a passive majority can contribute to a culture by doing nothing; by "not getting involved." Unless the majority acts, the minority can rule. The majority can act not only by doing what it considers right in financial matters and in terms of trust and honesty. The majority can also act by enforcing on others the norm of trust and honesty. This norm then becomes a *meta-norm.*

What Is a Meta-Norm?

A meta-norm is an aspect of a culture. It is the kind of behavior that leads to a popular enforcement of an important social norm and accepted behavior. A meta-norm is distinguishable from other norms by the way it is enforced. This kind of norm is enforced not only by the police but also by the members of the society. Robert Axelrod defined a meta-norm as a pattern of behavior that *people feel compelled to enforce,* rather than stand by and let someone else deal with it. A meta-norm implies disapproval not only of the violators of the norm but also of those who do not act to prevent the violation [Axelrod, 55–56]. Therefore, a meta-norm expands monitoring and prevention of wrongs in society. It becomes part of the culture when it constitutes a social habit, when "everyone does it," and when it is the expected behavior, without debate.

Researchers have examined societies that have a meta-norm of trust. As Tom R. Tyler noted, "many groups subscribe to norms that build trustworthiness, and impose on members a duty to enforce the norms, rendering the norms powerful and the members credible."[26] In an Insurance Research Council survey, Elizabeth A. Sprinkel, who heads the organization, reported that when insurance policyholders understand that "little frauds" may result in rising premiums for everyone, the policyholders recommend prosecution of those who bring fraudulent claims.[27] This is the beginning of a meta-norm.

A 1986 study by Kahneman and Thaler found that two-thirds of the people who were tested were ready to sacrifice money in order to *punish* a selfish person who sought to free ride on the contributions of others without contributing and paying up his share. This large majority was willing to reward a generous person who gave money for the common good.[28] Thus, the majority acted to punish those who violated the norm, and reward those who followed the norm. This is how a meta-norm works.

Why Do People Adopt a Meta-Norm?

People may adopt a meta-norm for the same reasons they obey the law. They can internalize the norm because they were raised that way; no questions asked and no explanations necessary. They may follow the norm because they wish to belong to the group, which shares the same views. Or they may believe that the norm is important, regardless of the views of others. Or people may enforce a norm because they fear the punishments for standing by and doing nothing.[29] Robert E. Scott provides an example of "second-order" enforcement of a norm by members of a community. They will help its enforcement by joining in social disapproval of the violators.[30] As Richard McAdams notes, people enforce norms by withholding esteem from violators. In his opinion, people adopt this social sanction because withholding esteem is "relatively costless for them"[31] and can be very painful for the violators. In the words of Francis Fukuyama:

> In theory . . . rational people would have little interest in enforcing metanorms because they are public goods; it is very difficult for an individual to capture the benefits of his enforcement, so private individuals should have little incentive to do so. And yet, people go out of their way to see that metanorms

are enforced—or to put in plainer language, to see that justice is done—all the time, and in situations where they have no direct stake. They display . . . "moralistic aggression."[32]

Law Can Support a Meta-Norm

The recent congressional legislation supports a meta-norm, in that it not only requires obedience to the law but also *requires those who have information about violations of the law to do something about it.* The Sarbanes-Oxley Act imposes a duty on lawyers who have a valid suspicion of securities violations by their client organizations to notify the higher echelon within the organization.[33] This act may be against the self-interest of the lawyers. They consider some of the violators their clients. After all, these are the people who have hired the lawyers and usually gain the lawyers' confidential treatment. Even if they are not anxious to continue serving a particular client, lawyers may be concerned about retaining other clients who seek a full confidential relationship with their lawyers. And yet they must act. If the clients accept this new attitude, some confidence will be eroded; and if the lawyers adopt this attitude as a habit, a meta-norm will be established.

The legal duty to act as enforcers of the securities laws does not apply to investment bankers. Yet investment bankers can lend a hand to violations of the law by offering legitimate services. The investment banker may say: "This is not my business. I provide a service; what the client does with the service is not my concern." And to some extent, this is true. But what if the investment banker offers a service that helps, and is an integral part of, the illegal action of the client? What if the investment banker agrees to two transactions that look like a sale and a purchase of a note but are in fact a loan? What if the investment banker knows that his services are used to achieve an illegal purpose? The SEC's settlements with Citigroup and J. P. Morgan suggest that there is a point in this slippery slope at which the investment banker should not render the service. These settlements include a provision that does not relieve Citigroup and Morgan from responsibility for transactions of this sort. These institutions remain responsible for deals in which they were involved if the deals helped violate the law.[34] The settlement provisions signal support for a meta-norm of honesty.

Leadership can create or trigger a cascade, that is, a mass movement toward a meta-norm. A cascade is a mass movement of people who are not merely following a leader or the crowd but also ignoring their own information and judgment. In their analysis, Timur Kuran and Cass R. Sunstein note that cascades occur when people follow others without much questioning.[35] This attitude is similar to culture, in which people take for granted that things have to be done a certain way. Cascades may count as temporary cultures, because they can rise and change more easily than cultures. The 1990s stock market bubble can be viewed as a cascade.

Robert Axelrod describes how a new norm is introduced and entrenched by leadership and herd following, or a cascade. This method fits the corporations and the stock markets well. Many investors watch both the leaders and each other for signals, and then act on these signals. These signals can be represented by the aggregate prices of shares, by specific information from the corporations and other leaders, or by what the leaders do (whether they sell or buy the stock).

At the beginning of a new movement, Axelrod writes, the rebels who demand a change in a norm meet strong resistance. In line with this analysis, in the case of the current debate on fraud and abuse of trust, the critics of the existing cultural trend may be ridiculed, called naïve, idealists, liberals, or other pejorative names. Those who follow the current norm of self-interest as a guide to behavior have strong incentives to protect and elevate the norm by convincing the many that they too can benefit if they pursue the same route. The corporate CEO, who has collected over $20 million in a "bad" year, may try to convince the employees and the shareholders that they too have a chance of amassing such a fortune. Power holders can reward those who enforce their norms, and appeal for supportive theories and publications. These power holders can punish those who preach contrary norms.

But resistance weakens, Axelrod writes, when the incentive to punish the rebels weakens. As Axelrod predicts, the drive against the leaders of the criticized system strengthens. For a time, the guardians of the old regime resist. When the rebels persist, however, the vengeance of the old guard subsides, the rebels raise their heads again, "and the [contested] norm completely collapse[s]" [Axelrod, 62–64]. In our day and age, the mottoes of "self-interest over everything," "individual over society," "exchange over all forms of interactions," and "the markets over all other social structures" are under pressure. The guardians of the old regime are not relenting. Not yet. But if the pressure for change continues, these reigning ideas will give way to a better balance. Samuel Adams did not read Axelrod, but perhaps Axelrod read Adams, to whom the following quotation is attributed: "It does not require a majority to prevail, but rather an irate, tireless minority keen to set brush fires in people's minds."[36]

It takes everyone to create a meta-norm. It takes most people in a group to do something about enforcing a norm and preventing its abuse. If a class, within the larger group, withdraws its active support of the current way of doing things, others may follow. The old norm will lose its "punch." People might still disapprove of violating the old norm but will watch rather than try to stop a violation. In the words of Edmund Burke: "When bad men combine, the good must associate; else they will fall one by one, an unpitied sacrifice in a contemptible struggle."[37] America has been moving toward a culture of dishonesty. There are signs, however, that a reaction is setting in. The leadership and the people can redirect it toward honesty. To do that, honesty should become a meta-norm.

IS THE GOAL OF CHANGING AMERICAN BUSINESS CULTURE REALISTIC? I BELIEVE IT IS

Cultures can change direction. After all, the direction of today's culture differs from the direction of 25 years ago. Then, culture was not so hostile to law. It did not exalt the markets as much or put self-interest on such a high pedestal. This does not mean that people did not have the same views that are held today. But it means that these views and the behavior that followed from these views were not preached as loudly as they are today. Most important, these views were not on their way to becoming unarticulated, unspoken, generally understood *assumptions* of "what everyone does and what everyone should do." These views were not on their way to becoming the American culture. If these underlying assumptions and attitudes have changed in 25 years, then they can be redirected.

Assumptions draw on images, language, and theories. The images of markets, exchange, and self-interested behavior and the theories on which they are based have been shaping our culture. After all, the "business of America is business." What can substitute for these powerful images? Do we need to substitute for them something else?

A Paradox of a Detailed Social Design

A detailed social design or blueprint presents a paradox. It must be sufficiently simple and clear, or else people cannot easily follow it. Yet, if it is too simple and clear, it becomes unreal and false. Its influence can subvert the way we live. If we seek a short, concise book of "how-to" rules to lead to a more honest society, we face the paradox of the social design.

It is useful to think of the world as a market; people as self-interested; all relationships as exchanges; all transactions as contracts; all behavior of investors as uniformly rational. These views offer insights on the examination table. But as a blueprint to be implemented in real life, these views are pernicious. They can pave the road to deception and abuse of trust on a grand scale, even if their prophets do not preach these results. Markets without rules, fairness, and morality, are destined to fail. If they benefit the few at the expense of the many, they will not last long in a democratic society. At some point, the prey wakes up and flees the predators, or replaces them by the weight of sheer numbers, or joins them to overwhelm and crush the system under the weight of deception.

Self-interest, without compassion and self-control, is bound to raise a culture devoid of empathy for others; a culture destructive of trust. Exchange that applies to everyone and everything robs people of the joy of giving and other forms of more subtle reciprocity. It breeds meanness and dries up humanity. Rationality without reasonableness can bring very bizarre results. It can open the gates to treacherous, disloyal, and fraudulent behavior, seeping like sewage throughout society and contaminating everything in its way. Banishing morality, ethics, and emotions from public policy consideration, by exclusion or absorption, is wrong and unlikely to succeed. It is unclear whether even the sciences can excise and cut out moral considerations. Social sciences and law that ignore human traits and commitment to community are unreal.

A recent proposal by the Defense Advanced Research Projects Agency (DARPA), a renowned government-supported research organization, to create a "terror futures market" demonstrates the results of faith in a world that consists only of markets and of rational actors.[38] The proposal is based on the assumption that "talk is cheap, but money speaks the truth."[39] Or perhaps "money speaks louder than words." In this market, people will seek gain by predicting terrorist activities, based on their information and beliefs. The proposal follows the theory that the input of all the information represented in the betting will provide more accurate predictions than the predictions of experts. The *Economist* describes emerging research projects about "information markets." "The aggregated hunches of many people with money at stake are likely to be more accurate than the opinion of disinterested experts or of whoever happens to be at home when a pollster calls."[40] Indeed, as Cass R. Sunstein writes, some results of the research suggest that the predictions of numerous anonymous people are more accurate than the analysis of fewer identified experts.[41]

The DARPA proposal was rejected when it dawned on some people that terrorists and fraudsters could benefit greatly from this market, and the resulting prices may not represent accurate predictions. The terror futures market may help terrorists guess the public policy that will be shaped in reaction to the information. Terrorists may play the market and profit themselves or their organizations. After all, they can create the future better than anyone else, and are more likely to win. Also, dishonest persons may attempt to manipulate the market to their advantage.

The terror futures market is partially based on the assumption that people would bet on the basis of the information they have, not on the basis of the information that others have, or that others say they have. In addition, market prices will reflect no touting, no manipulation, and less bias. Yet in today's markets, solid true information is competing with betting, touting, and manipulation. It is unclear which of these motivates people to buy and sell stock or derivatives. The public market mechanism is therefore inappropriate for pooling the information people might have about possible terrorist attacks. As the *Economist* noted: "Information markets are also prone to imperfections. One is that they can exaggerate traders' misperception of risks"; they can be too optimistic, and they might be affected by "personal tastes."[42] As much as we seek the objective prediction, human nature can stand in the way. Under certain conditions, the predictions of many humans may not be more accurate than the predictions of the few, that is, when deviant motives are stronger than the quest for money.

If we reject a blueprint of society as markets, exchanges, and individual selfishness, what other options do we have? Any detailed social design would share the same characteristics of a simplistic world. Our proposal would have the same faults, even as it negates the substance and message of economics. To be popular and understood, the social design must offer a clear alternative world, with few nuances, approaches, categories, or contradictions. Yet humans and their societies cannot be packaged neatly. They are complex, messy, and continuously changing by actions and interactions among themselves and with their environments.

Society is populated by honest and dishonest persons; by selfless compassionate idealists and self-centered ruthless narcissists; by true victims and foolish or fake victims; by productive entrepreneurs and mimics of entrepreneurs who produce nothing. People behave inconsistently, change, and evolve. Moreover, truth, trust, and honesty are indeterminate. The differences among trust, gullibility, and faith are relative. They depend on the sources and cost of verifying the trusted persons' statements and the cost of monitoring the trusted persons' activities. They depend on the abilities of the people who rely on trusted persons to protect themselves against fraud. Protection against dishonesty is tricky. The very protection may undermine the trust we wish to foster in society. And the law, although helpful, is not the whole answer.

Therefore, a competing clear and specific blueprint to the one we have now will be as unreal and as misleading as the legal economics view of the world. An ideal world of truth, trust, and commitment to others as well as to one's own self is just as unrealistic. The closer our competing view will come to reflect the real complex world, the less understood it will become. Humans and their society cannot fit into a square box, or any box, for that matter.

Alternatively, we can continue to search for the simple and specific world that does not exist. A society with a strong sense of survival, like the American society, will swing from one such simple world to another. When a view supports an environment that has become too despotic and corrupt, like the one toward which we are heading, the pendulum could swing drastically in the opposite direction. Historically, America has been switching from one simplistic blueprint to another. As one blueprint has become intolerable, Americans have adopted another, which has become intolerable in turn. America experienced Puritanism with its despotic intrusion into private actions and thoughts, as well as the Wild West, the "roaring" twenties, and the rebellious sixties, with their attitude of "anything goes." Thus, after extreme authoritarian strictness came extreme permissiveness. After confining rules of behavior, dress, and personal moral rules came a revolt against any rule. Perhaps when the compulsion and corruption of the 1990s finally end, the pendulum will swing again, and the country will recede into intrusive regulation and strict authoritarian controls of deception and abuse of trust.

To avoid sharp swings of the pendulum from one simple vision of society to another, we could abandon the search, accept an unstructured world, and suffer the enormous anxiety and confusion that it produces. But such a solution may disintegrate and disorient communities and even individuals. It may also result in uncontrolled power, both governmental and private—a mix of benevolence and despotism, but with no principles and no guidelines.

Let us muddle through in search of a balance. Let America look for a balance. Let *self-interest* balance with *altruism,* let *taking* balance with *giving,* and commitment to the *self* balance with commitment to *society.* Moral self-limiting behavior is not stupid behavior. It offers rewards but does not condemn self-interest. Law is not the enemy of business. It is the enemy of crooked business. Law does not undermine free markets. It protects free markets but leaves them relatively free.

Society and its leaders reflect each other. In this strong democratic American society, followers can lead—that is, *if they get involved.* If Americans have had enough of what they have seen lately, if they want a society in which relationships are more honest and less cynical, more trusting and less doubting, then Americans can reject a culture dominated exclusively by the self and the market's self-protection. They can tell their leaders and themselves to move toward an honest society. Shareholders can tell management and themselves to move toward an honest corporate behavior. "Making capitalism work well will never be easy. To make it work, shareholders must be seen to play a wise and active role in governance. That would certainly be the best way to restore faith in top business bosses. To excel, good corporate leaders need good owners."[43]

JUST PICK AND FOLLOW THE GOAL OF HONESTY AND TRUST

Just aim at honesty and trust. We will disagree on the definition and argue about the details. This does not matter, so long as we care about trust and honesty generally, and so long as most people factor into their decisions the component of honesty and include in their considerations the society at large. The problem, as this book shows, is not that we cannot define honesty and trust with precision. We may argue about the precise definition. But most of us would agree on the basic concepts. The problem is that too many people and too many leaders have abandoned trust and honesty as a goal.

Aiming at honesty and trust could serve to control and mitigate the inhumanity, cruelty, despotism, and rational unreasonableness that any view of the world in vogue is likely to produce. Following this goal, we can maintain the insights of economics yet restrict manipulation, deception, and abuse of trust. The vision can pull us back from the culture of con artists toward which we have been sliding and lift us toward a truthful and more efficient culture.

The cynics may say: "Wake up! Be realistic! You are talking of people, not angels." That is true. But neither are most Americans cruel predators, self-centered beings lacking in empathy, and greedy to embezzle other people's savings by deception. Many Americans would like to see their corporate and financial world in the better light of trustworthiness. They may even be willing to receive lower, but true, returns on their money. The danger and damage of white-collar criminals to society can be abated if a sufficient number of people believe in an honest society, expect everyone to follow, and apply social sanctions on those that do not follow. Then, abusers of trust are likely to remain in the minority, always in the shadows, never emerging to lead in the light.

The critics would say: "This approach eliminates competition. It endangers America's prosperity and way of life." Yet Americans need not cease to compete.

The goal of honesty is not to reduce competitive ardor but to channel it in less destructive ways. Honesty encourages competition on the merits and prohibits competition by cheating. Honesty brings better quality of products and services and less shoddy products and fake services. If businesses do not compete on fraud, they can be more successful in gaining and retaining customers. More likely, the ambition toward an honest society will lead America to a better mix of preventive mechanisms, and to the middle of the road rather than to the extremes.

Yes, I am suggesting an unreachable goal. No competitive, dynamic society can be entirely honest. This goal cannot be achieved. Accepting and trying to reach an unreachable ideal is not new to America. American people have relentlessly aspired to the unachievable. And they have produced a free society and an economy that is the envy of the world. The real test for an honest and productive society is not what a society has achieved but what it aims to achieve. A society can put honest people on the pedestal, even if they do not maximize their personal benefits and preferences. A society can discard and shun as models of failure dishonest people who achieve their highest ambitions by fraud and abuse of trust. So what if this approach will not necessarily convert all people into honest people? It is the approach that matters. Like a toddler, we might even take a few steps toward this vision of a society, muddle through, and oscillate on the road to the world we will never reach.

If we substitute the word "honesty" in the statement of Senator Daniel P. Moynihan about crime in America, his words say it all: Honesty is not "revealed truth nor yet a scientifically derived formula. . . . It is simply a pattern that we observe in ourselves. Nor is it rigid." As we have been redefining honesty downward, we are "getting used to a lot of behavior that is not good for us." If the analysis in this book wins acceptance, and if the readers feel a sense of "genuine alarm" at what has been happening to our measure of trust and honesty, "we might surprise ourselves how well we respond to the manifest decline" of the American business morality.[44]

The one thing on which we need not compromise is the ambition to become an honest society and to have our society reap the rich rewards of honesty. This ambition is an ideal, yet it can shape and become a building block of our culture and our reality. Being an ideal, it is fully within our control—powerful and empowering. We can mold it any way we want. It is Utopia, which we cannot realize. But it can guide our life every day. "A man's reach should exceed his grasp," Robert Browning wrote. A society's reach toward honesty should exceed its grasp as well. It is not reaching that ideal but striving toward it that makes an honest society.

Notes

1. The Spreading Abuse of Trust and Deception

1. "When Something Is Rotten," *Economist,* U.S. ed., July 27, 2002, available online at: www.lexis-nexis.com.

2. "When Something Is Rotten."

3. Thomas A. Fogarty, "Freddie Mac Restates Its Earnings," *USA Today,* November 24, 2003, available online at: www.lexis-nexis.com.

4. Stephen Labaton, "MCI Faces Inquiry for Fraud on Fees for Long Distance," *New York Times,* July 27, 2003, available online at: www.lexis-nexis.com.

5. Peter J. Howe, "A T & T Nets a Share of Local Calls 4% of State Market Tallied in 6 Months; More Seen Next Year," *Boston Globe,* November 20, 2003, available online at: www .lexis-nexis.com.

6. Carrick Mollenkamp, "Two More HealthSouth Officials Plead Guilty in Fraud Inquiry," *Wall Street Journal,* August 1, 2003, available online at: www.westlaw.com.

7. Leslie Wayne, "Pentagon Brass and Military Contractors' Gold," *New York Times,* June 29, 2004, available online at: www.lexis-nexis.com.

8. Peter Pae, "Defense Dealing Too Close for Comfort?" *Los Angeles Times,* June 13, 2004, available online at: www.lexis-nexis.com.

9. Andy Pasztor and Rebecca Christie, "Boeing Ex-Officer Pleads Guilty in Hiring Case," *Wall Street Journal,* November 16, 2004, available online at: www.westlaw.com.

10. John M. Donnelly, "Debate Simmers on Contractor Ethics," *Defense Week,* November 24, 2003, available online at: www.lexis-nexis.com.

11. "Halliburton Inquiry Grows: FBI Investigating Deal Complaint," *Seattle Times* new service, October 29, 2004, available online at: http://seattletimes.nwsource.com/html/nationworld/2002076103_halliburton29.html.

12. Joel Brinkley and Eric Schmitt, "Halliburton Will Repay U.S. Excess Charges for Troops' Meals," *New York Times,* February 3, 2004, available online at: www.lexis-nexis.com.

13. "When Something Is Rotten," *Economist,* U.S. ed., July 27, 2002, available online at: www.lexis-nexis.com.

14. Mitchell Pacelle and Laurie P. Cohen, "J. P. Morgan, Citigroup Will Pay $305 Million to Settle Enron Case," *Wall Street Journal,* July 29, 2003, available online at: www.westlaw .com/; Tamsin Carlisle and Ann Davis, "CIBC's Penalty for Enron Role Is $80 Million," *Wall Street Journal,* December 23, 2003, available online at: www.westlaw.com.

15. John R. Wilke, "Price-Fixing Investigations Sweep Chemical Industry," *Wall Street Journal,* June 22, 2004, available online at: www.westlaw.com.

16. Scott Bernard Nelson, "Probes Raise Many Questions," *Boston Globe*, October 31, 2003, available online at: www.lexis-nexis.com.

17. Tom Lauricella, "Morgan Stanley Settles, but Woes Linger," *Wall Street Journal*, November 18, 2003, available online at: www.westlaw.com.

18. Peter Elkind, "Spitzer's Crusade," *Fortune*, November 15, 2004, 129, available online at: www.lexis-nexis.com.

19. David Wessel, "Venal Sins: Why the Bad Guys of the Boardroom Emerged en Masse,'" *Wall Street Journal*, June 20, 2002, available online at: www.westlaw.com.

20. David Haldane, "Podiatrist Billed for Amputees, U.S. Claims," *Los Angeles Times*, October 24, 2003, available online at: www.lexis-nexis.com.

21. Steven Quinn, "Tenet Faces Tough Road to Recovery," *Dallas Morning News*, 2nd. ed., January 2, 2005, available online at: www.lexis-nexis.com/., page 1D; also "Tenet Health-care Says It Faces Florida Medicaid Investigation," *New York Times*, August 9, 2003, available online at: www.lexis-nexis.com.

22. Christopher Windham, "Bogus Health Insurance Is Growing," *Wall Street Journal*, August 28, 2003, available online at: www.westlaw.com.

23. Alan Sager and Deborah Socolar, "Another Health-Care Crisis: Medical Theft Stings," *New York Newsday*, August 3, 2003, available online at: www.lexis-nexis.com; Reynolds Holding, "Medicare Bilked for Billions in Bogus Claims," *San Francisco Chronicle*, January 12, 2003, available online at: www.lexis-nexis.com.

24. United States General Accounting Office, *Health Care Fraud: Information-Sharing Proposals to Improve Enforcement Efforts* (Washington, D.C.: U.S. Government Printing Office, 1996; GAO/GGD-96-1011, May 1, 1996).

25. Coalition Against Insurance Fraud, *A Statistical Study of State Insurance Fraud Bureaus: A Quantitative Analysis—1995 to 2002*, available online at: http.insurancefraud.org/fraud_bureaus_study.intro.htm [February 9, 2004].

26. National Insurance Crime Bureau, *Insurance Fraud*, available online at the website of the National Insurance Crime Bureau, available on line at: www.nicb.org/public/publications/NICBinsuranceng.pdf (consulted February 9, 2004).

27. Coalition Against Insurance Fraud, "New Study: Convictions Double, but Gains Are Fragile," July 18, 2001, available online at: http://insurancefraud.org/releases_2001.htm, #091801.

28. National Insurance Crime Bureau, *Insurance Fraud*.

29. Insurance Research Council, "One in Three Americans Say It's Acceptable to Inflate Insurance Claims, but Public Acceptance of Insurance Fraud Is Declining," July 24, 2003, available online at the website of the Insurance Research Council: www.ircweb.org/news/200307242.htm.

30. New York State Insurance Department, "Department and Suffolk District Attorney's Office Announce 85 Indictments in No-Fault Insurance Fraud Scheme," August 12, 2003, available online at the website of the New York State Insurance Department: www.ins.state.ny.us/po308131.htm.

31. New York State Insurance Department, "Department and Suffolk District Attorney's Office Announce Eighty-Five Indictments."

32. Insurance Information Institute, "Auto Insurance," available online at the website of the Insurance Information Institute: www.iii.org/media/facts/statsbyissue/auto/ [June 7, 2004].

33. "Lie Detector Technology Catches False Claims," *Claims*, September 2003, available online at: www.claimsmag.com/Issues/Sep03/nationalreport.asp.

34. Insurance Research Council, "One in Three Americans Say It's Acceptable to Inflate Insurance Claims."

35. American Bankers Association, "Attempted Check Fraud Doubles to $4.3 Billion According to ABA Survey," available online at the website of the American Bankers Association: www.aba.com/Press+Room/111302checkfraud.htm [February 22, 2004]; also www .fraudban.com/content/FB-NL022703.pdf.

36. National Check Fraud Center, "Check Fraud Statistics," available online at the website of the National Check Fraud Center: www.occtreas.gov/checkfraud/chckfrd.pdf [February 10, 2004].

37. U.S. Department of Justice, Federal Bureau of Investigation, Financial Institution Fraud Unit, Financial Crimes Section, Financial Institution Fraud and Failure Report, Fiscal Year 2002, 1–2, available online at the website of the Federal Bureau of Investigation: www.fbi.gov/publications/financial/2002fif/fif02.pdf.

38. U.S. Department of Justice, Federal Bureau of Investigation, Financial Institution Fraud Unit, Financial Crimes Section, Financial Institution Fraud and Failure Report, Fiscal Year 2002, 1–2.

39. American Bankers Association, "Attempted Check Fraud Doubles to $4.3 Billion."

40. Office of the Comptroller of the Currency, *Check Fraud: A Guide to Avoiding Losses* (Washington, D.C.: U.S. Government Printing Office, 1996), available online at: www .cuesuplus.org/crse-lib/checkfra.html.

41. U.S. Department of Justice, Federal Bureau of Investigation, Financial Institution Fraud Unit, Financial Crimes Section, Financial Institution Fraud and Failure Report, Fiscal Year 2002, 1–2, available online at: www.fbi.gov/publications/financial/2002fif/fif02.pdf.

42. Federal Trade Commission, "FTC Releases Consumer Fraud Survey," August 5, 2004, available online at the website of the Federal Trade Commission: www.ftc.gov/opa/2004/ 08/fraudsurvey.htm [November 8, 2004].

43. Norman Jane, "Fake IDs a Snap, Informant to Say," *Des Moines Register*, September 9, 2003, available online at: www.lexis-nexis.com.

44. Trent Youl, "Phishing Scams: Understanding the Latest Trends," June 2004, available online at: www.fraudwatchinternational.com/internetfraud/phishing/report.pdf [November 8, 2004].

45. "Fraud May Start Next Door," *Internal Auditor*, December 1, 1999, available online at: www.investigation.com/articles/library/1999articles/articles3.htm.

46. KPMG, *Fraud Survey 2003*, available online at the website of KPMG: www.us .kpmg.com/RutUS_prod/Documents/9/FINALFraudSur.pdf; Ernst & Young, *Fraud: The Unmanaged Risk* (2002), 11, available online at the website of Ernst & Young: www.ey.com/ global/download.nsf/UK/Fraud_2002_Survey/$file/EY_8th_Global_Fraud_Survey.pdf.

47. KPMG, *International Fraud Report* (1996), 9–10, available online at: www.acsu.buffalo .edu/~evpatter/402SY/auddocs/ch2web/fraud.pdf.

48. "Retailers Should Brace for Sharp Increase in Shoplifting Activity, Checkpoint-Commissioned Studies Say," *Business Wire*, December 4, 2001, available online at: www.lexis-nexis.com.

49. Joel Kurth, "Underground Economic Signs Shadow Holidays," *Detroit News*, December 26, 2002, available online at: www.lexis-nexis.com.

50. Richard C. Hollinger and Jason L. Davis, *2001 National Retail Security Survey Final Report*, 12, University of Florida, 2002.

51. Ian Urbina, "As Energy Thieves Turn Crafty, Utilities Turn Up Battles of Wits," *New York Times*, May 5, 2004, available online at: www.lexis-nexis.com.

52. ADP Screening and Selection Services, *2002 Hiring Index;* "Employers Steadily Increase Candidate Screening in Hiring Process; ADP's Annual Study Highlights Increased Demand for Services," Automatic Data Processing, Inc., May 19, 2003, available online at: www.pressi.com/int/release/66619.html [March 1, 2004].

53. Automatic Data Processing, Inc., "Hiring Study Shows Many Resumes Misleading, over 40 Percent Have Information Difference in Employment and Educational History," April 1, 2002, available online at: www.investquest.com/iq/a/aud/ne/news/adpmisleading .htm [March 1, 2004].

54. Erich Swift, "Does That Position Require a Bachelor's Degree? We'll Sell You a REAL One!" March 14, 2004, available online at: www.digitas.harvard.edu/~hcssa/mailinglist/ archives/ad/msg00003.html.

55. Andrea Kay, "Background Checks Help Employers Steer Clear of Liability," *Gannett News Service,* January 16, 2003, available online at: www.lexis-nexis.com.

56. Jane Gross, "Exposing the Cheat Sheet, with the Students' Aid," *New York Times,* November 26, 2003, available online at: www.lexis-nexis.com.

57. Center for Academic Integrity, "CAI Research," available online at the website of the Center for Academic Integrity: www.academicintegrity.org/cai_research.asp [February 16, 2004].

58. Josephson Institute of Ethics, *Report Card 2002: The Ethics of American Youth* (2002), 2, 8, available online at: www.josephsoninstitute.org/Survey2002/Report-Card-2002_data-tables.pdf.

59. Center for Academic Integrity, "CAI Research."

60. John Leland, "Beyond File-Sharing: A Nation of Copiers," *New York Times,* September 14, 2003, available online at: www.lexis-nexis.com.

61. Ipsos, *Internet Piracy on Campus: American Students and Educators Share Their Attitudes toward Online Downloading, File-Sharing and Copyright Law* (September 16, 2003), available online at: www.bsa.org/resources/2, www.bsa.org/resources/11, and www.bsa.org/ resources/13.

62. Business Software Alliance, *Global Software Piracy Study* (June 2002), available online at the website of the Business Software Alliance: http://global.bsa.org/globalstudy/.

63. "Study: Colleges a Gateway to Software Piracy," *internetnews.com,* September 17, 2003, available online at: www.internetnews.com/article.php/3078651.

64. Dan Barry, Jonathan D. Glater, Adam Liptak, and Jacques Steinberg, "Correcting the Record; Times Reporter Who Resigned Leaves Long Trail of Deception," *New York Times,* May 11, 2003, available online at: www.lexis-nexis.com.

65. Sinead O'Brien, "For Barnicle, One Controversy Too Many," *American Journalism Review,* September 1998, available online at: www.lexis-nexis.com.

66. Elena Cherney and James Bandler, "Publishers Face Credibility Doubts; Inflated Circulation Data at Hollinger, Tribune Units Pose Issues for Advertisers," *Wall Street Journal,* June 21, 2004, available online at: www.westlaw.com.

67. Michael Stroh, "Bell Labs Fires Physicist for Faking Research Data," *Baltimore Sun,* September 26, 2002, available online at: www.lexis-nexis.com.

68. "Bell Fires Scientist for Falsified Data," *New York Newsday,* September 26, 2002, available online at: www.lexis-nexis.com.

69. R. Eugene Mellican, "From Fusion Frenzy to Fraud: Reflections on Science and Its Cultural Norms," *Bulletin of Science, Technology and Society* 12 (February 1992): 1–9.

70. Keay Davidson, "Berkeley Lab Found Research Fabricated; Scientist Accused of Misconduct Fired," *San Francisco Chronicle,* July 13, 2002, available online at: www.lexis-nexis.com.

71. David Labrador, "Damage Control," *Scientific American.com,* October 25, 2004, available online at: www.sciam.com/print_version.cfm?articleID=000C1F09–7778–1178–AD6883414B7F0000 [November 15, 2004].

72. Sandy Grady, "Just Say Yes to Pro Sports Drugs?" *USA Today,* December 2, 2003, available online at: www.lexis-nexis.com.

73. David Bjerklie and Alice Park, "How Doctors Help the Dopers," *Time,* August 16, 2004, available online at: www.lexis-nexis.com.

74. "Restoring Faith in America's Pastime: Evaluating Major League Baseball's Efforts to Eradicate Steroid Use," March 17, 2005, hearings before the House Committee on Government Reform, 109th Cong., 1st sess., available online at: http://reform.house.gov/GovReform/HearingsEventSingle.aspx?EventED=1637; "Track Chief Urges Zero Tolerance," *Chicago Tribune,* December 5, 2003, available online at: www.lexis-nexis.com; "Ramifications on . . ." *St. Petersburg (Florida) Times,* November 30, 2003, available online at: www.lexis-nexis.com; "Blue Cross and Blue Shield Association Survey Projects 1.1 Million Teens Have Used Potentially Dangerous Sports Supplements and Drugs," October 31, 2003, available online at:: www.healthycompetition.com/hc/news.html.

75. Alfred Lubrano, "Sportsmanship Apparently Does Not Begin at Home," *Charleston (West Virginia) Gazette,* September 23, 2001, available online at: www.westlaw.com.

76. "Fast and Faster," *Economist,* U.S. ed., July 31, 2004, available online at: www.lexis-nexis.com. See also Pat Butcher, *The Perfect Distance: Ovett & Coe: The Record-Breaking Rivalry* (London: Weidenfeld and Nicolson, 2004).

77. "Rowland's Resignation," *Wall Street Journal,* June 22, 2004, available online at: www.westlaw.com.

78. "Judges for Sale," *Economist,* U.S. ed., October 25, 2003, available online at: www.lexis-nexis.com.

79. Caroline Louise Cole, "Voter ID Bill Wins Backing; Cleaner Election Image Is Goal," *Boston Globe,* Northwest ed., September 18, 2003, available online at: www.lexis-nexis .com.

80. Donald E. Coleman, "Vote-Fraud Case Hits Valley Ex-Mendota Mayor, Former Employee Face Charges," *Fresno Bee,* September 17, 2003, available online at: www.lexis-nexis/com/.

81. CNN.com, "Report: Pentagon Auditors Altered Records," January 10, 2004, available online at: www.cnn.com/2004/US/01/10/watchdog.fraud.ap/.

82. Tom Campbell, "Three Guilty in Investing Scam," *Richmond (Virginia) Times-Dispatch,* February 19, 2004, available online at: www.lexis-nexis.com.

83. Dan Damon, "Turning the Tables on Nigeria's E-Mail Conmen," *BBC News,* U.K. ed., July 13, 2004, available online at:http://news.bbc.co.uk/1/hi/world/africa/3887493.stm. I am thankful to Professor Diego Gambetta for notifying me of this article.

84. *See* KPMG, *International Fraud Report* (1996), 8, available online at: www.acsu.buffalo .edu/~evpatter/402SY/auddocs/ch2web/fraud.pdf.

85. KPMG, *Fraud Survey 2003,* 1, 2.

86. KPMG, *Fraud Survey 2003,* 6.

87. Association of Certified Fraud Examiners, *2002 Report to the Nation: Occupational Fraud and Abuse,* 3–4, available online at the website of the Association of Certified Fraud Examiners: www.cfenet.com/pdfs/2002RttN.pdf.

88. James Chapman and David Hughes, "How Kinnock Failed to End EU Fraud," *London Daily Mail,* September 25, 2003, available online at: www.lexis-nexis.com.

89. Erik Portanger, "Parmalat' s Fallout May Be Wide," *Wall Street Journal*, December 23, 2003, available online at: www.westlaw.com.

90. PricewaterhouseCoopers, *Economic Crime Survey 2003*, 7, available online at: www.pwcglobal.com/gx/eng/cfr/gecs/PwC_GECS03_global%20report.pdf.

91. Wilmer, Cutler & Pickering, *Economic Crime: The U.S. Is Not Immune* (2003), 1, available online at: www.wilmer.com/post/news_items/Econ_Crime_US_Report.pdf.

92. KPMG, *Fraud Survey 2003*.

93. KPMG, *International Fraud Report* (1996), 3–4.

94. Wessel, "Venal Sins."

95. "New Report by Huron Consulting Group Reveals Financial Restatements Increase at Record Level in 2004," January 20, 2005, available online at: http://huronconsultinggroup.com/general01.asp?id=779&related ProfessionalID=563 [May 8, 2005]. See also "Corporate Regulation Must Be Working: There's a Backlash," *Wall Street Journal*, June 16, 2004, available online at: www.westlaw.com.

96. "New Report by Huron Consulting Group."

97. Theo Francis and Timothy Aeppel, "The Red Flag Called 'Self-Insurance,'" *Wall Street Journal*, March 15, 2004, available online at: www.westlaw.com.

98. Richard W. Stevenson and Jeff Gerth, "Web of Safeguards Failed as Enron Fell," *New York Times*, January 20, 2002, available online at: www.lexis-nexis.com.

99. Wessel, "Venal Sins.'"

100. This information was offered by Ann Ruthledge, principal, R & R Consulting, available online at: www.creditspectrum.com/.

101. "Arthur Andersen Agrees to Settlement Involving Connecticut Real Estate Firm," *Wall Street Journal*, May 5, 1993, available online at: www.westlaw.com; George Judson, "Accountants to Pay $10 Million to Victims of Real Estate Fraud," *New York Times*, April 24, 1996, available online at: www.lexis-nexis.com; United States v. Autuori, 212 F.3d 105 (2d Cir. 2000).

102. Associated Press, "Sued Accountants to Pay $90 Million," *New York Times*, June 29, 1999, available online at: www.lexis-nexis.com.

103. Gretchen Morgenson, "S.E.C. Puts Ban on Accountant over His Work on Tyco's Books," *New York Times*, August 14, 2003, available online at: www.lexis.com/.

104. Bloomberg News, "S.E.C. Accuses Three Accountants in Fraud Suit," *New York Times*, August 2, 2001, available online at: www.lexis-nexis.com.

105. KPMG, *International Fraud Report* (1996), 4, 8.

106. John C. Coffee, Jr., "Gatekeeper Failure and Reform: The Challenge of Fashioning Relevant Reforms," *Boston University Law Review* 84 (April 2004): 301–364.

107. Jacoboni v. KPMG LLP, 314 F. Supp. 2d 1172 (M.D. Fla. 2004) (dismissing one of the clients' complaints).

108. *In re* Bunsis, 243 A.D.2d 226 (N.Y. App. Div. 1998); Joseph P. Fried, "Financial Adviser Sentenced to Fifteen Months and Restitution," *New York Times*, Mar. 10, 1997, available online at: www.lexis-nexis.com; Joseph P. Fried, "Lawyer Pleads Guilty in Thefts of More than $1.5 Million," *New York Times*, May 1, 1996, available online at: www.lexis-nexis.com.

109. *Bingham v. Zolt*, 823 F. Supp. 1126 (S.D.N.Y. 1993), *aff'd*, 66 F.3d 553 (2d Cir. 1995), *cert. denied*, 517 U.S. 1230 (1996); "Verdict Favoring Singer's Estate Is Upheld," *New York Times*, September 30, 1995, available online at: www.lexis-nexis.com.

110. Paul W. Valentine, "Maryland Accountant Jailed on Probation Violation," *Washington Post*, October 23, 1992, available online at: www.lexis-nexis.com.

111. United States v. Karam, 201 F.3d 320, 323–24 (4th Cir. 2000); "Rockville Accountant Gets 2 Years in Fraud Case," *Washington Post*, March 20, 1998, available online at: www.lexis-nexis.com.

112. Sylvia Moreno, "Virginia Accountant Pleads Guilty in Loan Scheme; Arlington Man Stole from His Clients," *Washington Post*, September 9, 1998, available online at: www.lexis-nexis.com.

113. Lisa G. Lerman, "Blue-Chip Bilking: Regulation of Billing and Expense Fraud by Lawyers," *Georgetown Journal of Legal Ethics* 12 (winter 1999): 205–365.

114. Among the cases are United States v. Myerson, 18 F.3d 153 (2d Cir. 1994) (affirming the lower court's decision on mail fraud); *In re* Duker, 723 A.2d 410 (D.C. 1999) (William Duker disbarred after pleading guilty to mail fraud and related charges); Attorney Grievance Comm'n v. Hess, 722 A.2d 905 (Md. 1999) (Stanford Hess suspended three years for padding bills); Dresser Indus., Inc. v. Digges, No. JH-89–485, 1989 U.S. Dist. LEXIS 17396 (D. Md. Aug. 30, 1989) (awarding the plaintiff $3,124,414 in liquidated damages in case against former attorney, Edward S. Digges, Jr., for breach of contract and fraud).

115. "Merry Christmas, Wall Street," editorial, *Washington Post*, December 26, 2002, available online at: www.lexis-nexis.com; Conor O'Clery, "Wall Street Firms Agree to Pay $ 1.4bn in Fines," *Irish Times*, April 29, 2003, available online at: www.lexis-nexis.com.

116. Tom Lauricella, "NASD Orders Hefty Refunds on Fund Fees," *Wall Street Journal*, August 27, 2003, available online at: www.westlaw.com.

117. Herbert Lash, "U.S. Mutual Fund Scandal Widens, Putnam Chief Is Ousted," November 4, 2003, available online at: http//in.news.yahoo.com/031103/137/292ie.html [November 9, 2004].

118. Joseph B. Treaster, "Variable Annuities Inquiry Is Looking at Prudential," *New York Times*, May 31, 2003, available online at: www.lexis-nexis.com.

2. Old and New Concerns

1. State Street, "Investor Confidence Index Summary," 2004, 3–4. available online at: www.statestreet.com/investorconfidenceindex/ [February 3, 2004].

2. "SOM Study Shows Consumer Confidence in Stock Market Has Risen—But Not by Much," *Yale Bulletin and Calendar*, October 10, 2003, available online at the website of Yale University: www.yale.edu/opa/v32.n6/story12.html [June 9, 2004].

3. Faith Arner, "Can This Man Save Putnam?" *Business Week*, April 19, 2004, available online at: www.lexis-nexis.com.

4. Yuval Rosenberg, "Yield of Dreams," *Fortune*, July 12, 2004, available online at: www.lexis-nexis.com.

5. Ian McDonald, "Four Mutual Fund Firms See Cash Just Pouring In," *Wall Street Journal*, August 5, 2004, available online at: www.westlaw.com.

6. National Association of Securities Dealers, "Dispute Resolution Statistics," July 2004, available online at the website of the National Association of Securities Dealers: www.nasdadr.com/statistics.asp (citing Financial Retail Group).

7. "Independence Days," *Economist*, U.S. ed., Apr. 27. 2002, available online at: www.lexis-nexis.com.

8. Ruth Simon and Louise Story, "Independent Research Hits Wall Street," *Wall Street Journal*, July 27, 2004, available online at: www.westlaw.com.

9. "Making Companies Work," *Economist*, U.S. ed., October 25, 2003, available online at: www.lexis-nexis.com.

10. Kevin Peraino, "A Shark in Kid's Clothes," *Newsweek*, October 2, 2000, available online at: www.lexis-nexis.com; SEC v. Capital Gains Research Bureau, Inc., 375 U.S. 180 (1963).

11. H.R. Rep. No. 101–617, 10 (1990).

12. Securities Enforcement Remedies and Penny Stock Reform Act of 1990, Pub. L. No. 101–429, §§ 501–510, 104 Stat. 931, 951–58 (codified in scattered sections of 15 U.S.C).

13. George Sjostrom, "Sjostrom: Fraud Benefits from Our Lottery Mentality," *Ventura County (California) Star*, September 20, 2003, available online at: www.lexis-nexis.com.

14. Sjostrom, "Fraud Benefits from Our Lottery Mentality."

15. Timur Kuran and Cass R. Sunstein, "Availability Cascades and Risk Regulation," *Stanford Law Review* 51 (April 1999): 711.

16. Douglas Baird, "Enron and the Long Shadow of Stat. 13 Eliz.," *Northwestern University School of Law, Law and Economics Colloquium Series*, February 20, 2003, 1–5.

17. Gary Johns, "A Multi-Level Theory of Self-Serving Behavior in and by Organizations," *Research in Organizational Behavior* 21 (1999): 14.

18. Fred L. Smith, Jr., "More Regulations Do Not Inspire More Trust," *Wall Street Journal*, June 22, 2004, available online at: www.westlaw.com.

19. David Wessel, "Venal Sins: Why the Bad Guys Of the Boardroom Emerged en Masse,'" *Wall Street Journal*, June 20, 2002, available online at: www.westlaw.com.

20. Ron Kroichick, "Sports and Drugs; Cycle of Tragedy; Baseball Has BALCO, but Europe Is Plagued with Its Own Sports Drug Scandal: EPO and Bicycling," *San Francisco Chronicle*, May 9, 2004, available online at: www.lexis-nexis.com; Joe Posnanski, "Steroids Just Feel Too Good," *Hamilton (Ontario) Spectator*, November 24, 2003, available online at: www.lexis-nexis.com; Sharon Mathieson, "Robbin' Drug Cheats Drive Batman to the Brumbies," *Australian*, October 26, 2001, available online at: www.lexis-nexis.com.

21. Jere Longman, "Drugs in Sports Creating Games of Illusion," *New York Times*, November 18, 2003, available online at: www.lexis-nexis.com.

22. Kelly Heyboer, "Nearly Half of College Students Say Internet Plagiarism Isn't Cheating," *Newhouse News Service*, August 27, 2003, available online at: www.lexis-nexis.com; Kate Zernike, "Moral Boundaries Hazy for Internet Generation," *Salt Lake City Deseret Morning News*, September 21, 2003, available online at: www.lexis-nexis.com.

23. Wessel, "Venal Sins."

24. Wessel, "Venal Sins."

25. U.S. v. Causey, No. H-04–25 (s-2) (S.D. Tex. July 7, 2004), available online at: www.findlaw/.

26. Holman W. Jenkins, Jr., "Two CEOs, Two Trials," *Wall Street Journal*, July 14, 2004, available online at: www.westlaw.com.

27. P. Whittaker, "Investors Knew Risks, Says Loans Scheme Creator," *Queensland Courier-Mail*, May 8, 1998, available online at: www.lexis-nexis.com.

28. Jonathan R. Macey and Geoffrey P. Miller, "Kaye, Scholer, FIRREA, and the Desirability of Early Closure: A View of the Kaye, Scholer Case from the Perspective of Bank Regulatory Policy," *Southern California Law Review* 66 (March 1993): 1137.

29. Anthony Lin, "One Year after Sarbanes-Oxley Act, Many Officers See Need, but Grumble Nonetheless," *New York Law Journal*, July 31, 2003, available online at: www.lexis-nexis.com;

30. Lin, "One Year after Sarbanes-Oxley Act."

31. See, e.g., Alan C. Pritchard, "Self-Regulation and Securities Markets," *Regulation,* spring 2003, available online at: www.cato.org/pubs/regulation/regv26n1/v26n1–6.pdf.

32. See chapter 8.

33. See, e.g., "SEC Wants Grasso Payout Details," *Accounting Today,* September 22, 2003, available online at: www.lexis-nexis.com; "High Profiles in Hot Water," *Wall Street Journal,* June 28, 2002, available online at: www.westlaw.com.

34. Staff, "We All Can Help Build New State Economy," *Green Bay (Wisconsin) Press-Gazette,* September 10, 2003, available online at: www.lexis-nexis.com; Duncan Adams, "Domestic Furniture Manufacturers Can Still Compete, Say Analysts," *Roanoke (Virginia) Times,* March 9, 2003, available online at: www.lexis-nexis.com; Jo-Ann Johnston, "Executive Enforcement," *Tampa Tribune,* July 28, 2003, available online at: www.lexis-nexis.com.

35. Michael Schroeder, "Cleaner Living, No Easy Riches," *Wall Street Journal,* July 22, 2003, available online at: www.westlaw.com.

36. "The Case for Going Private," *Economist,* U.S. ed., January 25, 2003, available online at: www.lexis-nexis.com.

37. Kenneth Lehn, "How to Clean Up after Corporate Scandals," *Pittsburgh Post-Gazette,* October 6, 2002, available online at: www.lexis-nexis.com; George Melloan, "Give Thanks for the Resilience of Corporate America," *Wall Street Journal,* May 6, 2003, available online at: www.westlaw.com.

38. "Why Have an SEC?" *70 Research Reports* (no. 23, December 8, 2003), available online at: www.aier.org.2003pubs/RR23.pdf (Great Barrington, Mass.: American (Institute for Economic Research).

39. Associated Press, "Revamp S.E.C., Reagan Is Told," *New York Times,* January 23, 1981, available online at: www.lexis-nexis.com.

40. Cal. Corp. Code § 25140(a)(1)(B), (2)(B) (West Supp. 2004); Fla. Stat. Ann. § 517.111(1)(i) (West Supp. 2004); Tex. Rev. Civ. Stat. Ann. § 581–7(C)(2) (Vernon Supp. 2004).

41. "Independence Days," *Economist,* U.S. ed., April. 27, 2002, available online at: www.lexis-nexis.com.

42. Evan Cooper, "Washington vs. Albany, Boston," *On Wall Street,* August 1, 2003, available online at: www.lexis-nexis.com.

43. Sam Fulwood III, "It's Easy to Cheat a Greedy Investor," *Cleveland Plain Dealer,* February 25, 2002, available online at: www.lexis-nexis.com; Tom Dorsey, "New Co-Host Will Be Up," *Louisville Courier-Journal,* January 24, 2002, available online at: www.lexis-nexis.com.

44. Arthur Francel, "Greedy Investors: People's Expectations Have Been Set Too High," *Milwaukee Journal Sentinel,* August 2, 2002, available online at: www.lexis-nexis.com.

45. Cliff Slater, "Second Opinion," *Honolulu Advertiser,* August 5, 2002, available online at: www.lexis-nexis.com.

46. *CFO.com* staff, "Reader: Plenty of Blame to Go Around," *CFO.com,* February 4, 2002, available online at: www.lexis-nexis.com; Bob Schmerling, "Surviving Ups and Downs; Caught in Greed Trap," *Orlando Sentinel Tribune,* July 26, 2002, available online at: www.lexis-nexis.com; David Moon, "Investor Caution Will Do Better than New Government Regulations, Laws," *Knoxville News-Sentinel,* February 3, 2002, available online at: www.lexis-nexis.com.

47. "Analyze This," *Riverside (California) Press Enterprise,* May 23, 2002, available online at: www.lexis-nexis.com.

48. Seshadri Iyengar, "Telecom Services," *Chicago Tribune*, July 19, 2003, available online at: www.lexis-nexis.com. Jeffrey Silva, "Rally Killer," *RCR Wireless News*, May 27, 2002, available online at: www.lexis-nexis.com.

49. "New York Mayor Slammed for Rapping Greedy Investors," *Agence France Presse*, June 29, 2002, available online at: www.lexis-nexis.com.

50. Patrice Hill, "Congress Told Enron Cover-up 'Pervasive'; Fears Reverberate along Wall Street," *Washington Times*, February 5, 2002, available online at: www.lexis-nexis.com.

51. Bill George, "Wanted: Authentic Leaders," *Wall Street Journal*, December 16, 2003, available online at: www.westlaw.com.

52. Jill Goldsmith, "Congloms Looking Rumpled as Shareholders Press Suits," *Variety*, September 2–8, 2002, available online at: www.lexis-nexis.com.

53. "The Day the Bubble Burst," *Toronto Star*, March 11, 2003, available online at: www.lexis-nexis.com; George Pitcher, "Greed Is Not Enough for Arrogant Fund Managers," *Marketing Week*, February 6, 2003, available online at: www.lexis-nexis.com.

54. Daniel P. Moynihan, "Defining Deviancy Down," *American Scholar* 62 (winter 1993): 26.

55. Moynihan, "Defining Deviancy Down," 17–30.

56. Louise O'Brien, "How to Restore the Fiduciary Relationship: An Interview with Eliot Spitzer," *Harvard Business Review* 82 (May 2004): 72.

57. Moynihan, "Defining Deviancy Down," 19.

58. Stephen M. Bainbridge, "Precommitment Strategies in Corporate Law: The Case of Dead Hand and No Hand Pills," *Journal of Corporation Law* 29 (fall 2003): 30.

59. Martin Lipman and Steven A. Rosenblum, "Election Contests in the Company's Proxy: An Idea Whose Time Has Not Come," *Business Lawyer* 59 (November 2003): 71.

60. Roderick L Kramer, "Flawed Leaders: Their Rise and Fall," *Business Day* (*South Africa*), November 24, 2003, available online at: www.lexis-nexis.com.

61. *In re* Enron Corp., Investment Company Act Rel. No. 22,515 (February 14, 1997) (application); *In re* Enron Corp., Investment Company Act Rel. No. 22,560 (March 13, 1997) (order granted).

62. Enron Corp., Public Utility Holding Co. Act Rel. No. 24,428 (July 23, 1987) (order granted)

63. Consolidated Appropriations Act, 2001, Pub. L. No. 106–554, app. E, § 103, 114 Stat. 2763, 2763A-379 to 380 (2000) (codified at 7 U.S.C. § 2(d) (2000)).

64. Michael Schroeder and Greg Ip, "Out of Reach: The Enron Debacle Spotlights Huge Void in Financial Regulation," *Wall Street Journal*, December 13, 2001, available online at: www.westlaw.com.

65. "Perspectives," *Newsweek*, Feb. 4, 2002, available online at: www.lexis-nexis.com.

66. "Mutual Funds under Fire," October 28, 2003, available online at: www.onpointradio.org/shows/2003/10/20031028_a_main.asp [July 13, 2004].

67. Michael A. Carrier, "The Real Rule of Reason: Bridging the Disconnect," *Brigham Young University Law Review* 4 (1999): 1304.

68. E.g., Frederick M. Abbott, "Incomplete Rule Systems, System Incompatibilities and Suboptimal Solutions: Changing the Dynamic of Dispute Settlement and Avoidance in Trade Relations Between Japan and the United States," *Arizona Journal of International and Comparative Law* 16 (winter 1999): 187 n. 3.

69. Alan A. Fisher and Robert H. Lande, "Efficiency Considerations in Merger Enforcement," *California Law Review* 71 (December 1983): 1627 n. 174.

70. Matthew M. Sanderson, "A 'Basic' Misunderstanding: How the United States Supreme Court Misunderstands Capital Markets," *South Texas Law Review* 43 (summer 2002): 760.

71. Thomas H. Noe and Michael J. Rebello, "The Dynamics of Business Ethics and Economic Activity," *American Economic Review* 84 (1994): 531–547.

72. I am indebted to Professor Larry Cunningham, Boston College Law School, for this idea.

73. Michael Lewis, "Finding a Reason to Celebrate the Scandals," *Los Angeles Business Journal*, July 22, 2002, available online at: www.lexis-nexis.com.

74. Ian McDonald, "Mutual Funds Grateful for Automatic Pilots," *Wall Street Journal*, July 8, 2003, available online at: www.westlaw.com.

75. Merton H. Miller and Franco Modigliani, "Dividend Policy, Growth, and the Valuation of Shares," *Journal of Business* 34 (October 1961): 411–433.

76. Merton H. Miller and Franco Modigliani, "The Cost of Capital, Corporation Finance and the Theory of Investment," *American Economic Review* 48 (June 1958): 261–297.

77. Stephen A. Ross, "The Determination of Financial Structure: The Incentive-Signaling Approach," *Bell Journal of Economics* 8 (spring 1977): 23–40.

78. Sudipto Bhattacharya, "Imperfect Information, Dividend Policy, and 'The Bird in the Hand' Fallacy," *Bell Journal of Economics* 10 (spring 1979): 259–270; Kose John and Joseph Williams, "Dividends, Dilution, and Taxes: A Signaling Equilibrium," *Journal of Finance* 40 (September 1985): 1058–1070.

79. John A. Weinberg, "Accounting for Corporate Behavior," *Economic Quarterly* (Federal Reserve Bank of Richmond) 89 (summer 2003): 3.

80. Sarbanes-Oxley Act of 2002, Pub. L. No. 107–204, 2002 U.S.C.C.A.N. (116 Stat.) 745 (to be codified as amended in scattered sections of 15, 28 U.S.C.).

81. Charles Gasparino, "Merrill Lynch to Pay Big Fine, Increase Oversight of Analysts," *Wall Street Journal*, May 22, 2002, available online at: www.westlaw.com.

82. Kate Berry, "Grudging Compliance with Sarbanes-Oxley," *Los Angeles Business Journal*, June 23, 2003, available online at: www.westlaw.com.

83. Burton G. Malkiel, "Remaking the Market: The Great Wall Street," *Wall Street Journal*, October 14, 2002, available online at: www.westlaw.com/.

84. Alan Murray, "Can George W. Bush Save U.S. Capitalism from Its Excesses?" *Wall Street Journal*, Apr. 16, 2002, available online at: www.westlaw.com.

85. Martin Lipton, "The Millennium Bubble and Its Aftermath: Reforming Corporate America and Getting Back to Business," *M & A Lawyer*, July-August 2003, available online at: www.lexis-nexis.com.

86. Ken Brown, "Wall Street Plays Numbers Game with Earnings, Despite Reforms," *Wall Street Journal*, July 22, 2003, available online at: www.westlaw.com.

87. "Their Day in Court," *Economist*, U.S. ed., October 4, 2003, available online at: www .lexis-nexis.com.

88. John Braithwaite, "Challenging Just Deserts: Punishing White-Collar Criminals," *Journal of Criminal Law and Criminology* 73 (summer 1982): 723–763.

89. Braithwaite, "Challenging Just Deserts," 731–738. See also Donald J. Newman, "Public Attitudes toward a Form of White Collar Crime," *Social Problems* 4, 3 (1957): 228–232; Salomon Rettig and Benjamin Pasamanick, "Changes in Moral Values over Three Decades," *Social Problems* 6, 4 (1959): 320–328.

90. Joseph E. Scott and Fahed Al-Thakeb, "The Public's Perceptions of Crime: A Comparative Analysis of Scandinavia, Western Europe, the Middle East and the United States,"

in *Contemporary Corrections,* edited by C. Ronald Huff (Beverly Hills, Calif: Sage, 1977), cited in Braithwaite, "Challenging Just Desert," 737.

91. John Braithwaite, "White Collar Crime," *Annual Review of Sociology* 11 (1985): 4.

92. Braithwaite, "Challenging Just Deserts," 737–738.

3. Toward Abuse of Trust and Mistrust

1. "Ethics and the Professions," *CAP Electronic Bulletin,* October 19, 1999, available online at: www.collegepubs.com/elec_bulletin.shtml#EB99.4.

2. Joseph Dits, "Sled Race, Alaskan Culture Snare Hoosier," *South Bend (Indiana) Tribune,* March 11, 1995, available online at: www.lexis-nexis.com/ (trust and relationships are more important than business transactions).

3. Russell Hardin, "Distrust," *Boston University Law Review* 81 (June 2001): 503–506, 509.

4. Hardin, "Distrust," 503–506, 509–510, 511–514; Samuel Bowles and Herbert Gintis, "Social Capital and Community Governance," *Economic Journal* 112 (November 2002): F419–436; Steven N. Durlauf, "On the Empirics of Social Capital," *Economic Journal* 112 (November 2002): F459–479; Steven N. Durlauf, "Symposium on Social Capital: Introduction," *Economic Journal* 112 (November 2002): F417–418; Edward L. Glaeser, David Laibson, and Bruce Sacerdote, "An Economic Approach to Social Capital," *Economic Journal* 112 (November 2002): F437–459.

5. Carol M. Rose, "Trust in the Mirror of Betrayal," *Boston University Law Review* 75 (May 1995): 534–535.

6. David Shribman, "Reagan, All-American, Dies at Ninety-Three; Fortieth President Led a Revival of Conservatism," *Boston Globe,* June 6, 2004, available online at: www.lexis-nexis.com.

7. Timur Kuran and Cass R. Sunstein, "Availability Cascades and Risk Regulation," *Stanford Law Review* 51 (April 1999): 711.

8. Fabian Bornhorst, Andrea Ichino, Karl H. Schlag, and Eyal Winter, "Trust and Trustworthiness among Europeans: South-North Comparison," May 27, 2004, available online at: www.iue.it/Personal/Researchers/Bornhorst/files/northsouth12.pdf [November 19, 2004].

9. George A. Akerlof, "The Market for 'Lemons': Quality, Uncertainty and the Market Mechanism," *Quarterly Journal of Economics* 84 (August 1970): 488.

10. Robert Prentice, "Whither Securities Regulation? Some Behavioral Observations Regarding Proposals for Its Future," *Duke Law Journal* 51 (March 2002): 1397–1511.

11. E.g., Fox Butterfield, "This Way Madness Lies: A Fall from Grace to Prison," *New York Times,* April 21, 1996, available online at: www.lexis-nexis.com.

12. E.g., United States v. Bennett, 161 F.3d 171 (3d Cir. 1998).

13. Paul Whittaker, "Police 'Put Millions' into Failed Loans Plan," *South Australia Advertiser,* May 8, 1998, available online at: www.lexis-nexis.com.

14. First Empire Bank v. FDIC, 572 F.2d 1361, 1366 (9th Cir. 1978).

15. See, e.g., John Hawke, Jr., Melanie Fein, and David Freeman, Jr., "The Authority of National Banks to Invest Trust Assets in Bank-Advised Mutual Funds," *Annual Review of Banking Law* 10 (1991): 148.

16. See, e.g., Douglas C. Michael, "Federal Agency Use of Audited Self-Regulation as a Regulatory Technique," *Administrative Law Review* 47 (spring 1995): 224–226.

17. See, e.g., Benjamin Barton, "An Institutional Analysis of Lawyer Regulation: Who Should Control Lawyer Regulation—Courts, Legislatures, or the Market?" *Georgia Law Review* 37 (summer 2003): 1189 n. 74.

18. See chapter 4.

4. Toward Deception

1. A. R. J. Brown, "P. T. Barnum Never Did Say 'There's A Sucker Born Every Minute,'" *historybuff.com*, available online at: www.historybuff.com/library/refbarnum.html [November 7, 2003].

2. "Corporate Regulation Must Be Working: There's a Backlash," *Wall Street Journal*, June 16, 2004, available online at: www.westlaw.com.

3. Russell Gold, "Halliburton Settles SEC Probe into an Accounting Disclosure," *Wall Street Journal*, August 4, 2004, available online at: www.westlaw.com.

4. Charles Gasparino, "Merrill Lynch to Pay Big Fine, Increase Oversight of Analysts," *Wall Street Journal*, May 22, 2002, available online at: www.westlaw.com.

5. Stephanie Strom, "Double Trouble at Linda Wachner's Twin Companies," *New York Times*, August 4, 1996, available online at: www.lexis-nexis.com.

6. Jerry Knight, "Called to Account," *Washington Post*, October 30, 1996, available online at: www.lexis-nexis.com.

7. Ken Brown, "Wall Street Plays Numbers Game with Earnings, Despite Reforms," *Wall Street Journal*, July 22, 2003, available online at: www.westlaw.com.

8. Claire A. Hill, "Why Financial Appearances Might Matter: An Explanation for 'Dirty Pooling' and Some Other Types of Financial Cosmetics," *Delaware Journal of Corporate Law* 22, 1 (1997): 141–196.

9. "Illegal Pyramid Selling Schemes," available online at: www.crimes-of-persuasion .com/Crimes/Delivered/pyramids.htm [February 11, 2004].

10. "Capture Archives," episode of *America's Most Wanted*, July 9, 2001, available online at: www.amw.com/amw.html [July 10, 2004].

11. United States v. Gold Unlimited, 177 F.3d 472, 478 (6th Cir. 1999).

12. United States v. Gold Unlimited, 177 F.3d 472, 478 (6th Cir. 1999).

13. Bestline Products, Inc., Securities Act Release No. 33–5211 (1971); Harry M. Cochran, Jr., Note, "Dare to Be Great, Inc.! A Case Study of Pyramid Sales Plan Regulation," *Ohio State Law Journal* 33, 3 (1972): 676–704; *Prepared Statement of Debra A. Valentine, General Counsel for the U.S. Federal Trade Commission, on "Pyramid Schemes," Presented at the International Monetary Fund's Seminar on Current Legal Issues Affecting Central Banks* (May 13, 1998), available online at the website of the Federal Trade Commission: www.ftc.gov/ speeches/other/dvimf16.htm.

14. "Pyramid Schemes: Dare to be Regulated," note, *Georgetown Law Journal* 61 (May 1973): 1257, 1261–1262, 1293.

15. United States v. Gold Unlimited, 177 F.3d 472, 475 (6th Cir. 1999); *Prepared Statement of Debra A. Valentine on "Pyramid Schemes."*

16. "Illegal Pyramid Selling Schemes."

17. "Illegal Pyramid Selling Schemes."

18. "Top Business Leaders of the Second Millennium," *Chicago Sun-Times*, January 2, 2000, available online at: www.lexis-nexis.com.

19. Institute for Global Ethics, "Quote File," *Ethics Newsline*, quoting *Bill Bernbach Said* (New York: DDB Needham Worldwide, 1989), available online at the website of the Institute for Global Ethics: www.globalethics.org/newsline/members/quotes.tmpl [November 16, 2004].

20. These are samples on file with the author.

21. Chad Terhune, "Into the Fryer: How Coke Officials Beefed Up Results of Marketing Test," *Wall Street Journal*, August 20, 2003, available online at: www.westlaw.com.

22. See George A. Akerlof, "The Market for 'Lemons': Quality, Uncertainty and the Market Mechanism," *Quarterly Journal of Economics* 84 (August 1970): 488.

23. "With Surveys Like These, It's No Wonder Products Are Mis-Sold," *Financial Adviser*, December 18, 2003, available online at: www.lexis-nexis.com.

24. Randall Smith, "Pay to Play? Companies Put a New Squeeze on Their Investment Banks," *Wall Street Journal*, August 26, 2003, available online at: www.westlaw.com; Michael Siconolfi, "SEC Broadens 'Spinning' Probe to Corporations," *Wall Street Journal*, December 24, 1997, available online at: www.westlaw.com.

25. Charles Gasparino and Josh P. Hamilton, "Probe Launched on Pay-to-Play Involving Bonds," *Wall Street Journal*, May 22, 1998, available online at: www.westlaw.com.

26. U.S.C. § 6802(a) (2000); 12 U.S.C. §§ 3401 et seq. (2000 & Supp. I 2001).

27. Michael Freedman and Emily Lambert, "Will She Walk?" *Forbes*, July 7, 2003, available online at: www.lexis-nexis.com.

28. John Schwarz, "Enron's Many Strands: The Employees: In the Bunker, Andersen Crew Is Baffled but Happy for Hugs," *New York Times*, March 15, 2002, available online at: www.lexis-nexis.com.

29. Courtroom Television Network, "Al Capone, the Brilliant Brutal Chicago Crime Czar, and His Family History," available online at: www.crimelibrary.com/gangsters_outlaws/mob_bosses/capone/1_9.html?sect=15 [June 9, 2002].

30. Association of Certified Fraud Examiners, *2002 Report to the Nation: Occupational Fraud and Abuse*, available online at the website of the Association of Certified Fraud Examiners: www.cfenet.com/pdfs/2002RttN.pdf.

31. United States General Accounting Office, *Financial Statement Restatements: Trends, Market Impacts, Regulatory Responses, and Remaining Challenges* (Washington, D.C.: U.S. Government Printing Office, 2002; GAO-03-138, October).

32. KPMG, *Fraud Survey 2003*, available online at the website of KPMG: www.us.kpmg.com/RutUS_prod/Documents/9/FINALFraudSur.pdf.

33. KPMG, *International Fraud Report* (1996), 3–4, available online at: www.acsu.buffalo.edu/~evpatter/402SY/auddocs/ch2web/fraud.pdf.

34. Patricia M. Dechow, Richard G. Sloan, and Amy P. Sweeney, "Causes and Consequences of Earnings Manipulation: An Analysis of Firms Subject to Enforcement Actions by the SEC," *Contemporary Accounting Research* 13 (spring 1996): 30.

35. Robert Prentice, "Whither Securities Regulation? Some Behavioral Observations Regarding Proposals for the Future," *Duke Law Journal* 51 (March 2002): 1414–1415.

36. Ehsan H. Feroz, Kyungjoo Park, and Victor S. Pastena, "The Financial and Market Effects of the SEC's Accounting and Auditing Enforcement Releases," *Journal of Accounting Research* 29, supp. (1991): 108.

37. Laurie McGinley, "Los Alamos Lab Is Attacking Medicare Fraud," *Wall Street Journal*, June 17, 1997, available online at: www.westlaw.com.

38. Dee McAree, "'Blacklisting' of Patients, Tenants Draws Ire; Is Use of Web Court Data an Unfair Black Mark or a Good Way to Reduce Risk?" *National Law Journal*, April 19, 2004, available online at: www.lexis-nexis.com.

39. "New Pre-Employment Screening Service Helps Screen Out the Bad Apples," *ADP Advisor*, winter 1999, available online at: www.adp.com/home/advisor/vol9no4/6.html.

40. Theo Francis, "Some Insurance Is Costing Less at U.S. Businesses," *Wall Street Journal*, March 9, 2004, available online at: www.westlaw.com.

41. Joann S. Lublin, "In Era of Fraud, Board Prospects Probe for Dirt," *Wall Street Journal,* June 23, 2003, available online at: www.westlaw.com.

42. Akerlof, "Market For 'Lemons,'" 488–500. See also chapter 3, section entitled "The Economic Impact of Failure to Trust or Verify."

43. Akerlof, "Market For 'Lemons,'" 488.

44. Mass. Gen. Laws ch. 90, § 7N½ (2002).

45. Jacoboni v. KPMG LLP, 314 F. Supp. 2d 1172 (M.D. Fla. 2004).

5. *Toward a Different American Culture*

1. Merriam-Webster Online, *Online Dictionary,* available online at: www.m-w.com; *search* culture (May 21, 2004).

2. "When Something Is Rotten," *Economist,* U.S. ed., July 27, 2002, available online at: www.lexis-nexis.com/ (quoting Lawrence Weinbach, head of an information technology services firm); italics added.

3. Mark D. West, "Losers: Recovering Lost Property in Japan and the United States," *Law and Society Review* 37 (June 2003): 369–423; Norimitsu Onishi, "Never Lost, but Found Daily; Japanese Honesty," *New York Times,* January 8, 2004, available online at: www.lexis-nexis.com.

4. Charles Camic, "The Matter of Habit," *American Journal of Sociology* 91 (March 1986): 1051, quoting Emile Durkheim, *The Division of Labor in Society,* translated by George Simpson (1893; New York: Fredd Press, 1933; reprint, 1964), 159; Durkheim, *The Elementary Forms of the Religious Life,* translated by Joseph Ward Swain (1912; New York: Free Press, 1915), 103; Durkheim, *Professional Ethics and Civic Morals,* translated by Cornelia Brookfield (1898–1900; Glencoe, Ill.: Free Press, 1958), 90; Durkheim, *Moral Education,* translated by Everett K. Wilson and Herman Schnurer (1902; New York: Free Press, 1961), 52.

5. See, e.g., Ryan Chittum, "Retention Still an Issue at CB Richard Ellis; Some Foresee and Exodus of Brokers as Merged Firm Strives to Meld Two Cultures," *Wall Street Journal,* August 13, 2003, available online at: www.westlaw.com; Pui-Wing Tam, "H-P Designs Workshops to Break Post-Merger Ice," *Wall Street Journal,* July 11, 2002, available online at: www.westlaw.com.

6. Emile Durkheim, *The Division of Labor in Society,* translated by George Simpson (1893) (New York: Free Press, 1933; reprint, 1964), 241, quoted in Camic, "Matter of Habit," 1051.

7. Emile Durkheim, *Pragmatism and Society,* translated by J. C. Whitehouse (1913–1914) (Cambridge: Cambridge University Press, 1983), 79–80, quoted in Camic, "Matter of Habit," 1052.

8. Aaron-Andrew P. Bruhl, "Public Reason as a Public Good," *Journal of Law in Society* 4 (winter 2003): 261.

9. Bruhl, "Public Reason as a Public Good," 262 (footnotes omitted).

10. Bruhl, "Public Reason as a Public Good," 263 (footnotes omitted).

11. Bruhl, "Public Reason as a Public Good," 263–264 (footnotes omitted). See also Dan M. Kahan, "Trust, Collective Action, and Law," *Boston University Law Review* 81 (April 2001): 335–338; *Report to Congress: IRS Tax Compliance Activities* 3, July 15, 2003, available online at the website of the Internal Revenue Service: www.irs.gov/pub/irs-soi/03congressrpt.pdf (November 25, 2003).

12. Craig Haney, Curtis Banks, and Philip Zimbardo, "Interpersonal Dynamics in a Simulated Prison," *International Journal of Criminology and Penology* 1 (February 1973): 69–97. See also "The Stanford Prison Experiment," available online at: www.prisonexp.org.

13. Philip Zimbardo, *Congressional Testimony on the Need for Prison Reform*, hearings before Subcommittee no. 3 of the Committee on the Judiciary, House of Representatives, 92nd Cong., 1st sess., "On Corrections, Part II: Prisons, Prison Reform, and Prisoners' Rights, California," October 25, 1971 (Washington, D.C.: U.S. Government Printing Office): 112, 154.

14. Philip G. Zimbardo, A Situationist Perspective on the Psychology of Evil: Understanding How Good People Are Transformed in to Perpetrators," in *The Social Psychology of Good and Evil*, edited by Arthur G. Miller (New York: Guilford Press, 2004), 47.

15. Emile Durkheim, *The Division of Labor in Society*, 336, quoted in Camic, "Matter of Habit," 1053; Steven Lukes, *Emile Durkheim: His Life and Work* (Harmondsworth, England: Penguin, 1973), 164 (retranslation by Lukes).

16. Max Weber, *Economy and Society*, edited by Guenther Roth and Claus Wittich (1922; Berkeley: University of California Press, 1978), 326, 754, quoted in Camic, "Matter of Habit," 1059; Weber, *Wirtschaft und Gesselschaft*, edited by Johannes Winckelmann, 5th rev. ed. (1922; Tübingen: Mohr, 1976), 191, 442, cited in Camic, "Matter of Habit," 1059.

17. Weber, *Economy and Society*, 326, 754; Weber, *Wirtschaft und Gesselschaft*, 191, 442.

6. Rising Opportunities and Temptations

1. KPMG, *International Fraud Report* (1996), 4, available online at: www.acsu.buffalo.edu/~evpatter/402SY/auddocs/ch2web/fraud.pdf; italics added. PricewaterhouseCoopers, *Financial Fraud: Understanding the Root Causes* (2002), 3, available online at: www.pwcglobal .com/extweb/pwcpublications.nsf/4bd5f76b48e282738525662b00739e22/ada4d486d33ce44485256caf006911d8/$FILE/Financial%20Fraud%20report.pdf.

2. *Neighbors as Negatives: Relative Earnings and Well-Being*, KSG working paper no. RWP04–029, John F. Kennedy School of Government, Harvard University, August 2, 2004.

3. Equilar, Inc. The materials were offered by Tim Ranzetta of Equilar, Inc.

4. Quentin Letts, "Le Pretty Prince?" *Wall Street Journal*, November 19, 2004, available online at: www.westlaw.com.

5. Max Weber, *Economy and Society*, edited by Guenther Roth and Claus Wittich (1922; Berkeley: University of California Press, 1978), 67–68, 78, 89, 320, 335, quoted in Charles Camic, "The Matter of Habit," *American Journal of Sociology* 91 (March 1986): 1058.

6. David A. Weisbach, "Should Legal Rules Be Used to Redistribute Income?" *University of Chicago Law Review* 70 (winter 2003): 440.

7. Gail Snyder, "Consequence Change for CEO Crime," *PM*, September 24, 2002. available online at: www.pmezine.com/article_dtls.asp?NID=224 [December 29, 2003]; Lou Dobbs, "Toothless Tigers; Pols Talk Tough on Corporate Crime but Offer Weak Measures," *Money*, September 2002, available online at: www.lexis-nexis.com.

8. John Cassidy, "The Greed Cycle: How the Financial System Encouraged Corporations to Go Crazy," *New Yorker*, September 23, 2002, available online at: www.lexis-nexis.com.

9. Susan Adams, "Sitting Down with Sitting Bull," *AARP Modern Maturity*, November–December 2002, 28–30.

10. Bill George, "Why It's Hard to Do What's Right," *Fortune*, September 29, 2003, available online at: www.lexis-nexis.com/

11. Aric Press and Susan Beck, "Almost a Revolution," *American Lawyer*, May 2004, available online at: www.lexis-nexis.com.

12. Louis Lavelle, "A Payday for Performance: Compensation Is Less Outrageous This Year, except for CEOs Who Delivered," *Business Week*, April 18, 2005, available online at: www.lexis-nexis.com.

13. Joann S. Lubin, "Some Visiting CEOs Get Paid to Stay in Residences They Own," *Wall Street Journal*, May 6, 2005, B1, available online at: westlaw.com.

14. John Cassidy, "The Greed Cycle," *New Yorker*, September 23, 2002, available online at: www.lexis-nexis.com.

15. Martin Lipton and Steven A. Rosenblum, "Election Contests In the Company's Proxy: An Idea Whose Time Has Not Come," *Business Lawyer* 59 (November 2003): 90; Stephen M. Bainbridge, "Precommitment Strategies in Corporate Law: The Case of Dead Hand and No Hand Pills," *Journal of Corporation Law* 29 (fall 2003): 1–37.

16. Roderick L Kramer, "Flawed Leaders: Their Rise and Fall," *Business Day (South Africa)*, November 24, 2003, available online at: www.lexis-nexis.com.

17. Graham v. Allis-Chalmers Mfg. Co., 188 A.2d 125 (Del. 1963).

18. *In re* Caremark Int'l Inc. Derivative Litig. 698 A.2d 959 (Del. Ch. 1996).

19. Randall Smith, "Pay to Play? Companies Put a New Squeeze on Their Investment Banks," *Wall Street Journal*, August 26, 2003, available online at: www.westlaw.com.

20. See chapter 4, section entitled "Sliding into Deception: Pyramid Schemes."

21. Cassell Bryan-Low, "KPMG Didn't Register Strategy," *Wall Street Journal*, November 17, 2003, available online at: www.westlaw.com.

22. Steve Sjuggerud, "The Scariest Scenario Imaginable," *Daily Reckoning*, October 7, 2003, available online at: www.dailyreckoning.com/home.cfm.

23. Dunstan Prial, "IPO Outlook: Risky Business: Internet IPO Aftermarket," *Wall Street Journal*, May 17, 1999, available online at: www.westlaw.com; see also John M. Wingate, "The New Economania: Consumer Privacy, Bankruptcy, and Venture Capital at Odds in the Internet Marketplace," *George Mason Law Review* 9 (spring 2001): 926.

24. Randall Smith and Susanne Craig, "Firms Close in on Settlement of IPO Inquiry," *Wall Street Journal*, June 22, 2004, available online at: www.westlaw.com; Randall Smith, "Quattrone Found Guilty on Three Counts in Big U.S. Win," *Wall Street Journal*, May 4, 2004, available online at: www.westlaw.com; see also Jason Hubschman, "The 'Odd Duck Filing' and the Efficient Market Theory: Meeting SEC Registration Requirements for Internet Free Stock Programs," *New York Law School Law Review* 44, 3–4 (2001): 563.

25. David Wessel, "Venal Sins: Why the Bad Guys of the Boardroom Emerged en Masse,'" *Wall Street Journal*, June 20, 2002, available online at: www.westlaw.com (italics added).

26. Leslie Wayne, "Pentagon Brass and Military Contractors' Gold," *New York Times*, June 29, 2004, available online at: www.lexis-nexis.com.

27. Wayne, "Pentagon Brass and Military Contractors' Gold."

28. Wayne, "Pentagon Brass and Military Contractors' Gold."

29. Peter Pae, "Defense Dealing Too Close for Comfort? An Air Force Official's Relationship with Boeing Continues to Reverberate through the Company and the Military," *New York Times*, June 13, 2004, available online at: www.lexis-nexis.com.

30. Complaint, State v. Canary Capital Partners, LL.C. (N.Y. Sup. Ct. September 3, 2003), available online at: www.oag.state.ny.us/press/2003/sep/canary_complaint.pdf.

31. "Psst, Wanna Buy a Cheap Bracelet?" *Economist*, U.S. ed., July 3, 2004, available online at: www.lexis-nexis.com.

7. The Shift to Weaker Morality, Weaker Law, and Stronger Market Discipline

1. Emile Durkheim, *Moral Education*, translated by Everett K. Wilson and Herman Schnurer (1902; New York: Free Press, 1961), cited by Charles Camic, "The Matter of Habit," *American Journal of Sociology* 91 (March 1986): 1053.

2. Durkheim, *Moral Education*, 233, 28, and *L'éducation morale* (Paris: Alcan, 1934), 32, quoted by Camic, "Matter of Habit," 1054.

3. Durkheim, *The Evolution of Educational Thought*, translated by Peter Collins (1904–05; London: Routledge & Kegan Paul, 1977), 28–29, quoted by Camic, "Matter of Habit," 1055.

4. Matt Ridley, "What Makes You Who You Are," *Time*, June 2, 2003, available online at: www.lexis-nexis.com.

5. Kimberlin v. Dewalt, 12 F. Supp. 2d 487 (D. Md. 1998); State v. Starchman, 34 P.3d 1107 (Ct. App. Idaho 2001); Ayers v. Doth, 58 F. Supp. 2d 1028 (D. Minn. 1999); Thorgaard v. State, 876 P.2d 599 (Ct. App. Idaho 1994).

6. Rachel Zimmerman, "Medical Contrition Doctors' New Tool to Fight Lawsuits: Saying: I Am Sorry," *Wall Street Journal*, May 18, 2004, available online at: www.westlaw.com.

7. Zimmerman, "Medical Contrition Doctors' New Tool to Fight Lawsuits."

8. Zimmerman, "Medical Contrition Doctors' New Tool to Fight Lawsuits."

9. Alfred University, *Initiation Rites in American High Schools: A National Survey* 12 (2000), final report by Nadine C. Hoover and Norman J. Pollard, available online at: www .alfred.edu/news/hazing__study.pdf [June 15, 2004].

10. Philip G. Zimbardo, *A Situationist Perspective on the Psychology of Evil: Understanding How Good People Are Transformed into Perpetrators* (2003), available online at the website of Philip G. Zimbardo: www.zimbardo.com [June 14, 2004].

11. Zimbardo, *Situationist Perspective on the Psychology of Evil.*

12. Barbara Rose, "Motorola CEO Faces Anger, Call to Resign; Galvin Defends Firm's Progress," *Chicago Tribune*, May 6, 2003, available online at: www.lexis-nexis.com; Dave Carpenter, "Motorola Chief Stepping Down," *Chicago Sun-Times*, September 20, 2003, available online at: www.lexis-nexis.com.

13. Michael L. Benson and Francis T. Cullen, "The Special Sensitivity of White-Collar Offenders to Prison: A Critique and Research Agenda," *Journal of Criminal Justice* 16, 3 (1988): 211.

14. Don Jacobs, "Telemarketing Con Artists Do Not See Selves as Criminals; 47 Convicted of Fraud Subject of UT Study," *Knoxville News-Sentinel*, December 10, 2001, available online at: www.lexis-nexis.com.

15. Nava Ashraf, Iris Bohnet, and Nikita Piankov, *Is Trust a Bad Investment?* Faculty Research Working Papers Series, RWP03–047, John F. Kennedy School of Government, November 2003, available online at: papers.ssrn.com/5013/papers.cfm?abstract_id=47881.

16. Alan Greenspan, "Remarks by Chairman Alan Greenspan: Maintaining Economic Vitality," September 8, 1999, available online at the website of the Federal Reserve Board: www.federalreserve.gov/BoardDocs/speeches/1999/19990908.htm.

17. David Rynecki and Michael Shermer, "Has This Man Found the Root of All Evil?" *Fortune*, November 10, 2003, available online at: www.lexis-nexis.com.

18. Gerardo A. Guerra, "Crowding Out Trust: The Adverse Effects of Verification, an Experiment," *Department of Economics Discussion Paper Series* 98, March 2002, available online at: www.economics.ox.ac.uk/research/WP/PDF/paper098.pdf.

19. Christopher Koch, "IBM's New Hook," *CIO*, July 1, 2003, available online at: www .cio.com/archive/070103/hook.html.

20. Robert Prentice, "Whither Securities Regulation? Some Behavioral Observations Regarding Proposals for Its Future," *Duke Law Journal* 51 (March 2002): 1502.

21. 164 N.E. 545, 546 (N.Y. 1928).

22. George A. Akerlof, "The Market for 'Lemons': Quality, Uncertainty and the Market Mechanism," *Quarterly Journal of Economics* 84 (August 1970): 488 (Nobel Prize–winning article).

23. Securities Act of 1934, 15 U.S.C. §§ 77a–77aa (2000).

24. Maurice E. Schweitzer, "Trust but Verify: Monitoring in Interdependent Relationships," *Experimental and Empirical Studies* 5 (March 2004): 31.

25. I owe this example to Professor Kenneth Simons, Boston University School of Law.

26. For an extensive review of the literature relating to the connection between morality and economic analysis, see Robert Cooter, "Models of Morality in Law and Economics: Self-Control and Self-Improvement for the 'Bad Man' of Holmes," *Boston University Law Review* 78 (June 1998): 905–914.

27. Sergio G. Lazzarini, Gary J. Miller, and Todd R. Zenger, "Order with Some Law: Complementarity vs. Substitution of Formal and Informal Arrangements," April 2003, available online at: www.cbs.dk/department/ivs/event/complem-JLEO22.doc.

28. Alex Geisinger, "A Belief Change Theory of Expressive Law," *Iowa Law Review* (October 2002): 35–73.   Tom R. Tyler, "Trust and Law Abidingness: A Proactive Model of Social Regulation," *Boston University Law Review* 81 (April 2001): 361–406. Dan M. Kahan, "Trust, Collective Action, and Law," *Boston University Law Review* (April 2001): 335–338; *Report to Congress: IRS Tax Compliance Activities* 3 (July 15, 2003), available online at the website of the Internal Revenue Service: www.irs.gov/pub/irs-soi/03congressrpt.pdf [November 25, 2003].

29. See the discussion of meta-norms in chapter 10.

8. The Subtle Changes in Legal Doctrine and Interpretation

1. William C. Freund, "The 'Big Board' Lives On," *Wall Street Journal* (December 4, 1985), available online at: www.westlaw.com.

2. Jerry W. Markham and David J. Gilberg, "Stock and Commodity Options—Two Regulatory Approaches and Their Conflicts," *Albany Law Review* 47 (spring 1983): 743–744.

3. *In re* Daily Income Fund, Inc., Investment Company Act Release No. 10,451 (October 26, 1978) (exemption grated to a large number of firms); 17 C.F.R. § 270. 2a-7 (2003); Joseph A. Franco, "The Investment Company Act's Definition of 'Security' and the Myth of Equivalence," *Stanford Journal of Law, Business and Finance* 7 (autumn 2001): 38 n. 121.

4. 17 C.F.R. § 270.12b-1 (1980).

5. Senator Jim Saxton, *The Mutual Fund Industry: An Overview and Analysis* (H.R. Jt. Econ. Comm., 107th Cong., 2nd sess., February 2002): 3, 8–9, available online at: www .house.gov/jec/mutual2.pdf.

6. Jill E. Fisch, " From Legitimacy to Logic: Reconstructing Proxy Regulation," *Vanderbilt Law Review* 46 (October 1993): 1137.

7. Alon Brav and J. B. Heaton, "Market Indeterminacy," *Journal of Corporation Law* 28 (summer 2003): 517.

8. Homer Kripke, "The SEC, the Accountants, Some Myths and Some Realities," *New York University Law Review* (November 1970): 1145.

9. 15 U.S.C. § 77a et seq. (2000).

10. Plain English Disclosure, Securities Act Release No. 7497, 63 Fed. Reg. 6370 (Feb. 6, 1998) (codified at 17 C.F.R. § 230.421(d) (2003)).

11. Daniel R. Fischel and Frank H. Easterbrook, "Contract and Fiduciary Duty," *Journal of Law and Economics* 36 (April 1993): 425–446; see Wsol v. Fiduciary Mgmt. Assocs., No. 99 C 1719, 2000 U.S. Dist. LEXIS 955 (N.D. Ill. Jan. 27, 2000) (bench trial), *aff'd*, 266 F.3d 654 (7th Cir. 2001), *cert. denied*, 535 U.S. 927 (2002).

12. See, e.g., Tamar Frankel, "Fiduciary Law," *California Law Review* 71 (May 1983): 795.

13. Frankel, "Fiduciary Law," 795–836.

14. Moore v. Regents of the Univ. of Cal., 793 P.2d 479 (Cal. 1990).

15. Anne Barnard, "Board Says Surgery Halted for Bank Trip: Doctor Suspended for Leaving Patient," *Boston Globe*, August 8, 2002, available online at: www.lexis-nexis.com.

16. *In re* Walt Disney Co. Deriv. Litig., 825 A.2d 275 (Del. Ch. 2003).

17. *In re* Walt Disney Co., 2004 WL 550750 (Del. Ch. Mar. 9, 2004).

18. Steven Pearlstein and Peter Behr, "At Enron, the Fall Came Quickly; Complexity, Partnerships Kept Problems from Public View," *Washington Post*, December 2, 2001, available online at: www.lexis-nexis.com.

19. Gary Strauss, "Do Conflicts Cloud the Objectivity of Corporate Boards?" *USA Today*, March 5, 2002, available online at: www.lexis-nexis.com.

20. 15 U.S.C. § 80a-2(a)(19) (A) (iii), (B) (vii)(2000).

21. SEC v. Warde, 151 F.3d 42, 49–50 (2d Cir. 1998).

22. Snepp v. United States, 444 U.S. 507 (1980).

23. Daniel R. Fischel and Frank H. Easterbrook, "Contract and Fiduciary Duty," *Journal of Law and Economics* 36 (April 1993): 425–446.

24. Tamar Frankel, "Fiduciary Duties as Default Rules," *Oregon Law Review* 74 (winter 1995): 1212–1213.

25. Daniel R. Fischel, "The 'Race to the Bottom' Revisited: Reflections on Recent Developments in Delaware's Corporation Law," *Northwestern University Law Review* 76 (February 1982): 917.

26. See, e.g., Del. Code Ann. tit. 8, § 102(b)(7) (2001) (allowing in most cases a provision in the certificate of incorporation eliminating personal liability of directors for breach of fiduciary duty of care).

27. See, e.g., Richard A. Epstein, "Contract and Trust in Corporate Law: The Case of Corporate Opportunity," *Delaware Journal of Corporate Law* 21, 1 (1996): 13–24.

28. Unif. P'ship Act, § 21 (1914), 6 (pt. I) U.L.A. 275, 6 (pt. II) U.L.A. 194 (2001).

29. Unif. P'ship Act, § 21 (1997), 6 (pt. I) U.L.A. 1, 6 (2001).

30. Unif. P'ship Act, § 103 (1997), 6 (pt. I) U.L.A. 1, 73–74 (2001).

31. Unif. P'ship Act, § 103 cmt. 1 (1997), 6 (pt. I) U.L.A. 1, 74 (2001).

32. Wsol v. Fiduciary Mgmt. Assocs., 266 F.3d 654 (7th Cir. 2001), *cert. denied*, 535 U.S. 927 (2002). I consulted and was involved in a related case of *SEC v. Blizzard*, Initial Decisions Release No. 229, June 13, 2003.

9. The Shift from Professions to Businesses

1. Roscoe Pound, "The Professions in Society Today," *New England Journal of Medicine*, September 8, 1949, 351.

2. Pound, "Professions in Society Today," 352.

3. Pound, "Professions in Society Today," 352.

4. "Constance Fairfax's Commonplace Book: A Brief Introduction to British Academic Costume," available online at the website of the University of Chicago: http://home.uchicago .edu/~atterlep/costuming/academic%20clothing.htm [May 5, 2005].

5. Cynthia W. Rossano, "Reading the Regalia: A Guide to Deciphering the Academic Dress Code," *Harvard Magazine,* May–June 1999, available online at: www.harvardmagazine .com/issues/mj99/ner.reading.html

6. Noel Cox, "Academic Dress in New Zealand: The Hood," available online at: www .geocities.com/noelcox/Introduction.htm.

7. Walter T. Eccard, "A Revolution in White: New Approaches in Treating Nurses as Professionals," *Vanderbilt Law Review* 30 (May 1977): 841–842.

8. See, e.g., 17 C.F.R. § 270.3a-7 (2004).

9. 433 U.S. 350 (1977).

10. See Va. St. Bd. of Pharm. v. Va. Citizens Consumer Council, Inc., 425 U.S. 748, 773 n.25 (1976).

11. Shapero v. Ky. B. Assn., 486 U.S. 466, 491 (1988) (O'Connor, J., Rehnquist, C. J., and Scalia, J., dissenting).

12. Roscoe Pound, "The Professions in Society Today," *New England Journal of Medicine,* September 8, 1949, 353.

13. M. Gregg Bloche, "Trust and Betrayal in the Medical Marketplace," *Stanford Law Review* 55 (December 2002): 923.

14. Bloche, "Trust and Betrayal in the Medical Marketplace," 943.

15. Bloche, "Trust and Betrayal in the Medical Marketplace."

16. Warren Weaver, Jr., "U.S. Warns Doctors against Agreements on Fixing of Prices," *New York Times* (December 7, 1988), available online at: www.lexis-nexis.com.

17. David Wessel, "Venal Sins: Why the Bad Guys of the Boardroom Emerged en Masse," *Wall Street Journal,* June 20, 2002, available online at: www.westlaw.com.

18. Tom Herman, "As Crackdown on Abusive Schemes Widens, Wealthy Taxpayers Weigh Pros, Cons of Tough Settlement," *Wall Street Journal,* June 3, 2004, available online at: www.westlaw.com.

19. Cassell Bryan-Low, "KPMG Didn't Register Strategy," *Wall Street Journal,* November 17, 2003, available online at: www.westlaw.com.

20. Tom Herman, "As Crackdown on Abusive Schemes Widens," *Wall Street Journal,* June 3, 2004, available online at: www.westlaw.com.

21. Aric Press and Susan Beck, "Almost a Revolution," *American Lawyer,* May 2004, available online at: www.lexis-nexis.com.

22. ABA Section on Law Practice Management, "Beyond the Billable Hour," July 11, 2002, Fax Form 858 693–8969,.

23. Jathon Sapsford, "Lawyers Profit by Challenging Colleagues' Fees," *Wall Street Journal,* May 7, 2004, available online at: www.lexis-nexis.com.

24. Louise O'Brien, "How to Restore the Fiduciary Relationship: An Interview with Eliot Spitzer," *Harvard Business Review* 82 (May 2004): 72.

25. Schroeter and Cox, "Estimating the Distribution of Search Costs and Reservation Prices: An Application to Routine Legal Services Markets," paper given at Arizona State University, 1986), cited in Jim Rossi and Mollie Weighner, student authors, "An Empirical Examination of the Iowa Bar's Approach to Regulating Lawyer Advertising," *Iowa Law Review* 77 (October 1991): 230.

26. This brochure is on file with the author.

27. David M. Studdert, Michelle M. Mello, and Troyen A. Brennan, "Financial Conflicts of Interest in Physicians' Relationships with the Pharmaceutical Industry: Self-Regulation in the Shadow of Federal Prosecution," *New England Journal of Medicine,* October 28, 2004, 1891.

28. David Blumenthal, "Doctors and Drug Companies," *New England Journal of Medicine,* October 28, 2004, 1895.

29. Blumenthal, "Doctors and Drug Companies," 1888 n. 10, citing the concerns of the American College of Physicians.

30. David Labrador, "News Scan, Damage Control," *Scientific American,* November 2004, 18–19.

31. Labrador, "News Scan."

32. Helen Dewar, "Medical Liability Curbs Blocked; Senate GOP's Bill Targeted OB-GYNs," *Washington Post,* February 25, 2004, available online at: www.lexis-nexis.com.

33. David L. Hudson, Jr., "Professional Judgment: Courts Are Pondering Whether Consumer Fraud Laws Apply to Lawyers and Doctors," *ABA Journal,* July 2002, 14. The article cites Macedo v. Dello Russo, 819 A.2d 5 (N.J. Super. 2003).

34. Macedo v. Dello Russo, 819 A.2d 5, 9 (N.J. Super. 2003).

35. 15 U.S.C. §§ 77(d), (g), (j) (2000).

36. SEC v. Ralston Purina Co., 346 U.S. 119 (1953).

37. Doran v. Petroleum Mgmt. Corp., 545 F.2d 893 (5th Cir. 1977).

38. 17 C.F.R. §§ 230.501–.508 (2003). Rule 506 defines "accredited investors."

39. Frederick Schauer, "The Convergence of Rules and Standards," *New Zealand Law Review,* pt. 3 (2003): 303–328.

40. SEC v. Allaire, Litigation Release No. 18,174 (June 5, 2003); Stephanie Strom, "Foundation to Keep Leader Accused of Fraud at Xerox," *New York Times,* July 8, 2003, available online at: www.lexis-nexis.com.

41. Office of the Chief Accountant, United States Securities and Exchange Commission, *Study Pursuant to Section 108(d) of the Sarbanes-Oxley Act of 2002 on the Adoption by the United States Financial Reporting System of a Principles-Based Accounting System,* available online at the website of the Securities and Exchange Commission: www.sec.gov/news/studies/principlesbasedstand.htm (July 25, 2003)

42. Tom Baker, Alon Harel, and Tamar Kugler, "The Virtues of Uncertainty in Law: An Experimental Approach," version 4.3, November 11, 2002, available online at: http://ideas.repec.org/p/huj/dispap/dp310.html#download.

43. William C. Powers, Jr., Raymond S. Troubh, and Herbert S. Winokur, Jr., *Report of Investigation by the Special Investigative Committee of the Board of Directors of Enron Corp.* (February 1, 2002), 12–177; Robert Vosper, "GCs Weigh the Dangers of Engaging in Risky Business," *Corporate Legal Times,* September 2003, available online at: www.lexis-nexis.com.

44. Victor Brudney, "Contract and Fiduciary Duty in Corporate Law," *Boston College Law Review* 38 (July 1997): 617–618.

45. 15 U.S.C. § 80a-2© (2000). In enacting regulations, the SEC must consider the effect of the regulation on capital formation. National Securities Markets Improvement Act of 1996, Pub. L. No. 104–290, § 106)©, 110 Stat. 3416, 3425.

46. *In re* Enron Corp., Investment Company Act Rel. No. 22,515, Feb. 14, 1997 (application); *In re* Enron Corp., Investment Company Act Rel. No. 22,560, Mar. 13, 1997 (order granted). Enron Corp. Public University Holding Co. Act Rel. No. 24,428, July 23, 1987 (order granted).

47. Commodity Futures Modernization Act of 2000, Pub. L. No. 106–554, 114 Stat. 2763.

48. Michael Schroeder and Greg Ip, "Out of Reach: The Enron Debacle Spotlights Huge Void in Financial Regulation," *Wall Street Journal,* December 13, 2001, available online at: www.westlaw.com.

49. Quoted in "Perspectives," *Newsweek,* February 4, 2002, available online at: www.lexis-nexis.com.

50. Douglas Baird, "Enron and the Long Shadow of Stat. 13 Eliz.," *Northwestern University School of Law, Law and Economics Colloquium Series,* February 20, 2003, 1–5.

10. In Markets We Trust

1. Abrams v. United States, 250 U.S. 616, 630 (1919).

2. Roberta Romano, "Law as a Product: Some Pieces of the Incorporation Puzzle," *Journal of Law, Economics, and Organization* (Fall 1985): 225.

3. Daniel A. Farber and Phillip P. Frickey, "The Jurisprudence of Public Choice," *Texas Law Review* 65 (April 1987): 890–899.

4. Tamar Frankel, "The Managing Lawmaker in Cyberspace: A Power Model," *Brooklyn Journal of International Law* 27, 3 (2002): 859 (using an analogy to contestable markets theory).

5. Robert C. Ellickson, "The Market for Social Norms," *American Law and Economics Review* 3 (spring 2001): 1–49.

6. Richard A. Posner, "The Regulation of the Market in Adoptions," *Boston University Law Review* 67 (January 1987): 59; see also Tamar Frankel and Francis H. Miller, "The Inapplicability of Market Theory to Adoptions," *Boston University Law Review* 67 (January 1987): 99.

7. ABA Law Practice Management Section, in cooperation with Internet Bar Training, presentation of 120–minute live web seminar, "Beyond the Billable Hour," faxed on July 11, 2002; 17:13:28.

8. Pooled-income funds: I.R.C. §§ 170(f)(2)(A), 2522(c)(2)(A), 2955(e)(2)(A), 642(c)(5). Charitable Gift Annuities: I.R.C. § 170, Split-Interest Charitable Trusts: §§ 170(f)(2)(A), 2055(e)(2)(A), 2522(c)(2)(A).

9. Investment Company Act of 1940, § 3(c)(10), 15 U.S.C. § 80a-3(c)(10) (2000).

10. Armin Falk, "Charitable Giving as a Gift Exchange: Evidence from a Field Experiment," working paper series no. 1218, IZA Research Institute, June 2004, available online at: http://ssrn.com/abstract=560281.

11. Tamar Frankel, "The Legal Infrastructure of Markets: The Role of Contract and Property Law," *Boston University Law Review* 73 (May 1993): 389–405.

12. George W. Dent, Jr., "Gap Fillers and Fiduciary Duties in Strategic Alliances," *Business Lawyer* 57 (November 2001): 66.

13. Warren S. Grimes, "Antitrust and the Systemic Bias against Small Business: Kodak, Strategic Conduct, and Leverage Theory," *Case Western Reserve Law Review* 52 (Fall 2001): 236–237.

14. Matthew M. Sanderson, "A 'Basic' Misunderstanding: How the United States Supreme Court Misunderstands Capital Markets," comment, *South Texas Law Review* 43 (Summer 2002): 758.

15. William J. Brodsky, "New Legislation Permitting Stock Futures: The Long and Winding Road," *Northwestern Journal of International Law and Business* 21 (Spring 2001): 584.

16. E.g. Mass. Gen. Laws Ann. ch. 112, §§ 87PP–87DDD½ (St. Paul, Minn.: West, 2003). E.g. Mass. Gen. Laws Ann. ch. 140D, §4(e) (St. Paul, Minn.: West, 2002).

17. See Lisa Bernstein, "Opting Out of the Legal System: Extralegal Contractual Relations in the Diamond Industry," *Journal of Legal Studies* 21 (January 1992): 115–157; Roger Stard, "The Editorial Notebook; The Real Treasure of Forty-seventh Street," *New York Times*, March 26, 1984, available online at: www.lexis-nexis.com; Stanley Penn, "Don't Mention Name of Martin Rapaport in Diamond District—Or Stones May Start Flying," *Wall Street Journal*, February 13, 1986, available online at: www.westlaw.com.

18. NASD Regulation, *Statutory Disqualification Process*, available online at: www.nasdr .com/sd_process.asp (December 1, 2003).

19. Tamar Frankel, "Trusting and Non-Trusting on the Internet," *Boston University Law Review* 81 (April 2001): 472.

20. "E-Commerce Sites Lose Customers When the Color Isn't Correct, According to Online Shopper Study Commissioned by Imation," *Business Wire*, March 14, 2002, available online at: www.lexis-nexis.com.

21. Square Trade is available online at: www.squaretrade.com.

22. Shannon Henry, "Networking without the Wine and Cheese," *Washington Post*, January 15, 2004, available online at: www.lexis-nexis.com.

23. John C. Coffee, Jr., "Understanding Enron: 'It's about the Gatekeepers, Stupid,'" *Business Lawyer*, August 2002, available online at: www.lexis-nexis.com.

24. Kevin Mitchell, "Antitrust Analysis: A Roadmap for Election Reform under the First Amendment," *CommLaw Conspectus* 10, 1 (2001): 158.

25. See George A. Akerlof, "The Market for 'Lemons': Quality, Uncertainty and the Market Mechanism," *Quarterly Journal of Economics* 84 (August 1970): 488 (Nobel Prize–winning article).

26. Michael M. Phillips, "The Economy: Fed Chief Sees More Profit Revision," *Wall Street Journal*, July 18, 2002, available online at: www.westlaw.com.

27. "World Business Briefing Europe: Spain: Telecom Payout Planned," *New York Times*, April 11, 2003, available online at: www.lexis-nexis.com.

28. Marcia Vickers, "The Quest for Quality," *Business Week*, June 28, 2004, 112.

29. Yuval Rosenberg, "Yield of Dreams," *Fortune*, July 12, 2004, available online at: www.lexis-nexis.com.

30. See Hollinger International, Inc. v. Black, 844 A.2d 1022 (Del. Ch. 2004).

31. George J. Stigler, "Economics: The Imperial Science?" *Scandinavian Journal of Economics* 86, 3 (1984): 311.

11. *Why Did Legal Enforcement Fail to Stem the Avalanche of Fraud?*

1. 15 U.S.C. § 77q (2000) (Securities Act); 15 U.S.C. §§ 78i(a)(4), 78j(b), 78o(c)(1), (2) (2000) (Securities Exchange Act).

2. 18 U.S.C. §§ 1956–1957 (2000).

3. 18 U.S.C. § 1341 (2000).

4. Mass. Gen. Laws ch. 266, § 34 (2002).

5. "When Something Is Rotten," *Economist*, U.S ed., July 27, 2002, available online at: www.lexis-nexis.com.

6. Gordon Tullock, "Does Punishment Deter Crime?" *Public Interest* 36 (1974): 103–111.

7. Peter Fimrite, "Did He Have a Deal for You," *San Francisco Chronicle*, February 15, 1998, available online at: www.lexis-nexis.com.

8. Fimrite, "Did He Have a Deal for You."

9. See Timothy D. Lane, "Can Market Forces Discipline Government Borrowing?" *Finance and Development,* March 1993, available online at: www.lexis-nexis.com.

10. "The Fall of Enron: How Could It Have Happened?" January 24, 2002, hearings before the United States Senate Committee on Governmental Affairs, 107th Cong., 2nd sess., (Washington, D.C.: U.S. Government Printing Office, 2002).

11. "Investors Psychology and Asset Pricing," *Journal of Finance* 56 (August 2001): 1533.

12. Donald C. Langevoort, "Selling Hope, Selling Risk: Some Lessons for Law from Behavioral Economics about Stockholders and Sophisticated Customers," *California Law Review* 84 (May 1996): 627.

13. Stephen J. Choi, "Regulating Investors Not Issuers: A Market-Based Proposal," *California Law Review* 88 (March 2000): 279–334. See also Stephen J. Choi and A. C. Prichard, "Behavioral Economics and the SEC," *Stanford Law Review* 56 (October 2003): 1.

14. Robert Prentice, "Whither Securities Regulation? Some Behavioral Observations Regarding Proposals for Its Future," *Duke Law Journal* 51 (March 2002): 1397.

15. Donald C. Langevoort, "Theories, Assumptions, and Securities Regulation: Market Efficiency Revisited," *University of Pennsylvania Law Review* 140 (January 1992): 851.

16. John A. Weinberg, "Accounting for Corporate Behavior," *Economic Quarterly* (Federal Reserve Bank of Richmond) 89 (summer 2003): 2.

17. "New Report by Huron Consulting Group Reveals Financial Restatements Increase at Record Level in 2004," January 20, 2005, available online at: http://huronconsultinggroup .com/general01.asp?id=779&related ProfessionalID=563 [May 8, 2005]; Stephen Bryan et al., "Undoing the Past: The Implications of Earnings Restatements," *Financial Executive,* March 1, 2005, available online at: www.lexis-nexis.com; see also "Long and Short: Corporate Regulation Must Be Working," *Wall Street Journal,* June 16, 2004, available online at: www.westlaw.com.

18. Theo Francis and Timothy Aeppel, "Moving the Market," *Wall Street Journal,* March 15, 2004, available online at: www.westlaw.com.

19. David Wessel, "What's Wrong?" *Wall Street Journal,* June 20, 2002, available online at: www.westlaw.com.,

20. Dirks v. SEC, 463 U.S. 646, 650 n.4 (1983).

21. Dirks v. SEC, 681 F.2d 824, 830 (D. C. Cir. 1982), rev'd, 463 U.S. 646 (1983).

22. Dirks v. SEC, 463 U.S. 646 (1983). See also T.W. McGarry, "Funeral Home Accused of Routine Falsification of Death Certificates," *Los Angeles Times,* September 27, 1987, available online at: www.lexis-nexis.com.

23. See the unique example of the Enron employee who wrote to the CEO: Joann S. Lubin, "Saving Your Career after Earning a Name as a Whistleblower," *Wall Street Journal,* February 5, 2002, available online at: www.westlaw.com.

24. Lubin, "Saving Your Career."

25. Henny Sender and Gregory Zuckerman, "Behind the Mutual-Fund Probe: Three Informants Opened Up," *Wall Street Journal,* December 9, 2003, available online at: www .lexis-nexis.com.

26. Am. International Life Assurance Co. v. Bartmann (N.D. Okla. 1999) (No. 99-CV-0862-C)

27. Dirks v. SEC, 463 U.S. 646 (1983).

28. See, e.g., Edgar Sanchez, "Apartment Finder Leaves Clients Bereft," *Sacramento Bee,* May 20, 2003, B2.

29. Terry Greene Sterling, "The Moneychangers: A New Times Investigation; First in a Series," *Phoenix New Times*, April 16, 1998, available online at: www.lexis-nexis.com.

30. Scott P. Johnson and Christopher E. Smith, "White House Scandals and the Presidential Pardon Power: Persistent Risks and Prospects for Reform," *New England Law Review* 33 (summer 1999): 916 n. 54.

31. Wendy Ehrenkranz, "Whistle Blowing as a Rule 10b-5 Violation: Dirks v. SEC," *University of Miami Law Review* 36 (September 1982): 987.

32. Robert L. D. Colby and Michael J. Simon, "The National Market System for Over-the-Counter Stocks," *George Washington Law Review* 55 (November 1986): 99–100; David C. Worley, "The Regulation of Short Sales: The Long and Short of It," *Brooklyn Law Review* 55 (winter 1990): 1283–1284.

33. 15 U.S.C. § 78p (1982) (section 16 of the Securities Exchange Act of 1934).

34. Roy A. Schotland, "ReExamining the Freedom of Information Act's Exemption 8: Does It Give an Unduly 'Full Service' Exemption for Bank Examination Reports and Related Material?" *Administrative Law Journal* 9 (spring 1995): 70.

35. Sharon Reece, "Enron: The Final Straw and How to Build Pensions of Brick," *Duquesne Law Review* 41 (fall 2002): 142–148; Michael Duffyet al., "What Did They Know . . . When Did They Know It? Meet Sharon Watkins, Who Sounded the Alarm on Enron Long before Its Collapse," *Time*, January 28, 2002, available online at: www.lexis-nexis.com.

36. U.S. Department of Justice Programs, Office for Victims of Crime, *Providing Services to Victims of Fraud: Resources for Victim/Witness Coordinators I-1*, July 1998.

37. U.S. Department of Justice Programs, Office for Victims of Crime, *Providing Services to Victims of Fraud;* "Regulators Sound Alarm on Affinity Scams," *Canada NewsWire*, January 29, 2002, available online at: www.lexis-nexis.com.

38. Lori Pugh, "Heartland Case a Warning to Investors," *Indianapolis Business Journal*, August 21, 2000, available online at: www.lexis-nexis.com.

39. Jonathan R. Macey, "Efficient Capital Markets, Corporate Disclosure, and Enron," *Cornell Law Review* 89 (January 2004): 394.

40. Ken Brown and Mark Heinzi, "Nortel Board Finds Accounting Tricks behind '03 Profits," *Wall Street Journal*, July 2, 2004, available online at: www.lexis-nexis.com.

41. Fimrite, "Did He Have a Deal for You."

42. Clifton Leaf, "White-Collar Criminals: They Lie, They Cheat, They Steal and They've Been Getting Away with It for Too Long," *Fortune*, March 18, 2002, available online at: www.lexis-nexis.com.

43. Dorreen E. Iudica, "Sting in Hotel Criticized by Aldermen," *Boston Globe*, May 13, 1990, available online at: www.lexis-nexis.com.

44. Leaf, "White-Collar Criminals."

45. "Savings and Loan Scandal," *In the 80s*, available online at: www.inthe80s.com/sandl.shtml [December 14, 2004].

46. Michael Waldman, "The S & L Collapse: The Cost of a Congress for Sale," *Stanford Law and Policy Review* 2 (spring 1990); Paulette Thomas, "GAO Puts Cost of S & L Rescue at $285 Billion," *Wall Street Journal*, May 22, 1989, available online at: www.westlaw.com.

47. This data is cited from SEC and Thomson Financial by Gail Snyder, "Consequence Change for CEO Crime," *PM*, September 24, 2002. available online at: www.pmezine.com/article_dtls.asp?NID=224 [December 29, 2003].

48. Fimrite, "Did He Have a Deal for You."

49. Jennifer Wells, "The Small Price of Big-Time Fraud," *Toronto Star,* May 22, 2002, available online at: www.lexis-nexis.com.

50. Michael L. Benson and Francis T. Cullen, "The Special Sensitivity of White-Collar Offenders to Prison: A Critique and Research Agenda," *Journal of Criminal Justice* 16, 3 (1988): 207.

51. Benson and Cullen, "Special Sensitivity of White-Collar Offenders to Prison," 214.

52. Gordon Tullock, "Does Punishment Deter Crime?" *Public Interest* (summer 1974): 103–111.

53. Tullock, "Does Punishment Deter Crime," 105. See also Robert Cooter, "Models of Morality in Law and Economics: Self-Control and Self-Improvement for the 'Bad Man' of Holmes," *Boston University Law Review* 78 (June 1998): 915.

54. Tullock, "Does Punishment Deter Crime,"110.

55. Louise O'Brien, "How to Restore the Fiduciary Relationship: An Interview with Eliot Spitzer," *Harvard Business Review* 82 (May 2004): 75.

56. Richard A. Posner, "Optimal Sentences for White-Collar Criminals," *American Criminal Law Review* 17 (1980): 410.

57. Cooter, "Models of Morality in Law and Economics," 905–914.

58. Thad A. Davis, "A New Model of Securities Law Enforcement," *Cumberland Law Review* 32, 1 (2001–2002): 111.

59. Ronald J. Gilson and Reiner Kraakman, "Reinvesting the Outside Director: An Agenda for Institutional Investors," *Stanford Law Review* 43 (April 1991): 863–904.

60. See 15 U.S.C. § 77t(e) (2000) (Securities Act); 15 U.S.C. § 78u(d)(2) (2000) (Securities Exchange Act). In the mutual fund area, at least 40 percent and in most cases 50 percent of the directors must be independent of the advisor whom they supervise. The definition of independence is quite broad, and includes close connections with the advisors and underwriters of the funds' shares. In this case, disqualification is partial. A disqualified director may still sit on the board, but not as an independent director. See Investment Company Act of 1940, § 2(a)(19), 15 U.S.C. § 80a-2(a)(19) (2000).

61. William D. Harrington, "Business Associations," *Syracuse Law Review* 46 (1995):272.

62. Sarbanes-Oxley Act of 2002, Pub. L. No. 107–204, § 1105, 2002 U.S.C.C.A.N. (116. Stat.), 745, 809–10 (to be codified at 15 U.S.C. §§ 77h-1(f), 78u-3(f)) (the SEC is authorized to issue a cease and desist order against any person who violated section 10(b) and the rules thereunder, prohibiting such a person from serving as an officer or a director of any issuer of securities registered under section 12 of the Securities Exchange Act of 1934).

63. The list is on file with the author.

64. SEC v. Allaire, Litigation Release No. 18,174 (June 5, 2003).

65. Stephanie Strom, "Foundation to Keep Leader Accused of Fraud at Xerox," *New York Times,* July 8, 2003, available online at: www.lexis-nexis.com.

66. Gary Johns, "A Multi-Level Theory of Self-Serving Behavior in and by Organizations," *Research in Organizational Behavior* 21 (1999): 14.

67. Patrick Barta, John D. McKinnon, and Jon E. Hilsenrath, "Board's Revolt at Freddie Mac Led to Ousters," *Wall Street Journal,* June 23, 2003, available online at: www.westlaw .com/; Patrick Barta, John D. McKinnon, and Gregory Zuckerman, "Freddie Mac Probe Examines New CEO's Role," *Wall Street Journal,* July 11, 2003, available online at: www .westlaw.com.

68. Constance L. Hays, "Former Chief of ImClone Is Given Seven-Year Term," *New York Times,* June 11, 2003, available online at: www.lexis-nexis.com.

69. Kurt Eichenwald, "Former Enron Treasurer Enters Guilty Plea," *New York Times*, September 11, 2003, available online at: www.lexis-nexis.com.

70. Kurt Eichenwald, "Former Enron Executive Pleads Guilty," *New York Times*, October 31, 2003, available online at: www.lexis-nexis.com.

71. Mike France, Julia Cosgrove, and Susann Rutledge, "Heiress in Handcuffs," *Business Week*, November 24, 2003, available online at: www.lexis-nexis.com.

72. "The Ex-Bosses Fight Back," *Economist*, U.S. ed., April 12, 2003, available online at: www.lexis-nexis.com.

73. "CNN Lou Dobbs Moneyline," *CNN.com*, May 14, 2003, available online at: www.coloringthenews.com/html/cnn_lou_dobbs_moneyline_on_c.html [May 5, 2005].

74. This data is cited from SEC and Thomson Financial by Snyder, "Consequence Change for CEO Crime," *Performance Management Magazine*, September 24, 2004.

75. "Executives on Trial," *Wall Street Journal Online*, available online at: http://online.wsj.com/page/0,,2_1040,00.html?mod=home_in_depth_reports (last modified July 22, 2004) [July 24, 2004].

76. John R. Emshwiller, "Enron Ex-Official Pleads Guilty to Fraud, Agrees to Aid Probe," *Wall Street Journal*, August 2, 2004, available online at: www.westlaw.com.

77. Securities and Exchange Commission, "2004 Annual Performance Plan and 2002 Annual Performance Report, March 2003," available online at the website of the Securities and Exchange Commission: www.sec.gov/about/gpra2004_2002.pdf; Federal Deposit Insurance Corporation, "2003 Annual Report," available online at the website of the Federal Deposit Insurance Corporation: www.fdic.gov/about/strategic/report/2003annualreport/index.html.

78. Securities and Exchange Commission, "2004 Annual Performance Plan."

79. Securities and Exchange Commission, "2004 Annual Performance Plan."

80. "The Ex-Bosses Fight Back."

81. Brooke A. Masters, "Banker Pleads Not Guilty; Quattrone Arraigned on Obstruction Charges," *Washington Post*, May 28, 2003, available online at: www.lexis-nexis.com.

82. O'Brien, "How to Restore the Fiduciary Relationship," 76.

83. Bob Keefe, "WorldCom Settlement Approved; $750 Million Deal Lets Firm Survive, Reimburses Investors," *Atlanta Journal and Constitution*, July 8, 2003, available online at: www.lexis-nexis.com.

84. Rob Kaiser, "Motorola CEO Galvin Resigns," *Chicago Tribune*, September 20, 2003, available online at: www.lexis-nexis.com; Dan Reed, "Carty Resigns as Two Unions Agree to New Concessions," *USA Today*, April 24, 2003, available online at: www.lexis-nexis.com; Jesse Drucker and Joann S. Lublin, "Motorola Searches for a New CEO," *Wall Street Journal*, September 22, 2003, available online at: www.westlaw.com.

85. Reed, "Carty Resigns."

86. Patrick Barta, John D. McKinnon, and John R. Wilke, "Freddie Mac Gives Large Parachutes," *Wall Street Journal*, June 12, 2003, available online at: www.westlaw.com.

87. Kate Kelly and Susanne Craig, "Weakened NYSE Must Face Challenges," *Wall Street Journal*, September 18, 2003, available online at: www.westlaw.com.

88. Stephanie Kang, "Callaway Golf Chairman and CEO Drapeau Resigns," *Wall Street Journal*, August 3, 2004, available online at: www.westlaw.com.

89. Mitchell Pacelle and Monica Langley, "Citigroup's Weill Taps a Top Aide as His Successor," *Wall Street Journal*, July 17, 2003, available online at: www.westlaw.com.

90. This list is on file with the author.

91. Matthew Boyle, "When Will They Stop?" *Fortune*, May 3, 2004, available online at: www.lexis-nexis.com.

92. Ruth Simon and Louise Story, "Independent Research Hits Wall Street: Starting Today, Major Firms Must Provide Clients with Stock Recommendations by Outsiders," *Wall Street Journal*, July 27, 2004, available online at: www.westlaw.com.

93. Susanne Craig and Randall Smith, "Last Stock-Case Holdouts to Pay," *Wall Street Journal*, July 14, 2004, available online at: www.westlaw.com.

94. Paul Schott Stevens, "America's Mutual Funds: The Road Ahead," National Press Club Luncheon speech, June 15, 2004, available online at the website of the Investment Company Institute: www.ici.org/statements/remarks/04_npc_stevens_speech.html#TopOfPage.

95. John M. Donnelly, "Debate Simmers on Contractor Ethics," *Defense Week*, November 24, 2003, available online at: www.lexis-nexis.com.

96. Don Van Natta, Jr., "Enron's Collapse: The Politicians," *New York Times*, January 21, 2002, available online at: www.lexis-nexis.com.

97. Omnicare, Inc. v. Healthcare Inc., 818 A.2d 914 (Del. 2003); MM Cos. v. Liquid Audio, Inc., 813 A.2d 1118 (Del. 2003); Saito v. McKesson HBOC, Inc., 806 A.2d 113 (Del. 2002); Levco Alternative Fund Ltd. v. Reader's Digest Ass'n, 803 A.2d 428 (Del. 2002); Telxon Corp. v. Meyerson, 802 A.2d 257 (Del. 2002).

98. *In re* Walt Disney Company Derivative Litigation, 825 A.2d 275, 291 (Del. Ch. 2003).

99. Sarbanes-Oxley Act of 2002, Pub. L. No. 107–204, § 1105, 2002 U.S.C.C.A.N. (116. Stat.), 745, 809–10 (to be codified at 15 U.S.C. §§ 77h-1(f), 78u-3(f)).

100. Russ Mitchell, "White Collar Criminal? Pack Lightly for Prison," *New York Times*, August 11, 2002, available online at: www.lexis-nexis.com.

101. Act of October 12, 1984, Pub. L. No. 98–473, § 218(a)(5), 98 Stat. 1837, 2027.

102. 18 U.S.C. § 3624(a); "The Unconstitutionality of Determinate Sentencing in Light of the Supreme Court's 'Elements' Jurisprudence," note, *Harvard Law Review* 117 (February 2004): 1250.

103. Sarbanes-Oxley Act of 2002, Pub. L. No. 107–204, §§ 902, 116 Stat. 745, 805 (codified at 18 U.S.C.A. § 1349 (Supp. 2004).

104. Sarbanes-Oxley Act of 2002, Pub. L. No. 107–204, §§ 903–904, 116 Stat. 745, 805 (codified at 18 U.S.C.A. §§ 1341, 1343 (Supp. 2004)).

105. Sarbanes-Oxley Act of 2002, Pub. L. No. 107–204, §§ 805, 905, 1104, 116 Stat. 745, 802, 805–06, 808–09.

106. United States Sentencing Commission, Sentencing Guidelines for United States Courts, 68 Fed. Reg. 3080 (January 2, 2003); United States Sentencing Commission, Sentencing Guidelines for United States Courts, 68 Fed. Reg. 36,960 (May 16, 2003).

107. Craig and Smith, "Last Stock-Case Holdouts to Pay."

108. Jonathan Weil, "Win Law Suit—and Pay $300 Million," *Wall Street Journal*, August 2, 2004, available online at: www.westlaw.com.

109. Suzanne Vranica, "Nike Stands by Jones, Not Her Man," *Wall Street Journal*, August 6, 2004, available online at: www.westlaw.com.

12. *Toward an Honest Society*

1. Harold Garfinkel, "A Conception of, and Experiments with, 'Trust' as a Condition of Stable Concerted Actions," in *Motivation and Social Interaction*, edited by O. J. Harvey (New York: Ronald Press, 1963): 187–238.

2. Matt Ridley, "What Makes You Who You Are," *Time*, June 2, 2003, available online at: www.lexis-nexis.com.

3. "Famous Quote from Sir Winston Churchill," *Liberty-Tree.ca*, available online at: http://quotes.liberty-tree.ca/quotes.nsf/quotes5/fcc18d1e19d8e5e385256a7e001bfeae [December 14, 2004].

4. Charles Camic, "The Matter of Habit," *American Journal of Sociology* 91 (March 1986): 1058–1059, quoting Max Weber, *Economy and Society,* edited by Guenther Roth and Claus Wittich (1922; reprint, Berkeley: University of California Press, 1978), 31, 312, m.t.; and Weber, *Wirtschaft und Gesselschaft,* edited by Johannes Winckelmann, 5th rev. ed. (1922; reprint, Tubingen: Mohr, 1980), 16, 182.

5. National Center for State Courts, *Examining the Work of State Courts,* 2003, available online at the website of the National Center for State Courts: www.ncsconline.org/D_Research/csp/2003_Files/2003_Main_Page.html; Administrative Office of the U.S. Courts, *Federal Judicial Caseload Statistics,* Mar. 31, 2003, available online at: www.uscourts.gov/caseload2002/contents.html.

6. U.S. population in 2003 estimated at 291 million. U.S. Census, "Population Estimates Program," available at: http://eire.census.gov/popest/estimates.php.

7. U.S. Dept. of Justice, Office of Justice Programs, Bureau of Justice Statistics, *Criminal Offenders Statistics 2001,* available online at: www.ojp.usdoj.gov/bjs/crimoff.htm.

8. David E. Francis, "The Rocky Road to Mutual-Fund Morality," *Christian Science Monitor,* June 28, 2004, available online at: www.lexis-nexis.com.

9. Francis, "The Rocky Road."

10. "When Something Is Rotten," *Economist*, U.S. ed., July 27, 2002, available online at: www.lexis-nexis.com/ (citing Lawrence Weinbach).

11. See Alex Geisinger, "A Belief Change Theory of Expressive Law," *Iowa Law Review* 88 (October 2002): 35–73.

12. Geisinger, "Belief Change Theory of Expressive Law."

13. Gordon Tullock, "Does Punishment Deter Crime?" *Public Interest* 36 (summer 1974): 103–111.

14. See, e.g., David Overlock Stewart, "Raising the Stakes: Resisting the Upward Transformation of Antitrust and Fraud Charges," *American Journal of Criminal Law* 20 (winter 1993): 210.

15. Dan M. Kahan, "Trust, Collective Action and the Law," *Boston University Law Review* 81 (April 2001): 335–338.

16. Kahan, "Trust, Collective Action and the Law," 335–338; Tom R. Tyler, "Trust and Law Abidingness: A Proactive Model of Social Regulation," *Boston University Law Review* 81 (April 2001): 361–406.

17. Tyler, "Trust and Law Abidingness."

18. William H. Donaldson, chairman of the SEC, remarks to the National Press Club, July 30, 2003, available online at the website of the Securities and Exchange Commission: www.sec.gov/news/speech/spch073003whd.htm.

19. Leo Herzel and Laura D. Richman, "Delaware's Preeminence by Design," foreword to R. Franklin Balotti and Jesse A. Finkelstein, *The Delaware Law of Corporations and Business Organizations* 1, F-1, 4th ed. (New York: Aspen, 2003).

20. *In re* Walt Disney Co., 825 A.2d 275, 289–290 (Del. Ch. 2003); *see also* Omnicare, Inc. v. NCS Healthcare, Inc., 818 A.2d 914, 939 (Del. 2003); MM Cos., Inc. v. Liquid Audio, Inc.,

813 A.2d 1118, 1132 (Del. 2003); Levco Alternative Fund, Ltd. v. Reader's Digest Assn., Inc., 803 A.2d 428 (table) 2002 WL 1859064 at *1 (Del. August 13, 2002).

21. Gary Young, "Fifty Law Firms Subpoenaed in Enron Inquiry," *National Law Journal*, March 10, 2003, available online at: www.westlaw.com.

22. See, e.g., Henry A. McKinnell, "Bad Medicine for Good Governance," *Wall Street Journal*, October 21, 2003, available online at: www.westlaw.com.

23. Kenneth A. Bamberger, "Blurring Boundaries: Regulated First, Discretion and Accountability in the Administrative State," working draft, 2004 (on file with the author; cited with the permission of Kenneth A. Bamberger), 5.

24. "Boeing Fires CEO over Relationship," cnn.com, March 7, 2005, available online at www.lexis-nexis.com; J. Lynn Lunsford and Andy Pasztor, "New Boss Struggles to Lift Boeing above Military Scandals," *Wall Street Journal*, July 14, 2004, available online at: www.westlaw .com.

25. Bill George, "Why It's Hard to Do What's Right," *Fortune*, September 29, 2003, available online at: www.lexis-nexis.com.

26. Tyler, "Trust and Law Abidingness."

27. Insurance Research Council, "One in Three Americans Say It's Acceptable to Inflate Insurance Claims, but Public Acceptance of Insurance Fraud Is Declining," July 24, 2003, available online at the website of the Insurance Research Council: www.ircweb.org/news/ 200307242.htm.

28. Daniel Kahneman, Jack L. Knetsch, and Richard H. Thaler, "Fairness and the Assumptions of Economics," *Journal of Business* 59 (October 1986): S285–300.

29. Melvin A. Eisenberg, "Corporate Law and Social Norms," *Columbia Law Review* 99 (June 1999): 1253 n. 10; Elizabeth S. Scott, "Social Norms and Legal Regulation of Marriage," *Virginia Law Review* 86 (November 2000): 1922 n. 48.

30. Robert E. Scott, "The Limits of Behavioral Theories of Law and Social Norms," *Virginia Law Review* 86 (November 2000): 1610–1611.

31. Richard H. McAdams, "The Origin, Development, and Regulation of Norms," *Michigan Law Review* 96 (November 1997): 366, 372.

32. Francis Fukuyama, "Differing Disciplinary Perspectives on the Origin of Trust," *Boston University Law Review* 81 (April 2001): 492–493.

33. *Sarbanes-Oxley Act of 2002*, Pub. L. No. 107–204, § 307, 116 Stat. 745, 784 (2003).

34. Mitchell Pacelle and Laurie P. Cohen, "J. P. Morgan, Citigroup Will Pay $305 Million to Settle Enron Case," *Wall Street Journal*, July 29, 2003, available online at: www.westlaw .com.

35. Timur Kuran and Cass R. Sunstein, "Availability Cascades and Risk Regulation," *Stanford Law Review* 51 (April 1999): 711.

36. "Famous Quote from Samuel Adams," *Liberty-Tree.ca*, available online at: http://quotes .liberty-tree.ca/quotes.nsf/quotes5/d336d397bf6233fa85256a8b002624fe [December 15, 2004].

37. Thinkexist.com, available online at: http://en.thinkexist.com/quotes/edmund_burke [May 15, 2005].

38. Carl Huse, "Congress Shuts Pentagon Unit over Privacy," *New York Times*, September 20, 2003, available online at: www.lexis-nexis.com.

39. "Economics Focus, Guessing Games, Economists and Policymakers Are Just Beginning to Understand the Use of Information Markets," *Economist*, U.S. ed., November 20, 2004, available online at: www.lexis-nexis.com.

40. "Economics Focus, Guessing Games."

41. Cass Sunstein, "Group Judgements: Deliberation, Statistical Means, and Information Markets," *New York University Law Review,* forthcoming (2005).

42. Sunstein, "Group Judgements."

43. "Making Companies Work," *Economist,* U.S. ed., October 25, 2003, available online at: www.lexis-nexis.com.

44. Daniel P. Moynihan, "Defining Deviancy Down," *American Scholar* 63 (winter 1993): 19.

Bibliography

American Psychiatric Association. *Diagnostic and Statistical Manual of Mental Disorders.* 4th ed., text revision. Washington, D.C.: American Psychiatric Association, 2000.

Avolio, Bruce J. *Full Leadership Development: Building the Vital Forces in Organizations.* Thousand Oaks, Calif.: Sage, 1999.

Axelrod, Robert. *The Complexity of Cooperation: Agent-Based Models of Competition and Collaboration.* Princeton: Princeton University Press, 1997.

Barber, Bernard. *The Logic and Limits of Trust.* New Brunswick, N.J.: Rutgers University Press, 1983.

Bebchuk, Lucian, and Jesse Fried. *Pay without Performance: The Unfulfilled Promise of Executive Compensation.* Cambridge, Mass.: Harvard University Press, 2004.

Bok, Sissela. *Lying.* New York: Vintage Books, 1979.

Bonner, John Tyler. *Life Cycles: Reflections of an Evolutionary Biologist.* Princeton: Princeton University Press, 1993.

Bourdieu, Pierre. *Outline of a Theory of Practice.* Translated by Richard Nice. Cambridge: Cambridge University Press, 1977.

Brin, David. *The Transparent Society.* New York: Perseus Books, 1998.

Callahan, David. *The Cheating Culture: Why More Americans Are Doing Wrong to Get Ahead.* Orlando, Fl.: Harcourt, 2004.

Cass, Ronald A. *The Rule of Law in America.* Baltimore: Johns Hopkins University Press, 2001.

Ceraso, John, Howard Gruber, and Irvin Rock. "On Solomon Asch." In *The Legacy of Solomon Asch: Essays in Cognition and Social Psychology,* edited by Irvin Rock. Hillsdale, N.J.: Erlbaum, 1990.

Cialdini, Robert B. *Influence: The Psychology of Persuasion.* New York: Morrow, 1993.

Clinard, Marshall B., and Peter Yeager. *Corporate Crime: The First Comprehensive Account of Illegal Practices among America's Top Corporations.* New York: Free Press, 1980.

Cook, Fred J. *The Corrupted Land: The Social Morality of Modern America.* New York: Macmillan, 1966.

Corbin, Arthur Linton. *Corbin on Contracts.* Edited by John E. Murray, Jr., and Timothy Murray. 2004 spring cumulative supplement, rev. ed. Newark: LexisNexis Matthew Bender, 2004.

Deal, Terrence E., and Allan A. Kennedy. *The New Corporate Cultures.* New York: Perseus, 1999.

de Botton, Alain. *Status Anxiety.* New York: Pantheon Books, 2004.

DeMey, Dennis L., and James R. Flowers, Jr. *Don't Hire a Crook!* Tempe, Ariz.: Facts on Demand Press, 1999.

Dirks, Raymond L., and Leonard Gross. *The Great Wall Street Scandal.* New York: McGraw-Hill, 1974.

Drew, Daniel. *The Book of Daniel Drew.* New York: Frontier Press, 1969.

Frank, Robert H., and Philip J. Cook. *The Winner-Take-All Society.* New York: Free Press, 1995.

Frankel, Michael E. S. *Mergers and Acquisitions Basics.* New York: Wiley. 2005.

Frankel, Tamar, and Ann Taylor Schwing. *The Regulation of Money Managers.* 2nd ed. New York: Aspen, 2001 (supp. 2005).

Friedman, Milton. *Capitalism and Freedom.* Chicago: University of Chicago Press, 1962.

Fukuyama, Francis. *Trust: The Social Virtues and the Creation of Prosperity.* New York: Free Press, 1995.

Gambetta, Diego. *The Sicilian Mafia.* Cambridge, Mass.: Harvard University Press, 1993.

Giddens, Anthony. *The Consequences of Modernity.* Stanford: Stanford University Press, 1990.

Golomb, Elan. *Trapped in the Mirror.* New York: Morrow, 1992.

Goodman, Walter. *All Honorable Men: Corruption and Compromise in American Life.* Boston: Little, Brown, 1963.

Hayek, Friedrich A. *Law, Legislation and Liberty.* Chicago: University of Chicago Press, 1978.

Hoffman, Martin L. *Empathy and Moral Development.* Cambridge: Cambridge University Press, 2000.

Homans, George C. *The Human Group.* Somerset, N.J.: Transaction, 1951; reprint, 1992.

Hyde, Lewis. *Trickster Makes This World: Mischief, Myth, and Art.* New York: North Point Press, 1999.

Kaplow, Louis, and Steven Shavell. *Fairness versus Welfare.* Cambridge, Mass.: Harvard University Press, 2002.

Lifton, Robert Jay. *The Nazi Doctors: Medical Killing and the Psychology of Genocide.* New York: Basic Books, 1986.

Linden, Eugene. *The Parrot's Lament.* New York: Penguin Putnam, 2000.

Loewy, Arnold H. *Criminal Law.* 4th ed. St. Paul, Minn.: West, 2003.

Loss, Louis, and Joel Seligman. *Securities Regulation,* 3rd rev. ed. New York: Aspen, 2004.

Lowenstein, Roger. *Origins of the Crash: The Great Bubble and Its Undoing.* New York: Penguin Books, 2004.

Loye, David. *Darwin's Lost Theory of Love: A Healing Vision for the New Century.* New York: toExcel Press, 1998.

Lukes, Steven. *Emile Durkheim: His Life and Work.* Harmondsworth, U.K.: Penguin, 1973.

Lynn, Michael, and C. R. Snyder. "Uniqueness Seeking." In *Handbook of Positive Psychology,* edited by C. R. Snyder and Shane J. Lopez. Oxford: Oxford University Press, 2002.

Malloy, Michael P. *Banking Law and Regulation.* New York: Aspen, 1994.

Mansfield, Edwin. *Microeconomics: Theory/Applications.* New York: Norton, 1997.

McGovern, William M., Jr., and Sheldon F. Kurtz. *Wills, Trusts and Estates.* 2nd ed. St. Paul, Minn.: West, 2001.

McNeill, Daniel. *The Face.* Boston: Little, Brown, 1998.

Merriam-Webster's Collegiate Dictionary. 10th ed. Springfield, Mass.: Merriam-Webster, 1999.

Milgram, Stanley. *Obedience to Authority: An Experimental View.* New York: Harper and Row, 1974.

Misztal, Barbara A. *Trust in Modern Societies.* Cambridge: Polity Press, 1996.

Mitchell, Lawrence E. *Stacked Deck: A Story of Selfishness in America.* Philadelphia: Temple University Press, 1998.

Newman, John Q. *Identity Theft: The Cybercrime of the Millennium.* Port Townsend, Wash.: Loompanics Unlimited, 1999.

Offer, Avner. "The Mask of Intimacy: Advertising and the Quality of Life." In *In Pursuit of The Quality of Life,* edited by Avner Offer. New York: Oxford University Press, 1996.

Parker, Donn B. *Fighting Computer Crime.* New York: Scribner's, 1983.

————. *Fighting Computer Crime.* New York: Wiley, 1998.

Partnoy, Frank. *Infectious Greed.* New York: Times Books, 2003.

Ponzi, Charles. *The Rise of Mr. Ponzi.* New York: Charles Ponzi, 1935.

Posner, Richard A. *Overcoming Law.* Cambridge, Mass.: Harvard University Press, 1995.

Pound, Roscoe. *The Lawyer from Antiquity to Modern Times.* St. Paul, Minn.: West, 1953.

Radin, Margaret Jane. *Contested Commodities.* Cambridge, Mass.: Harvard University Press, 1996.

Restatement (Second) of Contracts § 208 cmt. d (1981).

Restatement (Third) of Trusts § 2 cmt. b (2003).

Ridley, Matt. *The Origins of Virtue: Human Instincts and the Evolution of Cooperation.* New York: Penguin Books, 1998.

Rushkoff, Douglas. *Coercion: Why We Listen to What "They" Say.* New York: Riverhead Books, 1999.

Schein, Edgar H. *Organizational Culture and Leadership.* 2nd ed. San Francisco: Jossey-Bass, 1992.

Schelling, Thomas C. *Micromotives and Macrobehavior.* New York: Norton, 1978.

Schulman, Michael. "How We Become Moral." In *Handbook of Positive Psychology,* edited by C. R. Snyder and Shane J. Lopez. Oxford: Oxford University Press, 2002.

Schwartz, Eugene. *Breakthrough Advertising: How to Write Ads That Shatter Traditions and Sales Records.* Englewood Cliffs, N.J.: Prentice-Hall, 1966.

Scott, Wakeman Austin, and William Franklin Fratcher. *The Law of Trusts.* 4th ed. Boston: Little, Brown, 1987.

Shleifer, Andrei. *Inefficient Markets: An Introduction to Behavioral Finance.* New York: Oxford University Press, 2000.

Smith, Adam. *The Theory of Moral Sentiments* (1759). New York: Garland, 1971.

Snelling, John. *The Buddhist Handbook.* Rochester, Vt.: Inner Traditions International, 1991.

Stotland, Ezra, et al. *Empathy, Fantasy, and Helping.* Beverly Hills, Calif.: Sage, 1978.

Sutherland, Edwin H. *White Collar Crime: The Uncut Version.* Edited by Gilbert Gott (1949). New Haven: Yale University Press, 1983.

Swartz, Mimi, and Sherron Watkins. *Power Failure: The Inside Story of the Collapse of Enron.* New York: Doubleday, 2003.

Tidwell, Gary L. *Anatomy of a Fraud: Inside the Finances of the PTL Ministries.* Hoboken, N.J.: Wiley, 1993.

Trebilcock, Michael J. *The Limits of Freedom of Contract*. Cambridge, Mass.: Harvard University Press, 1993.

Uniform Commercial Code § 2–302 cmt. 1 (2003).

Walsh, James. *You Can't Cheat an Honest Man*. Los Angeles: Silver Lake, 1998.

Weber, Max. *Economy and Society*. Edited by Guenther Roth and Claus Wittich (1922). Berkeley: University of California Press, 1978.

Werner, M. R. *Barnum*. New York: Harcourt, Brace, 1923.

Williston, Samuel. *Williston on Contracts*. Edited by Richard A. Lord. 4th ed. Rochester, N.Y.: Lawyers Cooperative, 1990.

Wilson, David Sloan. *Darwin's Cathedral: Evolution, Religion, and the Nature of Society*. Chicago: University of Chicago Press, 2002.

Young, Michael. *The Metronomic Society: Natural Rhythms and Human Timetables*. Cambridge, Mass.: Harvard University Press, 1988.

Index

Abuse of trust. *See also* Acceptance, of fraud; Fiduciary; Management
  acceptance of, 27
  barriers to, 20, 82
  cost/benefit analysis: punishment for, 73
  culture of, 87
  dangers of, 20
  fiduciaries, by, 115, 119, 122
  lawyers, by, 15, 23
  management, by, 11, 16
  opportunities for, 83, 87, 102
  physicians, by, 106
  teachers, by, 125, 153
  view of, as natural, 40
Academia
  academic credentials, false, 15
  academic hood, professional, 137
  affecting social change, 196
  attitudes of, 47, 130
  recognizing immoral rules as legal, 130
  redefining wrongs, 37
Acceptance. *See also* Fraud; Justifications for fraud
  of abuse of trust, 3, 27
  of broad consensus, 29, 37: "everyone does it," 40
  continuous: to culture, 83; to habit, 89
  of fraud, 30, 45
  of system, 141
  of view of abuse of trust as natural, 40

Accounting
  corporations, fraud by, 9, 43, 45, 176: changing the rules, 61, 62; Enron, 21, 72, 99; objective of raising stock prices, 180
  firms, 14, 19, 20: deceptive, 163; fraudulent, 22, 141; violation of duties, by, 97
  issues, 19
  management (*see* Management)
  profession, purpose of, 21
  rules, 62: detailed, 148; innovative, 162; principle-based, 148; relaxed, 33
  "tricks," 171
Advertising, 66–67
  corporate financial statements, 70
  focus on: latent wishes of customers, 67; products, 67
  use of: celebrities, 68; "objective" polls and surveys, 69
  puffing, 70
Affinity groups
  peer groups, 29, 30, 195
  vulnerability to deception, 54, 99
American Psychiatric Association, 91
Analysts of securities, 20–22, 26, 43–44, 62, 93, 98, 125, 162
  mistrust of, 183
  reporters of fraud, 162
Aspiration, 5
  of power, 37
  of professionals, 137, 144
  of society, to honesty, 205

243

DATE DUE

Demco, Inc. 38-293